THE WEALTH OF THE NATION

The Wealth of the Nation

AN ECONOMIC HISTORY
OF THE UNITED STATES

STUART BRUCHEY

HARPER & ROW, PUBLISHERS, New York

Cambridge, Philadelphia, San Francisco,
Washington, London, Mexico City, São Paulo
Singapore, Sydney

1817

FIRST EDITION

Designer: Sidney Feinberg

Copy editor: Ann Finlayson

Indexer: Sylvia Farrington

Library of Congress Cataloging-in-Publication Data

Bruchey, Stuart Weems.
  The wealth of the nation.

  Includes index.
  1. United States—Economic conditions.   I. Title.
HC103.B78855   1988   330.973   87-45602
ISBN 0-06-015854-9   88 89 90 91 RRD 10 9 8 7 6 5 4 3 2 1
ISBN 0-06-091455-6 (pbk.)   88 89 90 91 RRD 10 9 8 7 6 5 4 3 2 1

To Eleanor, with love
The thirty-one years seem more like thirty-one days

Contents

Preface

I have written this book not only for students who are not specialists in economic history but also for the general public. The absence of explicit hypotheses and equations may disqualify the
work for the attention of economists, for whom the theoretical and
quantitative modes are de rigueur for serious work in the field.
Nevertheless, I daresay that many men and women trained in
economic science will not find the book beneath their notice. For
it rests upon an attempt to cope with much of the literature that
they have produced over the last thirty years.

Yet this book goes well beyond that literature. In brief, it
represents an effort to place economic change in a broad frame-
work of social change. It seems to me that a history of the nation's
economic development requires emphasis upon the mutual inter-
play of values, social structure, and the legal system. Accordingly,
I have examined the forces behind the making of the United States
Constitution and its interpretation by the major Supreme Courts
of the nineteenth century, in particular—an emphasis that is justified by the importance of that century in laying the foundations
for the modern, if not the present-day, American economy.

In this two hundredth anniversary year (1987) of that remarkably flexible document, interest may well be piqued by my sugges-
tions about the underlying social purposes of John Marshall's

Supreme Court, especially in the areas of contract and corporation law. Is it not possible that the great jurist sought a regime of stability in which a traditional elite might maintain its social, political, and economic dominance? Is it not possible that this too was a fundamental objective of Alexander Hamilton, the financial genius whose programs are commonly associated with goals of economic growth and the development of manufactures? If so, the disruptive forces leading to the increased economic, social, and legal egalitarianism of the age of Andrew Jackson and Roger B. Taney take on an added meaning. Many decades of slow economic growth and of relative social stability gave way to what John Higham has well called an "age of boundlessness."

The reader will note the brevity with which our early history is treated—not least because of the recent publication of John J. McCusker and Russell Menard's monumental *Economy of British America.* I nevertheless try in these early chapters to call attention to the significant underlying forces bearing upon the economy. The detail becomes more abundant in the chapters devoted to the last century or so, years which saw the completion of the first Industrial Revolution and the gradual emergence of our present service and information economy. I have written in some detail about the period of the Second World War, although not about other American wars, not only because government intervention in the economy was then far more extensive than ever before but also because this period had a strong impact on the Great Depression of the 1930s and on the structure of the postwar economy.

Finally, I have in the concluding chapter sought to identify some of the underlying technological and demographic forces at work in the recent past, and have discussed the grievous problems created by our present-day budget and trade deficits. What the future will bring nobody knows. But of one thing we can be sure: It will bear some relationship to the forces which have moved us from the past into the present. In this book I have tried to identify those forces.

THE WEALTH OF THE NATION

I

In the Beginning

HISTORY is important to us all because of the influence of the past in making us what we are. The values we hold and the knowledge we bring to bear upon the problems arising out of our social and physical environments become central to our culture. And these cultural traits not only help shape the character of individuals; they also help distinguish us from other cultural groups. Two such groups could hardly have been more different than the English and the native Indians they encountered in their effort to establish settlements in North America in the early seventeenth century. (Late twentieth-century historians have taken to calling this a "resettlement" by invading Europeans. The real invaders, however, were bacteria brought to America by hundreds of explorers and traders before the early seventeenth century. The invasion was so "successful" that it killed off more than 90 percent of the natives in the area that was to become the United States. An estimated aboriginal population of 10 to 12 million had fallen to some 850,000 by the time the Pilgrims landed on Plymouth Rock in 1620.)

The Indians were a Stone Age people lacking in written language, and those encountered by English settlers lived as seminomadic hunters and farmers. Their skilled craftsmen made such artifacts as canoes, moccasins, buckskin clothing, and bows

1

and arrows. Archaeological evidence for periods after A.D. 800 shows that they were practicing agriculture even that early. Luckily for the colonists, the Indians not only introduced them to such crops as maize, pumpkins, squash, beans, sweet potatoes, and melons, but also showed them how to cultivate these vegetables and prepare them for the table. Their knowledge of the properties of plants is evidenced by the fact that more than 200 indigenous drugs used by Indian tribes for curative purposes have been included at one time or another in *The Pharmacopoeia of the United States of America* or in the *National Formulary*. The disadvantages under which they suffered become apparent only in relation to advantages possessed by the English.

Firearms, and the ability to supply initial beachheads by means of ocean-going ships, furnished with charts and instruments of navigation, were surely some of these advantages. So too—at least in the New England settlements—was the Puritans' religious conviction that Satan was the ruler of the howling wilderness of America and that it was their duty to convert the Indian "savages" to Christianity: There was resolute staying power in that stern sense of religious duty. Ability to write was another advantage, especially for its help in wresting land from its former possessors: Indians could be overawed by strange black marks on deeds they could not read. But in the long run other things were even more important.

Perhaps above all, the reach of the English exceeded their grasp. Because they wanted more than they had it was necessary to calculate and plan. To be sure, these cultural attributes were not as fully developed as they would become under the imperatives of the Industrial Revolution. Even so, they thought of time in ways for which the Indians had no need. Provided with the necessities of human life by wildlife and by the products of the soil and the waters, the Indians had few additional wants. To some extent they traded in furs and obsidian, copper, textiles and other goods, but commercial activity played a relatively unimportant part in their lives. There was no need to parse the hours of daylight or think about the difference in value between consumer goods and capital goods, between what was ready to hand and what might be deferred for a larger return at a later time. Possessing in sufficiency (most of the time) nearly everything they desired, they lived, hand to mouth, in a continuing present. Indian levels of living in the seventeenth century were probably little changed from what they had been since time immemorial.

By contrast, in Europe a Commercial Revolution had occurred as long ago as the early fourteenth century. It was around that time that Italians invented a system of bookkeeping called double entry, a system unknown to the ancient world. Despite its name, it did not provide for a duplicate set of records, one truthful and hidden from prying eyes, the other for display purposes. All double entry meant was this: Since something was given (goods or services) and something received (goods, cash, or credit) every time a business transaction took place, the bookkeeping must reflect both sides of the transaction. Consider a man selling tobacco for cash. He must credit his tobacco account for the sale and at the same time debit his cash account the same amount. Every credit must be offset by an exactly equivalent debit. (The word "debit" means literally "debt." In other words, this account owes me, the proprietor, such and such an amount.) By strictly following the rule of double entry, the business proprietor was able to ascertain at any time just how much he owed others and others him, and precisely how much he had invested in goods of every kind. The system enabled him to keep track of change in the nature of his assets and liabilities, and to calculate his profit or loss.

The advent of double entry made it possible for the businessman to exercise a higher degree of rational control over his business decisions. An eminent economic historian in nineteenth-century Germany, Werner Sombart, went so far as to say that capitalism and double entry were "connected as intimately as form and contents." His even more distinguished contemporary, Max Weber, agreed.

Both of these champions exaggerated the importance of the Italian innovation—if only because the need for fresh news on prices and on supplies en route to various markets was more important in the preindustrial economy of the seventeenth and eighteenth centuries than were records permitting the calculation of profits or losses on past investments. Furthermore, at the time of the early emigrations to America, only the larger English mercantile firms found it worthwhile to exercise the care made possible by double entry. Nevertheless, even small traders in America used the forms of double entry in their record keeping—the long will or "apologia" of merchant Robert Keayne of mid-seventeenth-century Boston, for example, testifies unmistakably to this—and at least by the later decades of the eighteenth century, large-scale merchants in New York, Baltimore, and elsewhere were exploiting the possibilities of the system in detail.

Double entry was only one innovation brought by that early Commercial Revolution. Before then, business was conducted chiefly in partnerships organized for only a single venture. Now permanent units of enterprise began to replace these, and banking and insurance also appeared on the historical stage. Innovative offshoots of a commercial culture, they bespoke a degree of interest in controlling and improving the material conditions of life. And while some of these innovations had little or no impact on colonial America—commercial banking, for example, awaited the early 1780s before appearing for the first time in America—in time they were to join with other kinds of organizational and technological improvements to lift the levels of well-being of the average American.

Had white men never appeared on these shores, the culture of the Indians would probably have continued to shape its adherents in the same ancient ways. The America of A.D. 2000 would have been little different from the land of a thousand years before.

Whether that would have been "good" or "bad" depends upon one's point of view. Is a large population better than a small one? Surely not if it is set on a resource base too meager to support the average family decently.

Hopes of material improvement probably explain better than anything else why so many Europeans chose to come to the New World. In time, the values and the knowledge they brought with them, together with the more abundant resources of America, would make it possible for them to grow both in numbers and in well-being. The native Americans, on the other hand, can hardly have been expected to cheer on these developments. Satisfied with things the way they were before the arrival of the increasingly aggressive newcomers, they saw themselves as engaged in a just and valiant defense of their people, their environment, and their way of life.

While there were big differences between the values and the ways of the red man and the white, the latter's culture, once again, did not work its transformation overnight. Most colonial Americans were small subsistence farmers. Most of the food they grew and most of the goods they made were intended for their own use rather than for sale. Yet it was nearly impossible for any farm family to be entirely self-sufficient if only because such items as muskets and powder could not be made at home. To obtain them, farmers either bartered some of their produce or sold it for cash, the value of the goods involved being expressed in money prices. Where they sold their produce depended on their location and on the difficulty or ease of access to buyers. Farmers close enough to the coastal cities sold in the markets there. Those in the backcountry dealt with the storekeepers in their area, and those farther west did their bargaining with wandering peddlers. Wherever they sold, the prices received were strongly influenced by the prices at which goods were bought and sold in the major markets of the coastal cities. Certainly this was true by the mideighteenth century, and it was probably also true far earlier.

The arm of the market was long, but it did not lead most producers to try to maximize their earnings. The great majority followed a safety-first strategy. In the main, they avoided risk taking, specialization, and innovative behavior. Content to engage in mixed farming, they possessed what most had hoped to find in America—independence made possible by the ownership of land—for there were far more acres of land than there were people to work them. But while most families had relatively small farms, some held large estates, worked at first by indentured servants who had agreed to labor for three to six years in return for their passage to the New World, and increasingly toward the end of the seventeenth century, by slaves, particularly in the South.

These, then, were the main agricultural maximizers: the large-scale tobacco planters of tidewater Maryland and Virginia, the producers of naval stores (tar, pitch, masts, and other ship-building materials in North Carolina), and the growers of indigo and rice in South Carolina. It was they who possessed sufficient resources of land, labor, and capital to enable them to specialize on the production of staples destined for foreign markets. But the planters were not alone. Joining them as colonial maximizers were large-scale merchants in the coastal cities, men who owned ships or shares therein, who bought and sold insurance on vessels and their cargoes, sold at both wholesale and retail, lent and borrowed money at interest from other merchants—as well as receiving credits of up to a year's duration from English merchant bankers—had an interest in manufacturing (sometimes), and speculated in land. They were jacks-of-all-trades, men who earned something from supplying many goods and services rather than just one. Demand was not yet deep enough to warrant specialization. In the later decades of the eighteenth century, however, there is evidence that some had begun to specialize.

These merchants and planters were the movers and shakers of the exchange economy. It was they who organized colonial responses to widening markets in Europe, the West Indies, and elsewhere, responses which gradually pulled unemployed and underemployed resources out of subsistence agriculture and into the market sector. It was they who were the principal agents of economic growth, slow and gradual as it was, estimated to have occurred only at a rate between 0.3 and 0.6 percent per person per annum. And it was they who were the primary beneficiaries of a highly skewed distribution of wealth.

People in the lowest deciles of the distribution did not do very well. For example, by the middle of the seventeenth century the poorest 30 percent of the farmers in Maryland had accumulated estates consisting of miscellaneous livestock—about ten cattle, eight swine, two horses, and, for a quarter of the group, also an average of eight sheep—clothing, bedding, kitchen utensils, and a few work tools. The houses in which they lived were small one-story or one-and-a-half-story box frame structures which probably consisted of a single room. While we do not know how much land they owned, we do know that these poorer farmers were only a little better off at the end of the century, by which time the appraised value of their physical personal wealth had risen from an average of £11 Sterling at midcentury to £13 Sterling. In contrast, the wealth of the next group of 30 percent—the lower middle income group—rose from £37 to £45 Sterling. The wealth of the 30 percent following them—the upper middle group—went up from £108 to £164. That of the top 10 percent—the richest— rose most of all, from £349 to £630. This pattern continued in the eighteenth century, and by the eve of the Revolution more than half of the wealth held *in all thirteen* colonies was in the hands of the richest 10 percent of the population.

The owners of broad estates and rich mercantile capitals formed a colonial elite. Mature, static, homogeneous, and ingrown, their families dominated political, economic, and social life in dozens of counties in every colony from Massachusetts to South Carolina. Elegant and mannered, in possession of fine brick houses and furnishings, imported clothes, carriages, and other artifact badges of better folk, the elite expected to receive deference from lesser men and women, and it was accorded them. People believed that this was only right. Whether in England or America, a fundamental test of seventeenth-century social philosophy was a universal acceptance of social gradation and a complete belief in its rightness. Sailing in the vanguard of the Great Puritan Migration of 1630, John Winthrop had sketched the outlines of a tightly structured society in his lay sermon aboard the ship *Arbella:* "God Almightie in his most holy and wise providence, hath so disposed of the Condition of mankinde, as in all times some must be rich, some poore, some highe and eminent in power and dignitie; others meane and in subjection." Not surprisingly, then, colonists in the South as well as in New England persistently sought to reproduce in America stable, cohesive, and hierarchically structured communities.

In the countryside landed gentlemen emulated the ways of the English gentry. Often inheriting large estates and the slaves to work them, or, as in eighteenth-century Virginia, possessing superior access to the Colonial Secretary's office and the Privy Council, which controlled the land-grant process, they enjoyed sufficient wealth and leisure to pursue learning and the professions, especially law, and to indulge such amusements as horse racing, cock fighting, and wrestling. They donned the mantle of political leadership as the obligation of gentlemen.

In the cities, the social elite was made up of wealthy merchants and—probably far fewer—independently wealthy gentlemen. The latter were born rich, preferred safe investments to the risks of trade, lived off rents and interest, and devoted themselves to politics, civic affairs, public service, and genteel amusements. In Charleston, the great families of the eighteenth century included the Manigaults, Laurenses, Brewtons, and Gadsdens. Their counterparts in the maritime gentry were the Almys, Browns, Channings, and Collins of Newport, the Beekmans, Morrises, Rutgers, and Crommelins of New York, and the Hutchinsons and Hancocks of Boston, to name only a few. Separated from the Mother Country by 3,000 miles of water, long accustomed to managing their internal affairs, significant numbers of the colonial elite were unlikely to welcome an abridgement of the economic freedom which had enabled them to achieve such a striking degree of material success.

II

The Law of the Land

DURING most of the long years of colonial dependency, British law fell lightly over the external perimeter of the North American land. The purpose of the Navigation Acts, which were aimed at the Dutch, was to confine the shipping and trade of the empire to Englishmen, including those in colonial America. Vessels entering American ports must be English or colonial owned, and the nationality of the captain and three fourths of the crew must also be English or colonial. Thus favored, the imperial merchant marine was expected to serve as a nursery for seamen and ships, prize assets in the event of war. Requiring that naval stores be shipped only to the Mother Country or to another English port served the same purpose. But other articles were also "enumerated" so that some of the profits of imperial trade would go to Englishmen at home. Tobacco, the primary market for which was continental Europe, is a prime example. Finally, goods produced in continental Europe or in the East Indies must be shipped first to England, then reexported to America. The resulting addition of taxes, fees, commissions, insurance, and other extra shipping costs would, it was hoped, induce the Americans to prefer English-made to foreign goods.

All these laws, enacted by Parliament from time to time after 1660, are examples of the influence of "mercantilist" writers and policy advisers. Mercantilism, never a systematic body of thought, sought to increase the unity, wealth, and power of the state. To that end mercantilists argued that colonies should serve as sources of raw materials and look to the Mother Country for finished goods. Accordingly, Parliament provided for the payment of a bounty to colonial producers of such articles as indigo, source of a purple dye needed in England's growing textile industry, and naval stores. But while Parliament encouraged the production and export to the Mother Country of pig and bar iron, it prohibited the erection in the colonies of slitting mills and furnaces essential to the production of finished iron products. And it placed restraints on the colonial manufacture and sale of beaver hats and woolen goods.

Under the regime of the "old colonial system"—before the end of the Seven Years War in 1763—Americans only rarely complained about the Navigation Acts. Some smuggling went on, but the great bulk of colonial trade flowed in channels approved by law. The law and the conditions of trade were essentially in harmony. A great warehouse for the goods of the world and the initial home of the Industrial Revolution, England was both the preferred market for colonial produce and the best place to assemble return cargoes of diversified goods. While it is possible that some if not all Americans would have been better off under a regime of free trade—in all probability the tobacco growers would have been, for example—the lightness of the burden of the Navigation Acts is indicated by Benjamin Franklin's suggestion during the developing revolutionary crisis that the colonial legislatures themselves reenact the English laws.

The opposing interests of the British and Americans with regard to manufacturing is a different matter. Alarmed lest more rapid western settlement after 1763 should compel inland communities to manufacture for themselves, the British took measures to check or prohibit it. Manufacturing, noted a paper laid before the Board of Trade in 1768, was "a consequence which, experience shows, has constantly attended, in a greater or less degree, every inland settlement." On the eve of the Revolution, Franklin learned how adamant the British government had become on the point. Just before leaving England in 1775, he was drawn into informal negotiations with men closely connected with the ministry and asked to write out a set of propositions which he believed would lead to permanent union. One of his proposals was that all acts restraining manufactures be repealed. However, this proposition, Franklin relates, "they apprehended would meet with difficulty. They said, that restraining manufacturers in the colonies was a favorite here; and therefore they wish'd that article to be omitted, as the proposing it would alarm and hinder perhaps the considering and granting others of more importance." Had British policy remained the same, the future development of American manufacturing almost surely would have put the two peoples on a collision course. As it was, other events in the dozen years after 1763 mark the road to the American Revolution.

What set those events in motion was the British decision to enforce the Acts of Trade and Navigation more rigorously, to station 10,000 British troops in America, and to tax the colonies to help defray the cost of their support. More and more it seemed to leading Americans that the British intended to enslave them. They interpreted British actions after 1763 in terms of a tradition of antiauthoritarianism reaching back to the English Civil War— transmitted to Americans most directly by opposition politicians and radical publicists in early eighteenth-century England—and they became convinced that a deliberate assault was being launched against liberty in both England and America and that in the end the English constitution and all the rights and privileges imbedded in it would be destroyed. Few if any more precise statements of the relationship between the newly enforced commercial regulations and these deep-lying fears exists than one contained in a letter from Silas Deane to Robert Morris in June 1781: "The parliamentary regulations and restrictions on our commerce," wrote Deane, "were a principal cause of the unhappy contest between the two countries, and we were impatient under them because we were apprehensive, that they were part of a system to enslave us entirely. . . ."

The decade following the Declaration of Independence was filled with experiences which were to exert a profound effect upon the constitutional basis of the country's political economy. For the first time, Americans were forced to decide how much power to give to the federal government and how much to allow the states to retain. Their decision, embodied in the first American constitution, the Articles of Confederation, heavily favored local authority. The Articles explicitly affirmed the sovereignty of the states. And while numerous powers were assigned the federal government— to declare war and make peace, to send and receive ambassadors, for example—it was given little power to enforce its decisions. For most purposes, it had neither executive nor judicial authority. And for the most part, it had to act upon states rather than upon individuals. Denied the power to tax, it had to requisition the states for the funds essential to its operations. But it could not compel the states to pay. Nor could it compel them to adopt tariff and tonnage policies that would serve the national interest rather than that of each individual state. For the Articles also denied to it the power to regulate interstate and foreign commerce.

Flawed as these arrangements soon proved themselves to be, it would be surprising if the Americans had acted differently. Lacking experience in intercolonial government, it is remarkable they went as far as they did in the direction of central authority. They focused that authority on the Congress because both Locke and Blackstone, writers who deeply influenced leaders of public opinion, had exalted the legislative branch as preeminent. That they left real power at the local level is even more understandable. They had long been accustomed to being governed by provincial and town bodies under their own substantial control. And they had been rendered power-shy by what they regarded as abuses by the British government. The Constitution of 1787 was to alter the arrangements of the Articles in fundamental respects. De Tocqueville put his finger on the pulse of the American nineteenth century when he described the United States in the early 1830s as a country "in which every village forms a sort of republic, accustomed to govern itself."

The defects of the Articles, belatedly ratified by all thirteen states in 1781, became apparent during the Revolution. Grave difficulties were experienced in properly arming and equipping the troops. The reasons? Inadequate financial resources drawn by requisition from recalcitrant states. After the war, the government's inability to tax to raise the revenues required to pay interest on the national debt so destroyed public confidence that the price of the government's bonds fell to ten or fifteen cents on the dollar. American commercial interests abroad also suffered grievously. Throughout the colonial years, American trade with the British West Indies had provided immensely important outlets for the products of farm and forest. They had also been the major source of incoming cargoes of sugar, molasses, and other articles, and of bills of exchange that could be remitted to London to repay American indebtedness. The trade was also important to Britain, whose leaders recognized that the closeness of the continental colonies to the islands facilitated their supply. Indeed, after the war the British Prime Minister, William Pitt the Younger, proposed to Parliament that it continue to admit American vessels to West Indian ports as before.

Unhappily, Pitt's bill encountered opposition stirred by the publication in 1783 of Lord Sheffield's *Observations on the Commerce of the American States.* In his pamphlet Sheffield argued that "Our great national object is to raise as many sailors and as much shipping as possible. Parliament should endeavor to divert the whole Anglo-American trade to British bottoms." He went on to point out that the new American states lacked leverage in commercial bargaining with other countries. With individual states seeking commercial advantage over other states by lowering their tariff and tonnage duties, and Congress powerless to stipulate uniform rates throughout the union, the fledgling republic could offer neither inducement nor threat to the nations of Europe whose trade it sought on favorable terms. The precocious Alexander Hamilton saw the situation clearly. "Suppose, for instance," he wrote in 1787, "we had a government in America, capable of excluding Great Britain (with whom we have no treaty of commerce) from all our ports, what would be the probable operation of this step upon her politics? Would it not enable us to negotiate with the fairest prospect of success for commercial privileges of the most valuable and extensive kind in the dominions of that kingdom?" Unfortunately, Lord Sheffield was no less clear-eyed. "America," he pointed out, "cannot retaliate" against British policies. "It will not be an easy matter to bring the American states to act as a nation. They are not to be feared as such by us." Pitt's bill was lost.

With the West Indies closed to their vessels, the ability of American merchants to pay for their imports from Great Britain was severely diminished. Formerly they had been accustomed to ordering ship captains to proceed from the islands to Britain with West Indian products and bills of exchange received from the sales of their outgoing cargoes. They must now depend far more on specie shipments to Great Britain to pay for the difference between the value of their imports and exports. The difference in favor of imports was unusually heavy after the war, because American merchants responded to a long-pent-up demand by ordering large quantities of English goods. The upshot was that the loss of both specie and West Indian markets combined to exert strong downward pressure on prices and to make the decade after 1782 one of severe deflation.

A farmer who borrowed money at a time when he could sell his wheat at 50 cents a bushel found it difficult to repay the debt when wheat fell to 25 cents. In consequence, debts became extraordinarily burdensome, especially in Massachusetts. There, taxes, which Hamilton said were the highest in the nation, together with the execution of court orders for the sale of the property of delinquent debtors, created grave social tensions. Debtors importuned legislators to issue paper money to ease their tax payments and other obligations. Creditors, on the other hand, objected to being paid in paper that was worth less than specie.

To a lesser extent the same scenario was enacted in other states as well. When the paper money forces won out in seven states—with four of the seven declaring the bills legal tender in private payments—alarmed creditors and other property owners took action in defense of their interests. In Rhode Island, for example, merchants refused to accept paper, some closed their doors, and would-be buyers resorted to force and rioting, with farmers pledging to withhold produce from townsmen refusing to accept paper at par with specie. In 1786 armed attacks on creditors and tax collectors took place in Maryland, and a large band of armed men imprisoned the legislature in New Hampshire. That same year unrest in Massachusetts culminated in Shay's Rebellion, the well-known affair in which a Revolutionary War captain led a group of farmers into revolt against the government of the state.

In these circumstances, aggravated the more by state laws postponing the collection of debts or providing for their payment in installments or in commodities rather than in money, it is not surprising to find a growing concern over the insecurity of property rights. That concern began to dominate the criminal law of Massachusetts in the 1780s, especially after the end of the war, when the number of cases of prosecutions for theft and similar offenses more than tripled those of the war years. In Middlesex County alone there were four prosecutions for rioting and five for attacks on tax collectors between 1780 and 1785, and in the western counties attempts were made to prevent the courts from sitting and to rescue prisoners. A recent study of the legal history of Massachusetts concludes that postwar violence "undoubtedly heightened the fear of social breakdown and disorder" in the state.

Contemporaries saw clearly the connection between the commercial and the political and social situations and between these and the security of property. "Another unhappy effect of a continuance of the present anarchy of commerce," James Madison wrote in March 1786, "will be a continuance of the unfavorable balance on it, which, by draining us of our metals, furnishes pretexts for the pernicious substitution of paper money, for indulgences to debtors, for postponement of taxes. In fact, most of our political evils may be traced to our commercial ones. . . ." Madison vigorously defended a constitutional revision which would transfer the power of coining money from the states to the federal government and forbid the states to emit bills of credit (paper money). "A rage for paper money, or for any other improper or wicked object," he writes in *Federalist No. 10,* "will be less apt to pervade the whole body of the Union than a particular member of it. . . ." The "Monied Interest will oppose the plan of Government [the Constitution]," Gouverneur Morris says, "if paper emissions be not prohibited." Not surprisingly, the Constitution did prohibit the issuance of paper currency by the states; the states in addition were forbidden to coin money, make anything but gold and silver a tender in payment of debt, or pass any law impairing the obligation of contract (Article I, Section 10).

Years later Chief Justice John Marshall of the United States Supreme Court testified to the influence of the unsettled conditions of the 1780s on the inclusion of the above contract clause. It was "the prevailing evil of the times," he wrote in *Ogden* v. *Saunders* (1827), "which produced this clause in the constitution." Marshall defined this evil of the 1780s in terms of "the practice of emitting paper money, of making property which was useless to the creditor a discharge of his debt and changing the time of payment by authorizing distant installments." "[T]he power of changing the relative situation of debtor and creditor, of interfering with contracts," he added, "[was used by the states in pre-

Constitution days] to such an excess by the state legislatures as to break in upon the ordinary intercourse of society, and destroy all confidence between man and man." Had he then (1827) been alive, Hamilton would have agreed, for in the era of the Constitutional Convention and later as well, he expressed the conviction that the "relaxed conduct of the State Governments" had "undermined the foundations of Property and credit."

The concern is easily explained. It is not that the Framers were crass materialists but rather that they were Lockeians. No philosopher exerted upon their values a stronger influence than John Locke, and to Locke the security of one's material wealth was intimately linked with one's freedom. Indeed, he defined "property" broadly to embrace one's life, liberty, and estate. The framers appear to have conceived property more narrowly, synonymously with estate, but the association with liberty was inseparable. "[P]roperty must be secured," John Adams wrote, "or liberty . . . [cannot] exist." Hamilton saw it the same way: "Adieu to the security of property[,] adieu to the security of liberty."

Because the Framers were endeavoring to erect and defend a structure of fundamental law, it is the more understandable that they should have emphasized fundamental relationships rooted in the law of nature and described for them so clearly by Locke. One of the most basic was the relationship between property and liberty, and since legislative majorities in the states had threatened that relationship, the Framers decided that an increase in federal power was essential to its preservation. As a close student of our constitutional development once observed, "The problem of providing adequate safeguards for private rights and adequate powers for a national government were one and the same problem. . . ." The constitution met the problem head-on by its grant to the federal level of government of power sufficient to restrain the activities of the states in the crucial area of property rights.

In decision after decision, for example, in *Fletcher* v. *Peck* (1810) and in the *Dartmouth College case* (1819), Chief Justice

John Marshall used the contract clause to strike down state laws impairing the obligations of contract. Marshall was so adamant about the obligation to honor one's agreements that in *Ogden* v. Saunders (1827) he argued in dissent—the only instance in his thirty-four years on the bench when his reasoning failed to win a majority—that all state bankruptcy laws ought to be held unconstitutional. The Court had already ruled, in *Sturges* v. *Crowninshield* (1819) that bankruptcy statutes were invalid if they released a debtor from an obligation assumed *before* the passage of the law. In *Ogden* Marshall held that even a prospective law, one freeing a debtor from a contractual obligation entered into *after* passage of the law and in accordance with its provisions, ought also be held invalid. The prohibition in the contract clause was complete and total; there was no exception to it.

Why men like Marshall and Hamilton proved so adamant in defense of property rights may be sufficiently explained by their adherence to Locke's belief in the close association between property and liberty. But there is also another possibility to consider. Their emphasis upon vested property rights may also have originated in their determination to hold firm against social and economic forces threatening the stability of an older order and the dominance of that order by a traditional elite. Marshall's elitism, undoubtedly strengthened by his military experience during the Revolution, was initially imbibed in the culture of colonial Virginia, where everybody except "poor whites" looked to the "aristocratic element for ideals and standards of manners and conduct." Born on the frontier in modest circumstances, Marshall had the more reason to strive for acceptance by those "aristocratic elements." Hamilton's need was greater still, for he was born out of wedlock and in the West Indies.

The challenge to the old order may not have originated in the Revolution, but it certainly was greatly strengthened during those years. Looking back from the vantage point of 1792, Hamilton mused that the Revolution had "destroyed a large proportion of the monied and mercantile capital of the country and of personal property generally." A large part of the loss, probably most of it, must have fallen upon the older elite. In contrast, innumerable new men seized the abundant opportunities opened up by revolution and war to profit and rise in affluence. We have no numbers, but striking indications of what happen do exist.

As early as 1777 it seemed to Robert Treat Paine of Boston that "The course of the war has thrown property into channels, where before it never was, and has increased little streams to overflowing rivers. . . ." From the same city James Bowdoin wrote in 1783: "When you come you will scarcely see any other than new faces . . . the change which in that respect has happened within the few years since the revolution is as remarkable as the revolution itself." And so it went in city after city, testimony to topsy-turvy coming from John Jay in New York and from Pelatiah Webster in Philadelphia. New and bold traders had replaced the old in Charleston, David Ramsay wrote from that city, and "rapidly advanced their interests." "The men that had no money hardly, is now got the money," Dr. Joseph Orne said of society in Salem, Massachusetts. He added that they were called "the new Fangled Gentlemen." "Those who five years ago were the 'meaner people,' " declared an embittered Loyalist, Samuel Curwen, "are now, by a strange revolution, become almost the only men of power, riches and influence."

The distinction drawn in those days between the "better sort" and the "meaner sort," says a modern historian, David Hackett Fischer, was not between wealth and poverty but rather between those who had and those who hungered, between attainment and aspiration, respectability and ambition. Certainly, the protection of vested property rights behind the shield of the law represented a stronger force in defense of the status quo than of change. We shall later contrast with John Marshall's decisions the emphasis of the Court of Roger B. Taney.

This interpretation must confront the challenge of the traditional view of Hamilton as the Founding Fathers' leading champion of economic growth. Admittedly, the Secretary of the Treasury's famed *Reports to Congress on Public Credit, Manufactures, and a National Bank,* when taken together, do "constitute a theoretical plan," as Joseph Dorfman once claimed they did, for the development of the economy. But economic development was far from foremost among Hamilton's objectives. He sought above all the stability and staying power of the national government. He sought to prevent a retreat to state sovereignty and to the jeopardy to property rights which that sovereignty had entailed, and his instrumentality for these purposes was the restoration of the public credit.

It is true that in the *Report on Manufactures* Hamilton says that "manufacturing establishments . . . occasion a positive augmentation of the Produce and Revenue of the Society" by promoting diversified investment, division of labor, use of machinery, immigration, and a wider market for agricultural produce. But as John R. Nelson, Jr., has pointed out, Hamilton's "priorities did not lie with manufacturers." As everybody knows, he advocated that the state debts contracted during the Revolution be assumed by the national government, that the public debt of the Confederation be paid off at par and in specie, and that no discrimination be made between original and subsequent holders of government bonds. Since the price of a country's bonds was "the thermometre of its credit" he even went so far as to direct the cashier of the Bank of New York to enter the open market when necessary to support the price! Creation of a sinking fund would make possible a gradual retirement of the principal of the debt, but in the meantime there must be no interruption of interest payments. Since duties on imports were the principal source of the revenues needed to operate the government and service the debt, Hamilton opposed the manufacturers in their efforts to induce Congress to stem the flow of competing imports by enacting protective tariffs. Even the Society for Establishing Useful Manufactures was "largely prompted" by "security market problems." The SEUM represented an attempt not only to encourage manufacturing but also to draw mercantile capital away from speculation in the debt, its charter requiring that 50 percent of all subscriptions to its stock be payable in government securities. The upshot was this: Hamilton's "ties to manufacturers were first strained, then severed by conflicts between their interests and his program." "By the end of 1793 his pro-importer political economy was driving manufactures from Boston to Charleston into opposition to the Federalists."

Similar reservations have to be made about Hamilton's views on money and credit, easy access to which would certainly have made it possible for larger numbers of businessmen to get a piece of the action, so to speak. News that a third bank had "started up" in New York City in 1792 caused him "infinite pain."

> Its effects cannot but be in every view pernicious. These extravagant sallies of speculation do injury to the Government and to the whole system of public Credit, by disgusting all sober Citizens and giving a wild air to every thing. It is impossible but that three banks in one City must raise such a mass of artificial Credit, as must endanger every one of them & do harm in every view.

The relationships of the Secretary of the Treasury with the First Bank of the United States testify unmistakably to the primacy of public credit. It is true that Hamilton recommended in his *Report on a National Bank* that the institution be placed under private management to avoid the injury to its credit which would follow upon excessive loans to government. At the same time he also said forthrightly that "public utility is more truly the object of public banks than private profit." It proved so indeed. On the day of his resignation from the Treasury, total loans to government amounted to $4.7 million, virtually half the bank's authorized capital. Two early students of the bank, Holdsworth and Dewey, concluded that these large drains on the bank's funds "crippled its services to commerce and manufactures and made it difficult to facilitate the financial operations of the Government by temporary loans." Discovery of the bank's balance sheets for the period 1792–1800 enabled that institution's most recent student, James O. Wettereau, to make a stark numerical display of evidence supporting the view that the bank must indeed have been highly conservative in its loan and discount policy. For most of the years during that period the relationship between notes in circulation and reserves was close, ranging from a high of 4.93 to 1 in 1794 to a low of .96 to 1 in 1800. The average for the nine years was merely 1.95 to 1, less than $2 in banknotes for every dollar in specie. The Board of Directors clearly meant it when it said: "It must be Strikingly evident to those who have contemplated the Business of Banking, that its Resources & Advantages have their Limits. . . ." The best commentary on that conservative view is the fact that, within merely five years after the expiration of the bank's charter, state banks doubled in both numbers and capital stock. The volume of notes they placed in circulation tripled.

In sum, what happened was this: An economy whose rate of output growth and structural change had begun to exceed rates achieved during even the most vibrant years of the eighteenth century loosened the joints of a once more tightly structured society. An older elite, which had sat bestride that society and benefited from its relatively slow pace of change, began to lose its battle to hold back the future. To the nature of the forces quickening the pace of change and to a different kind of response to those forces on the part of the Supreme Court we now turn.

III

The Agricultural Republic

During the decades between the inauguration of Washington and the outbreak of the Civil War, two major forces, one demographic and the other economic, continued at an accelerated pace the unsettling of the older order in America. The former was by far the more important. Substantial immigration after the War of 1812 joined with processes of natural increase to swell the size of the population from fewer than 4 million in 1790 to over 31 million in 1860. By the end of the nineteenth century population exceeded 75 million. Had these added millions been compelled to occupy the same space in which far smaller numbers had lived, insufferable densities might have resulted, with consequences for disease and mortality comparable to those of nineteenth-century Asia. That these things did not occur was owing in part to an expansion in the size of the land space owned by the national government and subject to its control. Large territorial claims, based on the colonial charters of seven of the original thirteen states, were yielded up to the national government; what with this land and acreage added by subsequent purchase, diplomatic compromise, and cession in the wake of war, the public domain grew from roughly 233 million acres at the beginning of the nineteenth century to 1.423 billion acres in 1853 (see Table 1). By midcentury, in short, the federal government had title to nearly three of every four acres of land in the United States.

Table I. Acquisition of Public Domain, 1781–1853 (in thousands of acres)

Ceded by seven states to U.S. (1781–1802)	233,416
Louisiana Purchase (1803)	523,446
Florida (1819)	43,343
Oregon Compromise (1846)	180,644
Mexican Cession (1848)	344,479
Purchase from Texas (1850)	78,843
Gadsden Purchase (1853)	18,962
Total	1,423,133

Source: Bureau of Census, *Historical Statistics of the United States, Colonial Times to 1970.* Part I, 428 (Washington, D.C., 1975)

Government control of the land alone, however, was only one of the necessary conditions for the dispersal of the population to outlying areas. Favorable land disposal policies were also necessary. And if the Western settlements encouraged by those policies were to be united politically and economically with the rest of the nation, so too was the provision of improved transport facilities. However, even cheap land and available transportation to market for the products of the West were not in themselves enough to induce people to locate there. People move for many reasons, of course, but among them is an economic one that is not to be lost sight of: rising international and domestic market prices for the agricultural staples that could be grown on fertile Western soils promised a better living than the yield of worn out acres in the East. Finally, the channels in which people, products, and business transactions moved from state to state must be cleared of legal obstacles put in place by state governments seeking to protect local businesses from outside competition.

The demographic force loosening the joints of an older order is thus seen to have been one of many facets. The investment, technological, and occupational changes implied by an economic force—the early stirring of the American Industrial Revolution—are only less so, for industrialization was also promotive of population movement, although centripetally in the direction of urban growth in the East rather than of dispersal over the agricultural West. But the longer-term effects of the developing manufacturing sector are deserving of emphasis: It was this sector that served as the cutting edge of a more rapid rate of economic growth and structural change, especially after accelerated beginnings in the 1820s and 1830s. Before then, if we accept the words written in 1817 by an observant contemporary, Adam Seybert, the "brilliant prospects held out by commerce caused our citizens to neglect the mechanical and manufacturing branches of industry."

What made the prospects brilliant was a coupling of the outbreak of the wars of the French Revolution and Napoleon (1793–1815) with the fact that the merchants of the new republic were in possession of the largest fleet of neutral ships in the world. All during the colonial years the lush availability of forests had provided the masts, yards, bowsprits, and other materials needed by shipbuilders. Indeed, by the time of the Revolution one third of all the ships in the British empire had been constructed in America. As neutrals in wars that eventually enveloped much of Europe and even the United States (1812–1815), American shipowners were in a position to dominate the reexport and carrying trades following France's declaration of war against England in 1793.

Normally, the colonial empires of most of the European powers were closed in time of peace to the ships of other nations. After the Revolution, as we have seen, England excluded American ships from her ports in the West Indies, and although in the Jay Treaty of 1794 she conceded entry to small vessels of forty tons or less, an indignant Senate struck the article from the Treaty before ratifying it.

In 1784, France had opened seven of her West Indian ports to American shipping but on condition that they carry only rum, molasses, and French merchandise. The Spanish Empire was locked tight as a drum, at least insofar as law could succeed in doing so. (Bribery of colonial officials was a not unknown device for prying open the gates.) With the outbreak of war between England and France in 1793, all this began to change. France realized immediately that English naval superiority would interdict French shipping between her colonies and Europe, and so by a decree of February 1793 she opened the doors of her colonial empire, including the East Indies and the Isle of France and Bourbon as well as the West Indies, to American vessels. Spain did the same thing in 1797 under a special licensing system. Wartime conditions also resulted in the reopening of the British West Indies ports to American ships. In general, the war made such demands upon British shipping that her prohibitions against American vessels entering her West Indian ports were simply not enforced. Thus, by accident of war nearly the entire commercial world was thrown open to neutral American shipping.

Not right away, however, and not without exceptions. England's reaction to the war-born generosity of France was to invoke a regulation she had adopted during the Seven Years War (1756–1763)—the so-called Rule of 1756. According to this rule, in time of war no neutral nation might engage in a trade denied it in time of peace. England, after all, was the world's greatest sea power. She wished to bring that power to bear upon her enemies, to destroy their commerce and shipping. She also wished to achieve an economic blockade of France. Her strategy, therefore, was to capture the French West Indian Islands. She would also seize neutral vessels attempting to enter blockaded ports. Finally, she would take from neutral vessels any French goods found on board, and any contraband, i.e., goods such as munitions which nations agree at various peacetime conferences are such as aid enemy countries in time of war and which therefore cannot be supplied that country by a neutral. (The difficulty, of course, is that in wartime great naval powers trying to starve their enemies into submission tended to stretch the list of contraband goods to include even food.)

England's first impulse, therefore, was to construe narrowly the so-called rights of neutrals. During 1793 many American vessels were both seized and condemned by British Admiralty Courts. But in January 1794 came a British order-in-council which was to change the situation dramatically and in America's favor. The British decided to permit neutral vessels to buy goods from her enemies so long as they carried them to their neutral ports. England expected that Americans would buy French goods in Haiti, for example, take them to an American port, pay duty upon them, then unload and sell them. Some of them would no doubt be bought for American consumption, and some bought by a merchant intent upon reexporting them to Europe. What often happened in practice was quite different. American ships brought goods from Haiti and then, after touching at an American port, set sail for Europe without even the formality of unloading them! They paid duties on the imports, but American law permitted a refund of all such duties except 1 percent. Still, the Americans could argue that calling at an American port broke the voyage. It wasn't a *continuous* voyage between enemy colony and enemy homeland, and hence it was legal. The British agreed. In 1800 a British Admiralty Court ruled in the case of the ship *Polly* that the practice of breaking the voyage by calling at an American port legalized the voyage. What Americans were doing, then, was this: They were importing foreign goods and then reexporting them. This practice, of course, is known as engaging in the reexport or carrying trade.

Statistics on the reexport trade clearly show the result. In 1793, reexports were worth only $2 million. The next year they tripled in value. In 1796, they amounted to $26 million, a thirteen-fold increase in a period of three years. Then in 1797 the value of these reexported foreign goods exceeded that of domestic exports, an unusual phenomenon which continued every year from then on (except during the Peace of Amiens in 1802–1803) until the embargo virtually put an end to foreign trade in 1808.

American merchants imported such goods as coffee, cocoa, or other tropical products from the West Indies, or textiles, dyestuffs, coffee, and other goods from the East Indies, and then transshipped the bulk of them to Europe. From Europe, in turn, came return cargoes of clothing, hardware, and other goods for both colonial and American consumption. American merchants did not simply charge commissions—that is, a percentage of the value of the goods carried—for handling this trade. They also earned profits. That is to say, they purchased and sold both colonial and European products on their own account as well as for the account of some plantation owner, European merchant, or manufacturer. Precisely how high their profits were nobody knows, although we do know the results of shipments made by a few men. Others risked too much and failed—when values crashed during the Peace of Amiens, for example. But some grew rich.

The Wars of the French Revolution and Napoleon created the first American millionaires. There had been merchants during the colonial period, of course, who were better off than other members of their respective communities. A seaboard elite of wealth and social position existed in this country from at least the end of the seventeenth century and probably before. Colonel William Pepperell of Piscataqua, New Hampshire, was pretty well off in the 1690s, and he made his money in trade. In the eighteenth century, the Browns of Providence Plantations made significant earnings from foreign trade, rum distilling, iron making, and a variety of other enterprises. Other wealthy colonial families might also be mentioned, such as the Carrolls and Ridgelys of Maryland. But there does not seem to have existed a single colonial millionaire. Thomas Boylston of Salem was the richest man in colonial Massachusetts, and his wealth amounted to around $400,000. But at least three millionaires emerged from the period of the Napoleonic Wars. Elias Hasket Derby of Salem, Massachusetts, was one.

In 1799 he was worth a million and was reputed to be the richest man in America. Ten years later, Robert Oliver, a Baltimore merchant, was worth somewhat over a million, and by the end of the period of the wars, Stephen Girard of Philadelphia had perhaps between $7 and $9 million, which made him by all odds the richest man of his day. Around 1815 there may have been about a half-dozen millionaires in the country. But there were many, many men whose capital funds had been increased significantly in amount by profits from neutral shipping and trade.

The period of the French wars was an extraordinary one, and its larger economic significance for America lies in the fact that part of the earnings realized in international commerce went into savings and into investments in the kinds of enterprises that were gradually changing the structure of the economy: transport, banking, and manufacturing. Meanwhile, government policies rather than the coincidence of foreign war and American neutrality were impacting on migration to the agricultural West.

The early influence of those policies was negative. In part, this was because political leaders had another objective in mind, and in part because they differed on how to achieve that objective. Jefferson and Gallatin, as well as Hamilton, believed that the public domain should yield revenue to the government, especially for the purpose of retiring the public debt. Opinion divided, however, on how to maximize those revenues: sales to speculators or sales to settlers? Gallatin and Hamilton even disagreed on whether a high or low price per acre would appeal to speculators. Though political opposites, both men opposed speculation, but Gallatin believed a sales price of $2 an acre would discourage it, while Hamilton thought it would require a price as low as 20 or 30 cents.

As it turned out, neither settler nor speculator showed much interest in the terms finally settled on by a Congressional enactment of 1796. The law required a minimum purchase of 640 acres (one square mile) at a price of $2 an acre and offered the following credit terms: 5 percent down, with one half the balance in thirty days, the other half in a year. The terms were not nearly so generous as those commonly offered by landholding states and private owners. In effect, they favored the interests of Eastern landholders, who feared the depressing influence of widespread emigration on land values in the older states. It was in these states that the great bulk of the people lived, the first federal census of 1790 showing them distributed almost entirely along the Atlantic seaboard between Maine and Florida. Only 3 percent of the population lived west of the Appalachian Mountains.

Despite the unattractiveness of federal sales terms, the movement picked up its pace between 1790 and 1800, presumably under the stimulation of rival state and private offers (together with a disposition simply to "squat" on federal land), and by 1800 residents in the Western states and territories made up 7 percent of the total population. The movement became more rapid still after 1800, not least because Congress, disappointed with the sales results of the legislation of 1796, responded to spokesmen for the frontier and liberalized the land laws. The Act of 1800 made no concession on price, which remained at $2 an acre, but it reduced to 320 acres the minimum plot required to be purchased and made major changes in credit terms. Buyers were permitted to pay 5 percent of the total price at the time of purchase, one fourth in forty days, a second fourth in two years, and the third and fourth installments in three and four years. The year 1804 brought further liberalization, the minimum plot being halved to 160 acres, and by 1810, 15 percent of the population resided in the Western states and territories.

Despite this impressive early peopling of the West, the region was of limited economic significance to the rest of the nation. Large numbers lived at the level of subsistence or close to it. While some were able to produce more than was required for consumption needs and to exchange the surplus for goods provided by wandering peddlers or nearby country stores—often floating stores on Midwestern rivers—many represented an underemployed economic resource. As Congressman Porter of New York remarked in a speech in Congress in 1810, the "great evil . . . under which the inhabitants of the western country labor, arises from the want of a market." Western soils were so fertile that farmers had to spend only half their time in labor to fill their consumption needs. And since there was "nothing to incite them to produce more," they were "naturally led to spend the other part of their time in idleness and dissipation." The value of produce received at New Orleans, the port through which most of the trade of the West passed, was $5.37 million in 1807, and by 1816 it had risen to only $8.773 million. Those other evidences of expanding trade—flourishing towns and cities—were conspicuously few. In 1810, New Orleans, with a population of 24,562, was the only city of any considerable size in the West. Pittsburgh had 4,768 inhabitants, Lexington 4,326, and Cincinnati 2,540. Louisville, St. Louis, Nashville, and Natchez each had fewer than 1,000.

A principal deterrent to the growth of the West before the end of the War of 1812 was the high cost of transportation for the commodities of the region. The wheat, flour, butter, pork, tobacco, hemp, lead, and other products of the rich agricultural lands of the Ohio Valley were of low value in relation to their bulk. Because of this it was cheaper to ship them more than 3,000 miles by water—down the Ohio and Mississippi rivers to New Orleans, then by seagoing vessel up the Atlantic coast to Philadelphia, New York, or Boston—than 300 miles overland across the Appalachian Highlands to Philadelphia or Baltimore. Traffic, moreover, was for the most part a one-way flow—downriver—for shipments upriver against the current were almost prohibitively expensive. Textiles, hardware, hats, tea, and other commodities of high value relative to their bulk were imported from across the Appalachians rather than brought up the river. This was in the main another one-way flow of goods (one of the chief exceptions being cattle driven on foot over the mountains to the East Coast). This difficult pattern of interregional trade encouraged subsistence rather than commercial agriculture and depressed farm incomes in the West, as well as making Western food and raw materials more expensive in the East.

The appearance of steamboats on the rivers of the West after the War of 1812 marked the beginnings of significant change in the region's pattern of economic life. In 1817 only seventeen steamboats plied the Western rivers, and the total volume of freight carried amounted to only 3,290 tons; by 1855 these figures had increased phenomenally to 727 vessels and 170,000 tons. Steamboats made possible much more upriver traffic and reduced shipping costs both up and downstream. The reduction in upriver freight rates, far greater than in downstream charges, lowered the costs of imported merchandise. Just before the Civil War, downstream rates averaged 25 to 30 percent of their level in the years from 1815 to 1819, but upstream rates had fallen to 5 or 10 percent of those charged in the earlier period. The latter decline shifted the "terms of trade" in favor of the farmer—that is to say, it lowered the prices of goods farmers bought relative to those they sold. The net effect was to increase Western farm income substantially and to encourage both an increase in the settlement of the West and a shift from subsistence to commercial agriculture. Lowered freight rates promoted the rapid development of the trans-Appalachian frontier. Most of the decline took place in the early 1820s—it was in 1823 that the terms of trade began a long-term rise in the farmer's favor—and in 1828 and 1829 public land sales jumped from an annual average of 814,000 acres (1823–1827) to an average of 1,587,500 acres.

These results were helped along by increasingly generous federal land policies. In 1820, the government halved once again—to 80 acres—the minimum plot and adopted a cash price of $1.25 an acre, abandoning altogether sales on credit. And in 1832, the minimum plot was cut to 40 acres. For $50 cash a family could get a start in the West on a 40-acre farm. Thus encouraged, an increasing proportion of the American people chose to move to the West, the percentage of those remaining in the East declining each decade between 1810 and 1860 from 85 percent (1810) to 77 percent (1820), 71 percent (1830), 63 percent (1840), 57 percent (1850), and 50 percent (1860). On the eve of the Civil War every other American lived west of the Appalachians, in the East Central or West Central regions, with a handful of people in the Far West (see Table 2).

Table 2. Geographic Distribution of the Population, 1790–1860

Regions	1790	1800	1810	1820	1830	1840	1850	1860
I. East Coast	97%	93%	85%	77%	71%	63%	57%	50%
A. New England	26	23	20	17	15	13	12	10
B. Middle Atlantic	24	27	28	28	28	30	25	26
C. South Atlantic	47	43	37	32	28	20	20	14
II. East Central	3	7	14	20	26	32	34	35
A. North	0	1	4	8	12	17	19	22
B. South	0	6	10	12	14	15	15	13
III. West Central	0	0	1	3	3	5	8	13
A. North	0	0	0	1	1	2	4	7
B. South	0	0	1	2	2	3	4	6
IV. Far West	0	0	0	0	0	0	1	2
Total U.S.	100	100	100	100	100	100	100	100

Source: U.S. Bureau of the Census, *Historical Statistics of the United States from Colonial Times to 1957* (Washington, D.C.: Government Printing Office, 1960), pp. 12–13.

The Western movement cannot be explained fully as a response to increasingly attractive terms on which land could be acquired from the federal government. What must also be brought into the account is the prospective Western farmer's estimate of the problems he would face in getting his crops to market and, far from least, the influence of the price behavior of those crops upon his decision to move west and farm in the first place.

The market problem was essentially a transportation problem, but many political leaders questioned whether the Constitution allowed the federal government to use the resources available to it to promote "internal improvements," as they were known at the time. However, President Jefferson, a man of strict constructionist views—he made an exception when he acquiesced in the purchase of Louisiana Territory from France—did decide to invite Congress in 1806 to consider the application of surplus revenues "to the improvement of roads, canals, rivers, education, and other great foundations of prosperity and union, under the powers which Congress may already possess, or such amendment of the Constitution as may be approved by the states."

The Senate responded by directing Secretary of the Treasury Albert Gallatin to draw up plans for the use of federal funds. Gallatin's splendid report of 1810, while never implemented, specified ways in which a series of canals cut through geographic obstacles between Massachusetts and Georgia (for example, Cape Cod), together with a turnpike, would facilitate North–South transport that would be safe from enemy interdiction by sea, and ways in which river and road improvements could make it easier for Western products to reach the Atlantic coast via pairs of rivers close to one another, the one flowing down the Appalachians to the West, the other to the Atlantic (for example, the Monongahela and the Potomac). Gallatin also called for the construction of a canal that would connect the Hudson River with the Great Lakes—a project (the Erie Canal) which the state of New York was subsequently to undertake (1817–1825) wholly by the use of state funds.

While the federal government did construct the National Road, which reached the Ohio River at Wheeling in 1818 and Vandalia, Illinois, by midcentury, the main exception to the federal government's minimal role in the provision of funds for internal improvements took the form of Congressional authorizations of subscriptions to the stocks of three canal companies during the administration of John Quincy Adams. In 1824, however, Congress approved the first river improvement and harbor improvement bills, merged two years later in a long series of "rivers and harbors" measures. With the election of Andrew Jackson in 1828, federal funding of new improvements projects drew to a close, the President boasting in his Farewell Address that he had "finally overthrown—this plan of unconstitutional expenditure for the purpose of corrupt influence."

The existence of constitutional and other obstacles to the use of federal funds to aid internal improvements led to the suggestion that the federal lands be used instead. The Ohio Enabling Act of 1802 provided a precedent. That Act made available to Ohio 5 percent of the net proceeds from sales of public land in the state for use in the construction of roads. Three percent of the funds were to be spent on roads within the state and the other 2 percent on roads leading to Ohio, with permission from neighboring states being obtained to avoid the constitutional problem. The same policy was adopted later when Indiana, Mississippi, Alabama, and Missouri were admitted to the Union. In 1823 occurred the first of a long series of grants of public lands to the states for aid in the construction of specified projects. Between that year and 1866, when the grants ceased, 4.5 million acres were given in aid of canals, 3.5 million acres for roads, and 1.7 million acres for river improvements.

In addition, the Internal Improvements Act of 1841 made grants of land for general rather than specific purposes. Under this Act, not repealed till 1889, each public land state received 500,000 acres. Finally, we may mention two acts of 1850, the first of them the Swamplands Act, which provided that low-lying public lands unfit for cultivation be given to the states within whose boundaries they lay. The lands were to be sold, with part of the proceeds used to drain them and the rest for internal improvements. This Act and the Internal Improvement Act combined brought to the various states a total of 65 million acres. The second measure of 1850, the Illinois Central Land Grant Bill, initiated grants to railroads that proved even more generous, a total of 131 million acres being turned over between 1850 and 1872. From 1850 to 1862 the grants were made to the states and by the latter to railroad companies. Those made between 1862 and 1872 went directly to the railroads, which were then extending their lines through unorganized territories. Before 1862 the grants provided for a right-of-way 200 feet wide (i.e., the path of the railroad), and, in addition, alternate sections of land—a section being one mile square—on both sides of the right of way, to a depth of six square miles. Essentially, the pattern was that of a checkerboard, with the government granting one square mile of land for every mile of track laid and retaining the other square mile for later sale. The basic idea was that the land would serve as security for the bonds issued by the railroads, and that this would induce investors to purchase them. The proceeds of bond sales would then furnish the funds needed to build the railroad. Government, in turn, would recoup the value of some of its largesse, not only by requiring the railroads to carry government traffic free of charge, and mails at rates set by government, but by doubling the price of the alternate sections of land retained—on the theory that the railroad would enhance the value of the land.

Land grants were not the only federal aids to railroads. Under a law that was on the statute books between 1824 and 1838, federal engineers were authorized to make railroad surveys at government expense, i.e., to survey the land preliminary to the laying of track, building of bridges, etc. Finally, between 1830 and 1843 Congress lowered the duties on iron used for railroad construction, saving the railroads an estimated $6 million—until domestic iron manufacturers succeeded in convincing Congress that it ought to protect the iron interests instead of railroad interests!

All in all, the federal government made substantial contributions to the developing transportation system. Yet its promotional role tended to be a declining one in the later decades of the antebellum period. Democratic administrations predominated after 1829, and in these later years, if not during the first quarter of the century, Democrats adhered somewhat more closely to the Jeffersonian ideal of limited government. With respect to river and harbor improvements, Presidents Van Buren, Tyler, Polk, Pierce, and Buchanan were more strict constructionists than even Jackson had been. While it would be a mistake to discount the force of Old Republican values, especially in the case of Jackson, it is not primarily a growth in political idealism that explains this phenomenon. The most fundamental explanation is the maturation of conflicting sectional, state, and occupational interests. The sharpness of these differences made it difficult to reach agreements covering any wide area of national life. In fine, a diversity of local interests militated against decisive action on the part of the central government.

Two other strands enter into this developing centrifugal pattern. For one, with increasing accumulation of stocks of private capital, men and groups lacking the advantages bestowed by law upon older corporate groups turned against privilege sanctioned by the legal system. Secondly, as slavery edged ever closer to the center of the national stage, Southern leaders determined to contain federal authority within narrow bounds. As John Randolph of Roanoke, Virginia, observed during a debate on internal improvements during the 1820s: "If Congress possesses the power to do what is proposed by this bill, they may emancipate every slave in the United States."

In a basic sense, therefore, leading public issues that involved the constitutional power of the federal government also involved slavery. But questions concerning federally financed internal improvements—like those concerning land policy, the tariff, and the Bank of the United States—also possess an independent importance. The fear of emancipation cannot explain all presidential vetoes of internal improvements bills or public pronouncements of the unconstitutionality of direct federal action in this area. Opposition to logrolling, waste, local bickering, and corrupt use of patronage also played a part.

The South nearly always opposed internal improvements at federal expense. Not only was the region well supplied with rivers for carrying Western produce to the South and Southern cotton to the sea, but the construction costs would reduce federal funds and make necessary an increase in the tariff level to replenish them. In the earlier years of the century, furthermore, the greatest of the improvements were those designed to overcome the barrier of the Appalachian Mountains. But improved trade connections between East and West brought little benefit to the Southern states, and to the Lower South none at all. Henry Clay's American System, which called for tariff protection for the East and internal improvements for the West, posed the possibility of an East–West alliance that would threaten the political position of the South. Presiding over the Memphis Convention in 1845, John C. Calhoun, however, expressed Southern anxiety over the effects on Southern wealth of the great rise in direct shipments of Western produce to the East, and called upon the federal government to improve the navigation of the Western rivers. The West favored rapid settlement not only for its effects on land values, general business, and access to Eastern markets, but also because its growing population provided greater security against Indian attack. For the same reasons the region's spokesmen in Congress generally approved liberal land policies.

A constitutional amendment clarifying federal authority in the field of internal improvements therefore would not have addressed the underlying differences that impeded action at that level. Undoubtedly this helps explain why compelling popular pressure on behalf of a national program was lacking. It was also lacking, in part, because of a belief that the states were themselves well equipped to carry out the essential improvements. A writer in the *North American Review* argues well this point of view:

> The compass of each state is sufficiently narrow, and its legislative power sufficiently diffused, to render knowledge of its internal condition, wants, and resources easily attained. . . . Scarce any object of public utility is beyond the grasp of resources of the single states; so that, after all, the care of individual objects of public improvement is put into the hands of those most sure to be benefited by them

Even within the smaller arena of the state, however, distinct geographic and other interests made statewide agreements difficult, and they were often achieved only by the grant of costly or wasteful concessions to disaffected areas or groups. Intrastate conflicts were nevertheless more easily harmonized than differences between national regions, and, in consequence, the promotional activities of state and local governments far exceeded those of the federal government. With the role of the latter a declining one, advocates of roads and canals, and soon thereafter of railroads, pushed their projects in every state and in almost every locality. Some states, as the case of Virginia illustrates, institutionalized procedures for choosing between proposed projects.

"There never has existed a doubt but that it is a duty, as well as the interest of every good government to facilitate the necessary communication between its citizens. Next perhaps to the enjoyment of civil liberty itself are the blessings which governments can secure to the people by good roads, navigable rivers and canals." Justifying the details of its report in these words, the Virginia Assembly's Committee on Roads and Navigation recommended at the end of 1815 that the state contribute to the capital funds required for projects by subscribing to the stock of private companies—but only in such quantities and on such terms as would encourage private investment. Management of the projects should remain in private hands, the committee believed, with the state's only responsibility being that of preventing or correcting abuses.

The legislature responded in 1816 to this report by creating a Fund for Internal Improvements and placing it under the control of a newly established Board of Public Works. The latter was composed of such prestigious figures as the governor, treasurer, and attorney general of the state, together with ten citizens. So that the varying needs of different parts of the state would find representation on the board, three of the ten were to be selected from west of the Alleghenies, two from the Shenandoah Valley, three from the Piedmont, and two from Tidewater. The board was authorized to employ a principal engineer and with his aid to examine all proposals laid before it. Those approved for state aid were to be so recommended to the assembly. The law required the sponsors of each project approved by the assembly to raise by private subscription three fifths of the amount needed for construction, the state then subscribing the other two fifths and appointing its proportional share of directors on the board of the corporation chartered to build the project. Thus there existed no overall master plan for the state similar to that which Gallatin had drawn up for the nation in his report of 1808.

The system established by law in 1816 remained in effect, with some changes in its outline (e.g., regional members of the board were dropped in 1831, and the state's subscription later rose to three fifths), until the military operations of the Civil War put an end to it. In the main, the state raised the money it needed by borrowing, by issuing bonds, the proceeds of which it then used to purchase the stocks of the improvement companies. (Thus loans were based on the state's ability to tax rather than on a corporation's ability to earn profits.) Sometimes the state turned the bonds over to the companies to sell; usually it sold the bonds itself and turned over the money. In the late 1830s the state was turning over about $1 million a year to various companies engaged on approved construction projects. During the 1850s the amounts averaged $2 million a year.

Remarkable results were accomplished under the system. In 1851 the board reported that Virginia possessed 872 miles of "the most capacious and substantially constructed canals in the union," and about 3,000 miles of turnpikes. In 1860 the state owned an interest in twelve canals, ten plank road companies, and fourteen bridge companies. Twenty-five roads had been built entirely from state funds. Virginia also owned an interest in sixteen railroads in 1860. Miles of operation had risen from 147 in 1840 to 1,350 in 1860.

Virginia was by no means alone. Very few states failed to participate in one way or another in the drive for internal improvements. Sometimes the state built and operated a project entirely with state funds, as New York did in the case of the Erie Canal. Indeed, "in no other period of American history has the government been so active in financing and actually promoting, owning and controlling banks and public works, including turnpikes, bridges, canals, and railroads." Pennsylvania, for example, not only invested more than $6 million in some 150 "mixed" corporations, but spent over $100 million on the construction and operation of the Main Line canal and railroad system. By 1860, Massachusetts had invested more than $8 million in eight railroads, and by the same date Missouri had pledged some $23 million for a number of improvement projects. The states raised most of these sums by borrowing, with foreign lenders providing a large proportion of them. State governments could sell their bonds abroad because of the great prestige and strength given American public credit by the rapid payment of the national debt and its final extinction in 1832. "No other country had ever paid off a national debt, and it was felt that there could be little risk in lending money to a people whose resources were so great and whose disposition so frugal."

Thus state governments frequently used the private business corporation as an agency of the state for accomplishing public purposes. In doing so, they continued a practice that began soon after the Revolution. Of course, incorporation itself had been used long before then as a device for giving legal life to public or quasi-public associations. During the colonial period it had been used to establish towns, boroughs, and cities as well as organizations devoted to charitable, educational, and ecclesiastical purposes. But in all those years it had been employed only a half-dozen times for business organizations. In contrast, state governments created more than three hundred business corporations between the end of the Revolution and 1801. A brief examination will disclose their semipublic character.

Fully two thirds of them were established to provide inland navigation, turnpikes, and toll bridges. Thirty-two were empowered to underwrite insurance policies, a need deriving from expansion of the geographic area and the volume of foreign commerce, especially after the outbreak of European war in 1793 opened the commercial world to American neutral vessels, increasing their risks of loss. At the same time, the increased volume of trade gave rise to a need for the short-term credit facilities of commercial banks, with the result that no fewer than thirty-four were incorporated between 1781 and 1801 (twenty-seven of them between 1790 and 1801). Commercial expansion, by increasing the size of urban populations, also increased their needs for other services, so that thirty-two corporations for the supply of water and four for the erection of wharves were created in the six-year interval between 1795 and 1801. The greater need of urban communities for protection against fire losses was reflected in the organization of nearly a dozen mutual companies between 1786 and 1800. Most insurance companies, however, were permitted to underwrite both fire and marine risks.

The experience of Pennsylvania suggests that these early objectives of incorporation continued to predominate in the antebellum period. Of 2,333 business corporations chartered by special act between 1790 and 1860, 64.17 percent were in the field of transport, 11.14 percent in insurance, 7.72 percent in manufacturing, 7.2 percent in banking, 3.21 percent for gas, 2.79 percent for water, and 3.77 percent for miscellaneous categories. It is not difficult to visualize the semipublic character of early manufacturing corporations. Certainly in the troubled years preceding and during the War of 1812, some state governments appear to have adopted the view that the chartering of domestic manufacturing concerns was required by patriotism. Between 1808 and 1815 New York issued more charters (165) to joint-stock companies engaged in manufacturing than to all public utilities combined (164), a phenomenon that appears not to have happened again in any other period before the Civil War. But the larger truth is that, given the strength of the American desire for economic development, the scarcities of capital funds in the early years following independence, and the sharpness of competition from foreign suppliers, manufacturing was endowed with a quasi-public and not a private character, and given numerous encouragements by the state.

It is not only the functions of the corporations but the language of the laws creating them, the powers of government in which they were sometimes clothed, and their subsequent relation to the state that reveals their unmistakable semipublic nature. "Be it enacted by the Senate and House of Representatives in General Court assembled," reads a Massachusetts statute of 1818, that the following named individuals "hereby are constituted a corporation and body politic" for the purpose of erecting a flour mill. As bodies politic, corporations were accorded certain exclusive privileges to encourage the devotion of scarce private capital to public ends. Among these privileges were monopoly rights of way, tax exemption, the right of eminent domain, and the right granted to many nonbanking corporations to engage in banking and to hold lotteries in order to raise needed capital more easily. Many states established state-opened banks or invested in bank stock to provide funds or sources of credit for public enterprises. Sometimes the enterprises were private. Western and Southwestern states issued millions in bonds to provide capital for "property banks" specializing in loans to cotton planters. In Pennsylvania it was legislative practice to include in bank charters a requirement that specified transportation companies be given financial assistance.

Corporate charters also provided for strict regulation by the state, including, for example, detailed specifications relative to the size and power of boards of directors, the liability of officers and stockholders, the nature of capital structures, and operations to be undertaken. In addition, bank charters specified maximum interest rates, dividends were controlled by law, and public utilities were subjected to rate regulation. In this connection it should be noted that the significance of Marshall's decision in the *Dartmouth College case* (1819) is sometimes misapprehended. That decision, holding a corporate charter to be a contract, did not place such charters beyond the control of the state issuing them. The decision did not alter the established practice of including elaborate regulations in original charter acts, and even so far as subsequent regulations were concerned, "the inclusion of reservation clauses in charters and the pursuit of a strict construction policy by the state judicial severely limited the effect of anti-state barrier erected by Marshall."

Before approximately the 1830s and 1840s one general condition provides much of the explanation for the endowing of particular groups with a privileged status before the law. This was a shortage of private stocks of capital, together with a natural disinclination on the part of holders of such supplies as did exist to venture them in enterprises of high risk. Capital scarcities particularly affected needs for transport, where returns on investment were apt to be not only long deferred but to take the diffused form of enhanced land values, increased employment and business opportunities, and other external gains. With the major exception of railroads constructed in the Midwest in the 1850s, neither railroads nor canals, for the most part, were projected as links between settled points. They could not exploit opportunities for gain already in existence but had themselves to create those opportunities by affording ease of movement at reduced costs for people and products. They were "developmental" rather than "exploitative" in character. Public assistance, by lessening risks of loss, helped attract private funds to ventures they might not otherwise have supported.

The dominant role of state governments began to falter two years after the beginning of the Panic of 1837. Overextension, corruption, maladministration, and other factors accentuated a crisis in which five states temporarily defaulted on their interest payments, and one partially repudiated the principal of its debt. A wave of revulsion against state participation in internal improvements swept over the Old Northwest, and between 1842 and 1851 all six of its states bound themselves constitutionally not to make loans to improvements enterprises. In addition, Michigan, Indiana, Ohio, and Iowa also prohibited stock ownership, Maryland, Michigan, and Wisconsin prohibited state works, and Ohio, Michigan, and Illinois abandoned their extensive programs for state construction. Pennsylvania sold part of its state stock in 1843, Tennessee virtually abandoned her improvements program, and in the early 1840s even Virginia somewhat checked hers. The check to state enterprise was to prove only a temporary one, with a second wave of revulsion following in the 1870s, but it was sufficient to induce promoters of improvements projects to turn increasingly to local governments for aid. Their efforts were extraordinarily successful.

Municipal governments participated in improvements projects to an even greater extent than did the states, especially in the decade following the Civil War. No fewer than 2,200 laws passed by thirty-six states between 1830 and 1890 authorized the giving of local aid. In New York, 315 municipalities pledged approximately $37 million toward the construction of the state's roads between 1827 and 1875. Large as were the pre-Civil War commitments of Pennsylvania, state investment at its height was "of minor significance compared with investments by cities and counties." In Missouri during the 1850s it was the cities and counties along the routes of the railroads that bought most of the stocks of the state-aided railroads. In the antebellum South, cities and counties contributed $45,625,512.05 out of total Southern aids of $144,-148,684.92. Baltimore, Cincinnati, Milwaukee, and other cities also made generous contributions, subscribing to stock, purchasing railroad bonds, guaranteeing the credit of railroad companies, and even making donations. By 1879 outright gifts totaled nearly $30 million!

A contemporary historian has observed that "a persistent theme in the nation's economic development" has been "the incorrigible willingness of American public officials to seek the public good through private negotiations." One need add to this rich suggestion only its obverse: the equally incorrigible insistence of private citizens that government encourage or entirely provide those services and utilities either too costly or too risky to attract unaided private capital. It was especially on the undeveloped frontiers of the nation that capital needs and development needs conjoined most pressingly. Social overhead capital, especially in transport, was a frontier need and both a sign of economic development and a prerequisite for further growth. As these frontiers receded, private investment could flow in larger relative proportions into areas properly scoured of risk by community action. Government, therefore, typically played the role of pioneer. Because of wide popular demand that government do so, the roles of political man and private citizen are difficult to distinguish. If, therefore, waste and lack of scruple, political and private, sometimes appeared on stage, and if one also finds such subordinate elements as glib promoters reaching eagerly for public funds or hopeful administrators seeking state investments so profitable that taxes could be reduced, the play itself was in large part written by community consensus.

Once again, expansion of the public domain, increasingly favorable terms on which federal land might be acquired, and improvement in transport facilities all played a part in the settlement of the West. But so too did the lure of high prices for agricultural staples. For example, a rise in the price of wheat in the Philadelphia market from an annual average of $1.63 per bushel (1809–1814) to $1.94 in 1816 and to $2.41 the next year led to a doubling of sales from the public domain north of the Ohio River—geographic boundary between freedom and slavery—between 1815 and 1819. The impact of rising cotton prices on land sales in the South was even more impressive. Selling at an average annual price of 14.25 cents per pound in the New York market during the years 1809–1814, the price of "middling Upland" rose to 21 cents in 1815, then soared to 29.5 cents the next year. Such prices, together with anticipation of still higher ones, induced farmers and planters in Virginia and the Carolinas and other Southern states to abandon overcropped and outworn lands and move West, first to Kentucky and Tennessee, and then to Mississippi Territory. Resulting sales of public lands in Mississippi and Alabama rose from 27,000 acres in 1815 to 2.780 million four years later. Sales west of the Mississippi River also underwent large increases, 1,133,424 acres being sold in Missouri in the single year 1819.

It was cotton that led the Southern wing of the Western movement. Its rise to commercial prominence was a supply response to demand set in motion by the beginnings of the Industrial Revolution in England. Mechanization of the cotton textile industry greatly enlarged the output of yarn and cloth and the demand for the raw cotton essential to the production of that output. In possession of a favorable climate, abundant supplies of cheap and richly productive land, and an expandable plantation labor system with which to work it, the American South needed only the invention of the cotton gin to become the world's largest feeder of the English, and later its own, textile machines. A simple device—a cylinder fitted with wire teeth which drew the seed cotton through a wire screen that separated the seed from the lint, and with a revolving brush that removed the lint from the teeth of the cylinder—Eli Whitney's gin enabled the worker to raise his output of cleaned cotton from a single pound a day to fifty times that amount.

Cotton soon became the leading agricultural staple of an ever-widening portion of the Southern landscape, the tide of cultivation flowing inexorably to the West. By the mid-1820s South Carolina and Georgia began to lose their originally dominant positions, and by the Civil War they accounted for less than a quarter of the nation's output. Mississippi and Alabama had become the leading states, with Louisiana not far behind. New Orleans, the great central market for the cotton of the Western region, had received only 37,000 bales in 1816, but by 1822 the number had risen to 161,000, then to 428,000 in 1830 and 923,000 bales in 1840. Expressed in terms of changing proportions, the states and territories from Alabama and Tennessee westward increased their share of the nation's total output from one sixteenth in 1811, to one third in 1820, one half before 1830, and nearly two thirds in 1840. In 1791, cotton produced in the United States represented less than one half of 1 percent of world output. By 1840, 62.6 percent, nearly two out of every three bales produced in the world, originated in this country.

The producers, as everybody knows, were black men and women held in the bondage of chattel slavery. With regard to slaveholding, however, there are a number of popular misconceptions. When we look away to Dixieland, we are apt to see only vast plantations in which hundreds of slaves toiled "from day clean to first dark." To be sure, the large plantation is an essential part of the picture, but the part must not be mistaken for the whole. In 1860 there were in the South 1.516 million free white families, of whom only 385,000 were owners of slaves. Nearly three fourths of all free Southern families owned no slaves at all. The typical white Southerner was not only a small farmer but also a nonslaveholder. A large majority of the slave-owning families, moreover, owned only a few slaves. In 1850, as Table 3 reveals, 89 percent of the owners held fewer than twenty slaves, 71 percent, fewer than ten, and almost 50 percent, fewer than five. If we accept the usual definition of a planter as a man who owned at least twenty slaves, these proportions make it clear not only that the typical slave-holder was not a planter, but also that the typical planter worked only a moderate-sized gang of from twenty to fifty slaves. The planter aristocracy was made up of some 10,000 families living off the labor of gangs of more than fifty slaves. Yet it was on the large agricultural units that most of the slaves were to be found. Owner-ship was so highly concentrated that only one fourth of the slaves belonged to masters holding fewer than ten, considerably more than half lived on plantations holding more than twenty, and approximately a quarter belonged to masters owning more than fifty.

As is suggested by the fact that a large majority of the owners held only a few slaves, cotton was the crop of the little man as well as the big. Indeed, its cultivation required no slave labor at all, and

Table 3. Percentage Distribution of Slaveholding Families According to Number of Slaves Held, 1790 and 1850

Number of Slaves	Percentage of Families	
	1790	1850
1	24.5	17.4
2 and under 5	30.5	29.5
5 and under 10	22.0	24.4
10 and under 20	14.3	17.4
20 and under 50	6.4	9.1
50 and under 100	1.0	1.7
100 and under 200	0.2	0.4
200 and under 300	a	a
300 and over	a	
Unknown	1.0	

a = Less than one tenth of 1 percent.
Source: Compendium of the Seventh Census (Washington, D.C.: A. O. P. Nicholson, Public Printer, 1854), Table XC, p. 95.

it was accordingly grown on small-sized farms as well as on plantations. Unlike rice and sugarcane, which required large investments of capital for processing machinery, cotton was cheap to
grow. A small farmer could cultivate it with the assistance of his
wife and children, and he had little trouble getting it ginned and
prepared for market. As a rule, the value of cotton in relation to
its bulk was sufficiently high to bear the costs of transport over
considerable distances without jeopardizing the chance of profit.
Cotton stood abuse much better than many other farm commodities; it was nonperishable and hence suffered relatively little from
rough handling, exposure, long delays, and poor warehousing
while in transit to market. Smaller agricultural units were thus
enabled to make some contribution to each year's crop. Nevertheless, the great bulk of the crop came from the plantations, where
most of the slaves were concentrated.

Modes of operation and management, which varied with the
size of the agricultural units, may well have been more efficient
on large plantations. On small farms—the great majority of the
units in the South—masters usually gave close personal supervision to the unspecialized labor of a few slaves. Many were obliged
to work in the fields alongside their hands, although those owning
as few as a half dozen slaves sought a more elevated social status
by refraining from such labor. Small slave forces lacked skilled
craftsmen, and their masters found it necessary to repair tools, do
carpentry work, and perform other specialized tasks. At picking
time in the fall the master usually supplemented his small force
with his own labor.

Substantial farmers and small planters who owned from ten
to thirty slaves normally lived on their own land and devoted full
time to the management of their enterprise. They did not as a rule
employ overseers, although they might have the aid of a slave
foreman or driver, whose essential function was to urge on the
slave gangs by word or whip. Agricultural units of this size usually
benefited from some labor specialization. Besides the field hands

and driver, a few slaves might exercise manual skills or perform domestic work. Even so, the unit was too small for full-time carpenters or cooks, so that the latter often had to work in the fields as well.

Maximum specialization was possible for those planters who owned thirty or more slaves, although no more than one third of them used overseers. The latter were generally retained on a year-to-year basis under a written contract that could be terminated at will by either party, and as a rule each overseer made use of one or more drivers in working the slave gang. The "gang system" was one of two basic methods of labor management. Under the other—the less frequently used "task system"—each hand was given a specific daily assignment and could quit work when the task was completed. The planter who hired a full-time overseer was able to devote his own attention to problems of marketing, finance, and general plantation administration. He also enjoyed sufficient leisure to be able to absent himself from his plantation more or less at his own discretion. But absentee ownership was not characteristic of plantations of any size.

Plantations containing thirty or more slaves enjoyed a considerable degree of labor specialization. Household servants and field hands were clearly distinguished from each other, and the latter were divided between plow gangs and hoe gangs. On the larger plantations slaves were able to devote their full time to such occupations as ditching, tending livestock, driving wagons, and taking care of vegetable gardens. In 1854 one Virginia planter had eight plowmen, ten hoe hands, two wagoners, four oxcart drivers, a carriage driver, a hostler, a stable boy, a shepherd, a cowherd, a swineherd, two carpenters, five masons, two smiths, a miller, two shoemakers, five spinners, a weaver, a butler, two waitresses, four maids, a nurse, a laundress, a seamstress, a dairymaid, a gardener, and two cooks attached to the field service. The owner of a very large establishment employed a general manager or steward to help him run the estate. If several plantations were involved, he might run one himself, but as a rule he hired an overseer for each of them.

Regardless of the size of his plantation, no planter put all of his resources into cotton. He had good reason not to. Labor demand, which peaked at the time of the cotton harvest in the fall, was far more slack in other seasons. Putting the slave to work growing corn, beans, and sweet potatoes and raising pigs into hogs not only saved expenditures on outside food supplies but kept the labor force more fully employed in off-seasons than otherwise it would have been. And since land was cheap and rental demand for slaves thin, planters could grow corn without reducing cotton capacity, that is, at little real cost in terms of opportunities forgone. In sum, a substantial corn crop was not inconsistent with the largest cotton crop. On the whole, while the antebellum South specialized in cotton, it was also self-sufficient with respect to its human and animal requirements for food. Far from being dependent on external sources, Southern cotton farms were in a position to supply food to outsiders on an impressive scale.

The cotton sales of the typical planter, sometimes combined with income from sales or rentals of his slaves, brought profits to the individual and a calculated rate of growth in the per capita incomes of the region between 1840 and 1860 that exceeded the national average—even if the slaves are included in the population count. Yet these results are misleading, not least because the growth in world demand for cotton, which provided the fundamental underpinning for most of the income growth, was essentially a temporary phenomenon.

World demand had grown at the rate of 5 percent a year between 1830 and 1860, but in the 1860s it collapsed catastrophically. Output of the British textile industry began to decline in the early 1860s, and cotton demand had barely recovered its 1860 peak by the late 1870s. Between 1866 and 1895 demand ran at an enfeebled rate of less than 1½ percent per year. Measured from the peak year, the growth in demand was little more than 1 percent per year to the turn of the century.

What this means is that the economy of the prewar South was hitched to a falling star. The high prices of cotton and slaves in the late 1850s would almost certainly have declined drastically even if the Civil War had not occurred, dragging down land values and the profits of the planters with them. Ulrich B. Phillips was surely right when he called attention in the following words to the implications of the overpricing of slaves by the close of the fifties:

> Indeed the peak of this [slave] price movement was evidently cut off by the intervention of war. How great an altitude it might have reached, and what shape its downward slope would have taken had peace continued, it is idle to conjecture. But that a crash must have come is beyond a reasonable doubt.

And there would have been no early recovery.

Does this impending long-term collapse in values imply that the Civil War was an unnecessary war, that the institution of slavery would have fallen of its own economic deadweight had the politicians of the 1850s found ways of avoiding headlong confrontation? No one can say for sure, but it is doubtful this would have happened. The planters would have had to make severe, even cruel, adjustments in their living styles and material satisfactions. But it is arguable that they would have made an effort to hold on indefinitely to an institution bringing them other kinds of satisfactions. Eugene Genovese calls attention to deeper truths when he depicts the plantation system and slave-master relationship not so much as a way of organizing labor, investing wealth, or managing race relations as the basis for a regional social order and special way of life. Ownership of slaves imbued the master class with a "special set of values and interests incapable of being compromised." The master's "slaveholding psychology, habit of command, race pride, rural lordship, aristocratic pretensions, political domination, and economic strength militated in defense of the status quo." The weakening of the element of economic strength would have frayed most of the other categories, but one believes it would also have concentrated Southern energies more fully on the necessity for economic diversification—upon manufacturing, and not merely upon the growing of foodstuffs and export staples. After all, it was the *dependence* of the South on an ever-rising long-term demand curve for its major crop that made for the impermanence of its economic situation.

This is not to say that manufacturing and its concomitant, urbanization, were entirely absent from the antebellum South. They were not, but as Tables 4-a and 4-b make clear, they were present on a much smaller scale than in the North. The per capita value of the manufactures in New England in 1860 was nearly eight times that of the South. And whereas in the former region every third person lived in a city, fewer than one in ten did so in the South. The principle of comparative advantage heads the list of explanations offered for these contrasts: The South concentrated its resources on cotton because the region's total command of goods and services was greater than otherwise it would have been. But although it is true that the South's terms of trade improved during the years before the war—its consumption potential expanding more rapidly than its production—the existence of slavery was probably more fundamental. The use of rented slaves in Southern urban manufacturing was bitterly opposed by white artisans, tradesmen, and even unskilled workers who stood to lose economically by the presence of close substitutes. Not only did slaves tend to depress wages; they were also commonly used as strike breakers. Urban slavery therefore goes far to account for the low level of immigration of free white workers into Southern cities. Slave owners also had interests at odds with greater free labor immigration. Any increase in Southern labor might conceivably lower slave property values. More importantly, those values might be threatened by an influx of nonslaveholding outsiders whose antislavery political views might jeopardize the region's strength and unity in national politics.

Table 4-a. Manufacturing Investment and Output ($/capita)

Region	Manufacturing Capital		Manufacturing Value	
	1850	1860	1850	1860
New England	57.96	82.15	100.71	149.47
Middle States	33.50	52.21	71.24	96.28
South	7.60	10.54	10.88	17.09
Cotton South	5.11	7.20	6.83	10.47
United States	22.73	32.12	43.69	59.98

Source: 8th and 9th Census of Manufacturers, cited in Gavin Wright, *The Political Economy of the Cotton South* (New York: W. W. Norton, 1978), p. 110.

Table 4-b. Percentage of Population Living in Urban Areas

Region	1820	1830	1840	1850	1860
New England	10.5	14.0	19.4	28.8	36.6
Mid-Atlantic	11.3	14.2	18.1	25.5	35.4
East North Central	1.2	2.5	3.9	9.0	14.1
West North Central	—	3.5	3.9	10.3	13.4
South	5.5	6.2	7.7	9.8	11.5
East South Central	0.8	1.5	2.1	4.2	5.9

Source: Douglass North, *The Economic Growth of the United States*, 1790–1860 (Englewood Cliffs, N.J.: Prentice-Hall, 1961), p. 258.

Despite the opposition to slave workers on the part of white artisans, demand for them rose in most Southern cities in the 1850s. The supply response, however, fell short: Slaves were pulled out of the cities by strong agricultural demand rather than pushed out by disruption and fear. The urban demand for slaves was much more price elastic (price sensitive) than the rural demand: A small increase in rates for hiring slaves induced urban employers to switch to free workers. But because free labor was unwilling to work in gangs in the cotton fields, slave labor was unique in the rural sector and had no close substitutes. In short, it was the cotton boom of the 1850s that resulted in the pulling of urban slaves back into the countryside because of the impact of increasing demand for cotton and slaves on slave rental prices.

Slavery, in sum, was hostile to the growth of a labor supply in Southern manufacturing. But if enough slaveholders had had an incentive to encourage a more diversified development of their region—and of course some did—efforts to obtain labor-saving machinery would have been systematically made. At bottom, then, satisfactory returns from investments in slaves, together with fear of the disruptive influence of development on a highly valued way of life, stayed the regional hand. Lacking in a vigorous urban-industrial sector, the South was also deficient in its supply of innovation and native entrepreneurship. Its businessmen in the Atlantic and Gulf ports were either seasonal sojourners from the North and from Europe, or local agents of distant mercantile houses, which provided the shipping and financial services required by the cotton trade. In sum, it was outsiders who organized the exports to Liverpool or Boston, gave the planters credit in the form of advances on those shipments, and supplied the vessels to carry them. The South was a semicolonial appanage of England and the North, and the penalties for its undernourished development were to be severe, not only in imminent Civil War but also in its long aftermath. Long before a twentieth-century President declared it to be so, the South was the nation's number one economic problem.

While mainly a phenomenon of New England and the Middle States, manufacturing encountered early obstacles even there. When the Embargo and subsequent interruptions to international trade dimmed the "brilliant prospects" in commerce to which Adam Seybert referred, former merchants like Francis Cabot Lowell of Boston transferred their investments to textile and other industries. In 1813 Lowell joined with associates to incorporate a major cotton textile manufacturing enterprise, the Boston Manufacturing Company. Located at Waltham, Massachusetts, it built the first modern factory in the United States. And unlike numerous textile and other manufacturing firms, which had briefly flourished behind the protective wall afforded by embargo, nonintercourse, and war, it prospered and grew. Returning postwar competition from more experienced British manufacturers with lower production costs snuffed out most of the others.

The 1820s begin the telling of a different story, one whose principal theme—accelerating industrialization—continues to develop in the North in every decade before the Civil War and after the war as well. By 1830 the age-old system of home manufacturing was almost gone: wearing apparel for the family's own use, soap, candles, leather, maple sugar, and a wide variety of other such products. Shops and factories took its place. A number of manufacturing industries grew in the 1820s at decade rates far greater than the 35 percent increase in population. The number of spindles in operation in cotton textile mills, merely 191,000 in 1820, rose to nearly 1.25 million by 1831. In New England alone the output of cotton cloth increased from less than 4 million yards in 1817 to 323 million in 1840. And as in cotton textiles, so also in the production of woolen goods, carpets, paper, flint glass, lead, sugar and molasses, salt, iron, and steam engines. Between 1809 and 1839 manufacturing output climbed an average 59 percent per decade, soaring 154 percent in the 1840s before settling back to a more modest 60 percent in the 1850s. By 1860, the American manufacturing sector ranked second or third among the nations of the world. Making end products by putting together standardized interchangeable parts, and employing automatic machinery mainly driven by waterpower (but also to some extent by steam), factories were by then becoming important in practically every industrial field, including the manufacture of firearms, agricultural implements, sewing machines, and clocks and watches. The stage was set for their phenomenal expansion in the postwar years.

Surprisingly, prewar manufacturing industry was not, in general, capital-intensive. Analysis of information on Northeastern manufacturing firms collected by the Treasury Department in

1832 (the McLane report) shows that working capital—inventories and accounts receivable (credit extended to customers)—attracted a substantial share of the investments made by manufacturing firms. In only a few industries—cotton and woolen textiles and paper manufacturing—did fixed-capital shares heavily outweigh working capital, and only in cotton textiles was the capital invested in machinery and taxes a large fraction (nearly 30 percent) of total investment. In all other industries the value of the buildings, land, and fixtures far outweighed that of machinery and tools.

More generally, and even more surprisingly, industrialization did not increase the ratio between the value of capital and that of output (the capital–output ratio). Even early in the century the percentage of net national product devoted to capital formation was already high—between 6.2 and 7 percent in the years 1805–1840—and while this percentage rose to 12.1 percent between 1849 and 1858 (thus nearly doubling over the final decade before the war), the capital–output ratio performed much more modestly, increasing from 1.625 to 1 in 1840 to only 1.8 to 1 a decade later (figures for 1860 are unavailable). Once again, industrial output during these years of early modernization rose at a more rapid pace than did the fraction of real net national product devoted to investment in manufacturing capital. The capital–output ratios in heavy industries were not generally higher than those in the light industries. Capital deepening in American manufacturing that required masses of investment was a phenomenon of the decades following the Civil War.

One consequence was the ability of partnerships and single proprietorships to raise most of the capital sums needed by antebellum industry. Incorporation did undergo a significant expansion in the final decades before the war, however, and its growth then and after the war owed much to the Supreme Court presided over by Chief Justice Roger B. Taney. Rising hostility to the state marks the closing years of the prewar period, and while some of the suspicion and animosity is explicable in terms of economic depression (between 1837 and 1843) and defalcation on government bonds issued to finance internal improvements, the new attitude had a more basic source. As supplies of capital accumulated, new groups rose to challenge the privileged positions of vested corporations in possession of exclusive rights entrenched in law. Again and again the note of egalitarianism is struck in the discourse of the time and by no one more clearly than Taney.

Taney took his stand on the premise that the interests of the community override all special interests. To promote those interests, the state chartered corporations and gave them "peculiar privileges." But the gift must be carefully scrutinized to make sure that public interest really justified those privileges. And charter grants must be narrowly construed thereafter to prevent vested property rights from interfering with the right of the state to create additional corporations in the public interest. "Corporate egalitarianism" is the phrase which seems to describe best Taney's ideal of publicly sponsored free competition in the interest of community welfare. His essential contribution was so to adjust constitutional law to the needs of the corporation as greatly to stimulate its use in business.

Taney gave clear expression to his corporate egalitarianism even before his appointment as Chief Justice of the Supreme Court in 1836. A former director on the boards of Maryland banks, he spoke from knowledge when he declared: "There is perhaps no business which yields a profit so certain and liberal as the business of banking and exchange; and it is proper that it should be open, as far as practicable, to the most free competition and its advantages shared by all classes of Society." Believing that Nicholas Biddle's Bank of the United States restrained free enterprise in banking, he played, as Jackson's Secretary of the Treasury, a well-known key role in the "war" against that institution. While it is impossible to impute the subsequent increase in the number of state-chartered banks alone to the Jacksonian victory over the

Second Bank, that event does help explain why the number of banks rose from 506 in 1834 (the year in which federal deposits ceased to be made in the Second Bank) to 901 in 1840.

In one of his first statements as Chief Justice, an analysis written in June 1836 of an act providing for the rechartering of the banks in the District of Columbia, Taney vigorously stated his conviction that the power of the state must not be used to grant special privileges to any corporate group except for the purpose of promoting the public interest.

> Every charter granted by a state or by the United States, to a bank or to any other company for the purpose of trade or manufacture, is a grant of peculiar privileges, and gives to the individuals who compose the corporation, rights and privileges which are not possessed by other members of the community. It would be against the spirit of our free institutions, by which equal rights are intended to be secured to all, to grant peculiar franchises and privileges to a body of individuals merely for the purpose of enabling them more conveniently and effectually to advance their own private interests. No charter could rightfully be granted on that ground. The consideration upon which alone, such peculiar privileges can be granted is the expectation and prospect of promoting thereby some public interest, and it follows from these principles that in every case where it is proposed to grant or to renew a charter the interests or wishes of the individuals who desire to be incorporated, ought not to influence the decision of the government. The only inquiry which the constituted authorities can properly make on such an application, is whether the charter applied for is likely to produce any real benefit to the community, and whether that benefit is sufficient to justify the grant.

These principles inform Taney's decision in the *Charles River Bridge case* (1837), wherein he refused to uphold the claim that the bridge company's charter of incorporation gave it exclusive, monopolistic rights by implication. Were this precedent established, modern improvements would be at the mercy of old corporations. The country would "be thrown back to the improvements of the last century, and obliged to stand still, until the claims of the old turnpike corporations shall be satisfied; and they shall consent to permit these states to avail themselves of the lights of modern science, and to partake of the benefit of those improvements which are now adding to the wealth and prosperity, and the convenience and comfort, of every other part of the civilized world." The effect of Taney's decision was to free new businesses from the fear of monopolistic claims on the part of older corporations with ambiguously worded charters. In 1851 he applied the same principle to railroads in *Richmond Railroad* v. *Louisa Railroad* and served the public interest by opening another area of enterprise to free competition.

Other decisions of the Taney Court also stimulated corporate development. In *Bank of Augusta* v. *Earle* (1839) he held that a corporation might do business via its agents in states other than the one from which it had received its charter, provided those states permitted it to do so. In *Louisville, Cincinnati, and Charleston R.R. Co.* v. *Letson* (1844) the Taney Court extended to corporations the legal fiction of citizenship, thus assuring them the protection of federal judicial review of assaults upon them by the states. In *Briscoe* v. *The Bank of the Commonwealth of Kentucky* (1837), the Court upheld the constitutionality of banknotes. Finally, to abbreviate the list of instances that might be cited, in *Woodruff* v. *Trapnall* (1851), and *Curran* v. *Arkansas* (1853), Taney opposed attempts of banks or states to circumvent their legal obligations, thus increasing men's sense of security in transactions involving corporations and their instrumentalities.

Not only corporations but partnerships and proprietorships as well looked to the legal system for the adjudication and enforcement of claims and obligations arising out of contracts, bills of exchange, promissory notes, agency relationships, and other elements of private business transactions. Had not the law responded to the businessman's need for predictability in these matters, the development of national markets would surely have been obstructed. The problem was this: While rules for the settlement of claims and obligations had long been features of mercantile practice, and indeed had been incorporated in part in the common law, their interpretation by the courts varied from one state to another. What was required was uniformity, and this the Supreme Court provided in 1842. In *Swift* v. *Tyson* the Court established the principle that, in private suits arising between citizens of different states, federal judges possessed the power to determine what common law rule should decide the case—regardless of state law. The doctrine laid down in *Swift* remained the law of the land until 1938 and supplied the basis for "an enlarged national jurisprudence that was virtually a body of federal common law."

In sum, judicial interpretation at the federal level, together with state governments and their corporate agents, played major roles in the marshaling of the resources required by the developing economy. The importance of the federal judiciary is deserving of emphasis. In the earlier years of the century, the rulings of the Marshall Court had fallen on the side of vested property rights. A vehement absolutist with respect to contractual obligations, Marshall moved well beyond the intent of the Founding Fathers to confine contract impairment to private engagements. A legislative grant of land is an executory contract, he stated in his majority opinion in *Fletcher* v. *Peck* (1810), and it cannot be impaired by the rescinding act of a subsequent legislature. A corporate charter granted to individuals by government is also a contract, he ruled in the *Dartmouth College case* (1819), and its terms cannot be impaired by later legislation. Marshall was so adamant on the obligation to honor one's agreements that in *Ogden* v. *Saunders* (1827), as we have seen, he argued in dissent that not only state bankruptcy laws freeing debtors from contractual obligations assumed *before* the enactment of those laws but even laws releasing debtors from contracts entered into *after* their passage ought to be held unconstitutional.

It is unquestionably true, as Associate Justice Joseph Story wrote after the death of Marshall, that his revered master's doctrine was essential if individuals, rather than governments, were to be expected to provide capital for society in the form of roads, bridges, and other structures. The difficulty was that the same doctrine that secured investment from impairment by state legislatures also tended to preserve the status quo—unless the charter grant reserved to the legislature the right to change its terms. The preservation of attractive privileges, even of monopoly rights, was justifiable when savings were limited and the risk of loss a pronounced one, for otherwise private individuals would not have been willing to invest their money, and government would have been forced to resort to taxation, then as now a highly unpopular alternative, to raise the funds required. But while we have no figures to prove it, savings per capita were surely far more abundant by the time of Taney than they had been in the later colonial years. And the people doing the saving were far more numerous than earlier wealth holders. They had increased in numbers and affluence not only with the opening of opportunities in trade, privateering, and land speculation during the Revolution, but probably even more largely by those created during the wars of the French Revolution and Napoleon (1793–1815) and, after their conclusion, by those in banking, early industrialization, and agriculture, especially the growing of cotton. By the mid-1830s they were beating on the doors of legal privilege and demanding equal investment opportunity before the law.

Legal historian Morton Horwitz believes that "The *Charles River Bridge case* represented the last great contest in America between two different models of economic development. For . . . Justice Story of the Supreme Court, the essential elements for economic progress were certainty of expectations and predictability of legal consequences." The other model, that of the Taney Court majority, was that of a public policy promotive of free, fair, and open competition. There is another possible view of the matter, however, and that is that the contest was not between two different models of economic development at all, but rather between a model of development and an effort on the part of an older elite to hold back the forces making for change in the interest of preserving its place in a more stable society.

This older elite of original investors wanted the legal system to protect its exclusive monopoly rights to income from public utilities, and they maintained that, where exclusivity was not granted explicitly by the corporate charter, it was at least implied. Taney, on the other hand, wanted to apply brakes to exclusivity, to prevent it from running over and crushing competition. Once again, exclusivity was essential in earlier years if infrastructure (for example, canals, roads, and bridges) was to be provided by private investment rather than by the tax system. Now that population growth and increase in its urban density had made investment in bridge and other public utilities potentially profitable, the dead hand of an older elite must be struck off. Whenever the grant of monopoly was not explicit, this could be done by denying the validity of a grant that was merely implied. Where it *was* explicit, the government could use its power of eminent domain—the power to take private property (in the case of the Charles River Bridge, property in the form of tolls)—and to accord a just compensation to the proprietors for the taking.

The Taney Court provided the legal foundation for a democratized capitalism. Not only did it rule in favor of new and innovative investment while preserving the property rights of original investors, it also elaborated a constitutional basis on which the corporation as "citizen" could not only sue in federal court but also have standing in contract cases, rulings which paved the way for wider use of that increasingly essential mechanism for raising capital. State legislation would not be permitted to protect local business interests from outside competition by barring the activities of corporations chartered in other states. The battle against state protectionist policies was not a new one, nor would it end with the decisions of the Taney Court. Later in the century, as we shall see,

Justice Stephen J. Field would continue the judicial effort to keep uncluttered the channels of activity essential to the development of a national market whose geographic bounds paralleled the territorial limits of the United States.

IV

Beckoning Frontiers

T HE one economic fact that towers high above all others during the half century between the Civil War and the first World War is that Americans were able to achieve population growth and economic growth at the same time. This was an achievement rare in history, for as the Rev. Thomas Malthus explained in his famous *Essay on Population,* increases in the resources available to humankind from a series of good harvests or some other source are almost always followed by increases in marriages and births and the disappearance of the surplus. Certainly the American experience was not one to be seen in much of the rest of the world at the time. As the number of births went up in China and India and in most of the countries of Asia, Africa, Central America, and the Middle East, so too did the number of deaths from starvation and disease. In the United States, in contrast, while population more than doubled, rising from just under 40 million in 1870 to nearly 92 million in 1910, real per capita income, growing at an annual rate of 2.1 percent, nearly tripled.

How was this accomplished? What were the sources of the increases in the productivity of laboring men and women which made the growth possible? Did the growth entail hidden costs— paid by those same working men and women (and their children) and by immigrants, as distinguished from natives? We shall address these important questions as we go along, but first let us inquire into the sources of the population growth itself and trace the movement of the people over the continent and into the cities and onto the farms and ranches of the West.

A population increases when birth rates exceed death rates and when immigrants outnumber those who leave the country. Natural increase proved much the larger source of growth during these years, the annual birth rate averaging 34.7 per thousand and the death rate 20. The difference between the two, 14.7 per thousand, was more than twice as great as the contribution of 5.8 per thousand made by net immigration.

Little is presently understood about the factors underlying fertility and mortality in this period. The time patterns of declining birth rates, for example, vary from one country to another, and this makes it difficult to find an explanation that is both simple and universally applicable. We do know that both rates continued their historic declines, the birth rate falling from an annual average of 40.8 per thousand during 1870–1875 to 29.6 for the years 1905–1910. Presumably increasing urbanization and rising per capita incomes played important parts in this result. Certainly numbers of children under five years of age per 1,000 women twenty to forty-four years old have been larger in rural than in urban areas throughout the nation since at least 1800, and probably long before. Indeed, the fertility ratio of native white women living in rural areas was twice that of their urban counterparts between 1885 and 1909. There may well exist an inverse relationship between population density and fertility that would help explain these results, but the conditions under which the association appears have not yet been sufficiently explored to warrant generalization.

Rising incomes and standards of health care undoubtedly contributed to a decline in the death rate from 21.8 per thousand in 1870 to 16.6 per thousand in 1910. Approved medical and basic science schools increased in number during these years, from sev-

enty-five to 131, their graduates rising fivefold from 8,000 to 40,-
000. Professional nursing schools numbered fifteen in 1880 and
1,129 in 1910, their graduates rising from a mere 157 to 8,140. The
incidence of infectious disease declined, not only because rising
incomes improved housing conditions and diets but also because
of new public health measures adopted by the cities, especially the
installation of sanitary sewers and the provision of central supplies
of pure water. The discovery in the 1880s that several diseases
were water-borne led many cities to filter their water supplies. In
1875 fewer than 30,000 city dwellers had filtered water, but by
1910 over 10 million enjoyed it. In 1880, most American cities
lacked sanitary sewers, but by 1907 nearly all had them.

In consequence, life expectancy of urban males at birth rose
dramatically between 1880 and 1910, for example, from thirty-
seven to forty-six years in Boston and from twenty-nine to forty-
five years in New York City. The good luck of being born in rural
America, though, increased one's life expectancy at birth by ten
years. The bad luck of being born nonwhite meant a life expectancy sixteen years shorter than that of whites.

Whites predominated overwhelmingly, constituting 88 percent of the population in 1890, 55 percent of them being natives,
the rest either immigrants or the first generation of their descend-
ants. Rising wages and declining unemployment attracted a stun-
ning total of nearly 20 million immigrants to the United States
between 1870 and 1910. As before, Europeans predominated,
especially Germans, Englishmen, and Irishmen, and Scandinavi-
ans were numerous throughout. However, other nationalities
made significant contributions in particular years, for example,
Canadians in 1880–1883, Chinese in 1873, 1876, and 1882, and,
between 1890 and 1910, Russians, Italians, and others from eastern and southern Europe.

While thousands of the immigrants settled on farms in Minnesota, Wisconsin, and elsewhere, no less than 61 percent of net
foreign-born migration between 1870 and 1910 increased the

populations of Massachusetts, New York, New Jersey, Pennsylvania, Ohio, Illinois, and Michigan, the area of major industrial and commercial concentration in the United States. An even larger percentage, 71 percent, chose the states of the Northeast. Except for an upsurge of migration to California between 1900 and 1910, foreign-born movement to the West was numerically unimpressive, and to the relatively unurbanized South, least of all. The censuses for 1890, 1900, and 1910 show peoples of foreign white stock making up more than half the urban population of the United States.

Immigrants imparted momentum to the process of urbanization, but they did not initiate it. From the beginning of the United States as an independent nation, the urban population had increased at a higher rate than either the rural or total population—except for the decade 1810–1820. It was not till the 1860s, however, that the absolute number of persons added to the urban segment exceeded additions to those choosing the countryside. Thereafter, except for the years 1870–1880, it was invariably greater. Cities, defined by the Census as incorporated places of 2,500 or more inhabitants, increased in both number and size. While those in most class sizes tripled and quadrupled in number, people living in rural areas continued to form a precarious majority, one that dwindled from 74.3 percent to 54.3 percent between 1870 and 1910.

The Northeast was the most highly urbanized of the major regions, its urban proportion rising from 50 percent in 1880 to 71 percent twenty years later. Massachusetts and Rhode Island were 50 percent urban as early as 1850. New York became so by 1870, New Jersey by 1880, and Connecticut by 1890. While the growth of cities was relatively slow in the South, in both the North Central and Western regions, urbanization was approaching the 50 percent mark by 1910. In the former, it was the industrial states of the Middle West, especially Ohio, Illinois, and Michigan that conferred an urban character upon the region as a whole. In the West, it was the Pacific states, especially California, that urbanized most rapidly. Already in 1870 the population of that state was 37.2 percent urban; by 1910 the proportion reached 61.8 percent, and in Oregon and Washington the figures were 45.6 percent and 53 percent, respectively. The Western movement increased both the urban and rural population of the region but the growth of cities far outstripped that of rural areas. Above all, it was the rise of manufacturing that spurred the growth of cities. Industrial development, rather than mere commercial expansion, had played a primary role in urbanization since the early nineteenth century. Thereafter, the spatial redistribution of the population increasingly nationalized the process.

People fed the cities but rural America fed the people—and their machines. Above all, it was the vast Western reaches of the continent upon which Americans continually drew for the renewal of their rural resources.

On the eve of the Civil War, the frontier along the farms of the Western prairies had followed an irregular line of settlement falling between St. Paul and Fort Worth. Between that line and other settlements on the Pacific coast lay half of the continental domain, a vast area of nearly 1.25 billion acres of land awaiting exploitation, containing merely 1 percent of the nation's population. Some of this land was rich in minerals, notably in gold and silver, and over most of the Far West prospectors and miners pioneered innumerable pockets of settlement, many of them as ephemeral as the metallic mirages that drew them on.

Between the Rocky Mountains and a transition zone in the vicinity of the 100th meridian lay the Great Plains, stretching 1,300 miles from Canada to Texas and varying in width from 200 to 700 miles. Although it did contain islands of timber on the mountain tops in Colorado, Wyoming and elsewhere, this vast flat region was in the main a treeless area with a subhumid or arid climate. Home of the prairie dog, jackrabbit, coyote, and above all, the buffalo or American bison, the rich grasslands of the Plains supplied the physical basis for the rise of the Cattle Kingdom. Although the Great West was potentially rich agriculturally, only in Minnesota, Kansas, Texas, and California had any substantial number of farms been established on the eve of the Civil War. These states had respectively 18,181, 10,400, 42,891, and 18,710 farms. In all the rest of the West one found only 19,098 farms, containing a mere 7,437,819 improved acres out of a total of more than 1 billion acres. The story of these developing frontiers throws much light on the ways in which new slabs of resources essential to economic growth were made available to the American people.

Aside from explorers, hunters, and trappers who had been crossing the Far West for decades, it was prospectors and miners who pioneered the distant reaches of Cordilleran America. Colorado lay 600 or 700 miles from the Missouri frontier, California 2,000, with the intervening Great Plains essentially untenanted prior to the completion of the Pacific Railroad in 1869. The first of the mining frontiers opened in the Sierra Nevada region of northern California following the discovery of gold at Sutters Mill in 1848, with silver mining in Colorado and Nevada defining new frontiers for a number of years beginning in 1859. Then, in the 1870s came surges of population into Arizona and New Mexico and into the Black Hills of South Dakota. In consequence, California's population, excluding Indians, expanded from an estimated 14,000 in 1848 to 380,000 by 1860, while that of Colorado grew from 40,000 in 1870 to 194,000 a decade later. By no means had all these people come in search of precious metals. The Census of 1870 found only 36,339 miners in California and only 8,241 in Nevada. Most settlers formed parts of a service community called into being by the needs of the miners—storekeepers, innkeepers, saloonkeepers, traders, teamsters, bankers, and farmers, among others—not to mention gamblers and other desperate men. It was the output of precious metals that sustained them and diffused mineral wealth that raised per capita incomes in the Mountain states to the second highest level among the nation's regions in 1880.

If controversial estimates of output are to be believed, the gold mines of California yielded an astounding total of $81,294,-700 in 1852, and nearly $70 million in each of the next two years. After that the trend was steadily downward. For nearly twenty years after 1865, California produced between $15 million and $20 million a year, with output never falling below $11.2 million in any year in the remainder of the century. Silver and gold from Nevada's famed Comstock Lode proved far more valuable, the yield of sixty principal mines amounting to the huge total of $292,-726,310 between 1859 and 1882.

California's gold and Nevada's silver and gold are perhaps the most famous of the mining frontiers of the Far West, but they were not the only ones. Contemporaneously or later, silver, and later copper and zinc were found in Colorado—and, in the twentieth century, deposits of molybdenum, vanadium, tungsten, and uranium—gold and silver in Idaho and Montana, gold and lead in Utah, gold, silver, and copper in Arizona, gold and copper in New Mexico, and gold in the Black Hills of South Dakota. New mining frontiers opened in both the Northwest and Southwest between 1860 and 1880. What were the consequences of these developments? Some were local, others regional and national. Numbers of mining camps and towns sprang into life, attracting crowds of lawyers, small tradesmen, and mechanics besides encouraging hotels, restaurants, brothels, and hurdy-gurdy houses, only to decline and die off with the petering out of deposits that could be mined with the available technology, or yields that were economically infeasible in the face of discouraging trends in world silver prices. Regional service towns and cities fared better than the ghost towns and camps because their tributaries of supply and demand were larger and more diversified.

San Francisco became the Queen City of the California gold region almost from the beginning, "the great port where goods from the outside world were landed, bought and sold by merchants, and then loaded onto steamboats or small sailboats for carriage up the Sacramento and San Joaquin rivers to the principal commercial centers of the great interior valley."

Food, clothing, hardware, mining supplies, heavy mining equipment, whiskey, books, and newspapers were among common items dispatched to such leading interior distributing points as Sacramento, Stockton, and Marysville. From the latter, supplies were hauled by pack trains and wagons to the larger mining towns or to the hundreds of ephemeral camps. Under the stimulus of this trade San Francisco flourished, expanding from a population of fewer than a thousand in 1848 to 56,802 in 1860. The opening of the Comstock Lode refreshed the boom by opening a huge new market for the iron foundries and machine shops of the Queen City. Demand for mining machinery made San Francisco into an industrial town, with about two thirds of California's manufacturing concentrated there before the end of the 1860's. By 1868 its population numbered about 133,000.

What was the national impact? In the main the significance of large increases in supplies of the precious metals lies in their influence upon price levels as the metals were converted into coins and added to the reserves of the banking system. There was also a second impact: change in the relationship between the relative values of the metals. First, increased supplies of gold coins augmented the value of their silver counterparts, only to be followed by the reverse of this situation as Comstock poured forth its avalanche of silver. But changes in the balance of payments and worldwide demonetization of silver also contributed to this result. Some political consequences must also be noted, from the so-called crime of '73 to the formation of the Populist Party, and splinter movements in the major parties. These were not without influence on developments in an increasingly national political economy.

The second of the three Western frontiers to be opened to settlement was the cattlemen's frontier of the Great Plains. An area of devastating blizzards, hailstorms, and high winds sweeping uninterruptedly over the treeless grasslands, it was always prey to the threat of economic ruin to man, beast, and crop. The presence of no fewer than eleven Indian tribes, some of the most warlike on the continent, including the Comanche, Arapaho, Blackfoot, Crow, and Cheyenne, added immeasurably to problems of settlement and use. Some of these tribes, like the robber barons of feudal Europe, demanded tribute in the form of cattle before they would allow a herd to pass on to the grasslands. Nomadic and nonagricultural, they depended for their existence on the nearly countless numbers of bison that roamed the Plains.

The foundations of the Cattle Kingdom lay in Mexican herds, which were the offspring of Andalusian cattle brought to the New World by Spanish conquerors. These herds gradually spread throughout the vast pampas regions of Texas. By 1860, 3.5 million cattle were listed in that state for assessment purposes. As early as 1842 drovers had delivered cattle to New Orleans, and subsequent drives to Ohio, Chicago, the Territory of Colorado, and California all took place before the Civil War. By 1866 railway construction was pushing into the grazing areas of Kansas and connecting them with the great markets of St. Louis, Chicago, and the Atlantic seaboard. The arrival of 35,000 Texas cattle in Abilene the following year marked the beginning of the northbound Texas cattle trail. Millions of steers were to be driven over that trial in the next two decades and dispersed over the natural feeding grounds of the Great Plains.

The Texas Trail was no mere cow path; rather, it consisted of numerous paths and trails converging toward the northern part of the state before branching out into the grazing grounds of the Western plains. Abilene, where J. G. McCoy, an Illinois entrepreneur engaged in a large livestock shipping business, had built stockyards, pens, and loading chutes, was the original point where the north–south cattle trail intersected the east–west railroad, but the trail end shifted westward as the railroads advanced. For about ten years after the Atchison, Topeka & Santa Fe reached Dodge

City, Kansas, that town was the greatest cattle market in the world. Abilene, Dodge City, and other shipping points were more than loading points or stations where cattle could be held until a suitable Eastern market could be found. They were also entry points for cattle used to stock the great ranges of the Northern plains.

Between 1866 and 1880 nearly 5 million cattle were driven north from the plains of southwest Texas to Abilene and Northern and Western ranges. In addition, other herds were turned directly west to the ranges of New Mexico, Arizona and Colorado, while still others went to Montana, Wyoming and the Dakotas. Thus, in the space of fifteen years the range and ranch cattle industry spread over the Great Plains, an empire of grass whose formal proprietor was the federal government. The industry should be put in perspective, though. One large ranch on the Plains might produce as many cattle as 1,000 Eastern or Midwestern farms, but in the aggregate the numbers on the latter greatly exceeded those on the Plains. Nevertheless, growth on the Plains was much higher than elsewhere. In 1860, the Plains had only 1 percent of the national total but in just thirty years that percentage rose to 26 percent.

Before 1880 the cattle business of the Plains was largely a frontier industry. The open range system of ranching held full sway, so that, aside from the money needed for the purchase of cattle, the stockman's investment was slight. As a rule, he had only to select a site along some stream or water hole and obtain 160 acres under the Homestead Act to use as ranch headquarters. He then built a rude dwelling and a small stable for his horses. After purchasing a herd of cattle, he let them graze on the public domain, allowing them to run loose till spring, when they were rounded up and branded. Winter had brought him no added expense. Since winter winds generally blew away the light snow and exposed nutritious bunch grasses, very few cattlemen fed their cattle during that season. When fall came, the cattle were rounded up once again and shipped to market.

Rising beef prices around 1880 substantially altered this idyllic picture by inducing cattlemen to add to their herds and attracting others to the business. With the open range more and more crowded, stockmen sought, through purchase or lease, to gain control of their own parcels of land. Thanks to the invention of barbed wire by Joseph F. Glidden in the mid-1870s, they also began fencing in their land—in the process illegally including many acres of the public domain. In sum, the cattle industry, like manufacturing, as we shall see, began to undergo significant change around 1880. A regime in which herds were small and investments in land almost nil was increasingly replaced by one in which vast land areas, huge herds, and large amounts of capital were necessary. As in manufacturing, the livestock industry entered an era of consolidation. Small cattlemen were bought out by large incorporated companies better equipped to meet the swelling demand of a national market.

The open range became increasingly crowded as beef prices continued their rise in the early eighties—from $6.50 per cwt in 1880, cattle on the hoof in the Chicago market went to $7.50 in 1881 and to $9.35 the next year—the trend toward large companies increased, and capital flowed in from Eastern and European investors, especially English and Scotch. Stories of fabulous profits whetted the appetites of investors. In his book *Cattle Raising on the Plains of North America,* published in 1885, Walter Baron von Richtofen, a German who had been in the cattle business in Colorado, told of a Denver banker who earned a net profit of $120,000 over a six-year period. "An average yearly profit of twenty to thirty percent," an experienced livestock buyer of Minneapolis, E. V. Smalley, testified before a House Committee in 1885, "could ordinarily be expected on capital invested in the cattle business in Wyoming and Montana." Such accounts did not go unheeded. According to the *London Economist* of March 1886, eleven English and Scotch corporations operating in the Western states from 1883 to 1885 "owned" 2,016,883 acres as well as 672,-013 cattle, and paid dividends on a capital stock of $13,947,089 ranging from 6.7 percent to 10.5 percent. Unfortunately, many of the companies that bought cattle in the early eighties counted the increased value of their herds as profits. When beef prices fell after 1887 and herds decreased in value, these purported gains were converted into losses.

The bonanza did not last: Growth in the demand for beef did not keep up with increases in supply, and prices fell—to a low of $1 per cwt for cheaper grades in 1887. Not only were the ranges being overstocked and cattle marketed too soon, but cattlemen found themselves contesting with increasing bitterness with sheepmen and settlers for access to the grasses of the open range. The growth in the number of sheep on the Plains was almost as rapid as that of cattle. According to the Census of 1890, the Plains region held nearly 3 million more sheep than cattle that year, their number having increased by nearly 300 percent between 1870 and 1890. During the same interval the number of farms on the Plains grew from 49,424 to 145,878 and the number of acres devoted to farming from 16,219,086 to 47,282,233. The unusually severe winter of 1886–1887 dealt a lethal blow to the open range livestock business, with thousands of cattle perishing in severe and prolonged blizzards. Numerous firms went to the wall, among them many of the largest. Like the South Sea Bubble and Dutch tulip craze of earlier centuries, the Cattle Kingdom, built by men and millions attracted by the promise of tremendous profits and the myth of limitless free grass, fell into ruin and whimpered into history.

But not without a legacy of betterment. Meat-packing centers in such cities as Chicago, St. Louis, Kansas City, and Omaha had grown up to minimize the cost of transporting cattle and meat products from the ranges to the consumers. And with the decline of the open range and accompanying growth in barbed-wire fencing and winter feeding, it became possible to improve the quality of meat products. The era of longhorns grazing on the public domain gave way to an era of stocking with such improved European breeds as Herefords, Shorthorns, and Anguses. By 1900 the livestock industry of the post–Civil War West was producing nearly half of the nation's cattle, 56 percent of its sheep, and about 25 percent of its hogs.

The advent of barbed wire did more than hasten the decline of the Cattle Kingdom by changing the dominant occupation on the Great Plains from ranching to stock farming. It also made it possible for farmers to accelerate their march across the prairies and onto the Plains. But although cheap fencing enabled the homesteader to protect his agricultural unit from the grazing herds of cattlemen, this was not the only necessary condition for successful farming on the arid plains. The farmer also needed access to water. In the Great Plains region west of the 98th meridian—that is, a north-south line through the eastern Dakotas, Nebraska, Kansas, and Oklahoma—rainfall is spasmodic, varying from thirty to less than ten inches a year. In consequence, the runoff is large. In addition, there is much sunshine, comparatively little cloudiness, and great wind movement. Altogether, these conditions make the area even drier than the small amount of precipitation itself would suggest. Aside from dry farming, a technique for making crops with a minimum of rainfall, main reliance had to be placed on irrigation with underground water either via artesian wells if the geological structure was right or windmills to raise the water artificially. Neither method proved universally successful, but of the two, the windmill, first used extensively by the transcontinental railroads, contributed most to the advance of the agricultural frontier into the subhumid West.

That advance was slow before 1900, except in the main for an important wheat belt of bonanza farming in the Red River Valley of the North (Minnesota, North Dakota, and Manitoba). Yet without local markets provided by miners, freighters, and army posts, the advance would have been slower still. To be sure, land and agricultural booms promoted by railroads with lands to sell and by land companies, town-site promoters, and a host of land speculators of many kinds periodically encouraged a rush of settlers. For example, an advance into eastern Dakota between 1878 and 1887 raised the population of Dakota from 135,177 to 511,527 in ten years and increased the number of farms from 17,435 to 95,204. Many of these settlers, as on other frontiers, arrived with little equipment or capital, threw up a sod or cheap frame house, and with a team of horses or oxen, a wagon, and a plow, began to farm. Fortunately in the case of Dakota a series of good years during the decade before 1887 converted thousands of nearly penniless farmers into established operators.

Many did well, with bumper wheat yields of twenty-five to forty bushels an acre being realized in one Dakota county in 1882. But by 1887 the wheat and land boom in Dakota was over, destroyed by droughts so terrible that fields throughout the territory averaged between eight and nine bushels per acre that year. By the winter of 1889–1890 many families were in dire want. During the next seven or eight years periodic crop failures and low prices following the Panic of 1893 left many farmers in debt and barely able to make a living. By the late 1890s better crops and higher prices generated a new boom, and thousands of farmers settled on land west of the 100th meridian. But rainfall was meager and uncertain, and this made crop farming under current agricultural practices a highly risky business. Thousands succeeded in establishing decent homes, but few got rich.

Much the same story could be told of farming on other Western frontiers, for example, on the central Plains frontier represented by western Kansas and Nebraska and by eastern Colorado between 1878 and 1896. Boom periods were cut short by severe droughts only to be followed by renewals of the same alternating developments in the same or more western locales. Most of the settlers on the eastern Colorado frontier, like many on all the agricultural frontiers of the Great Plains, were poor and lacking in knowledge of the true geographic character of the region. Perhaps at best they survived on their traditional homesteads of 160 acres, "raised a few acres of corn or wheat, or both, owned a few heads of livestock and sold meagre quantities of dairy or poultry products." At worst, they failed, victims of nature and lack of understanding of the limitations and requirements for successful dry farming. In sum, the farmers who settled on the Great Plains in the 1880s endured tremendous hardships, but out of their experiences came a more accurate and realistic view of the region's true nature and a recognition of the kind of agriculture that could succeed there. As a result, a more stable and prosperous farming economy developed in the twentieth century.

The story of the bonanza wheat farms in the Red River Valley of North Dakota and Minnesota has a similar ending but its intervening chapters are dramatically different. Large farms of 1,000 acres or more were nothing new in American history, nor were they by any means confined in the later nineteenth century to the Red River Valley of the North. What is striking about the latter, however, is not only their rapid growth in the 1870s—from two to 145 in Minnesota and from none to seventy-four in Dakota Territory—but the fact that, as in the cattle industry on the Great Plains, they too are an agricultural reflection of contemporaneous developments in manufacturing. Often incorporated, owned and financed by Eastern and foreign investors but managed in the West, their extensive acreages required not only the employment of seasonal gangs of migratory workers, especially for harvesting operations, but also a degree of mechanization not found anywhere else in the United States except in the Central Valley of California.

As early as 1877 Oliver Dalrymple of Minnesota, who had been hired two years earlier by the Northern Pacific Railroad to establish a model large-scale farm that would demonstrate the productivity of the region and encourage sales of the railroad's land, had twenty-six breaking plows, forty plows for the turning of the broken sod, twenty-one seeders, sixty harrows, thirty self-binding harvesters, and five steam-powered threshers, each of the latter capable of threshing 1,000 bushels of wheat a day. By 1880 Dalrymple had 25,000 acres under a superintendent to overlook the work of foremen, to whom was entrusted the management of 2,000 acre plots into which the farm was subdivided, each of the subdivisions having its own farm buildings, boarding houses, stables, blacksmith shops and other structures.

Eventually, the Dalrymple interests amounted to about 100,-000 acres. Other notable bonanzas in North Dakota, which generally adopted the organizational and managerial practices of Dalrymple, included the Hillsboro Farm, 40,000 acres, the Cooper Farms, 34,000, the Amenia and Sharon Land Company, 28,350, the Spiritwood Farms, 19,700, the Mosher Farms, 19,000, and the Antelope Farm, 17,300. Drawn by the magnet of well-advertised success, thousands of small farmers rushed into the valley after 1875 in search of railroad and government land on which to establish wheat farms. Their output, combined with that of the bonanza tracts, catapulted the Red River Valley of the North into the nation's leading wheat region. In the decade ending in 1889 production rose from 2.5 million bushels to nearly 30 million.

By then, though, bonanza farming was on the decline, and large tracts were being broken up into small farms and leased or sold. Despite the efficiencies achieved by specialization and large-scale production, farmers were at the mercy of two uncontrollable forces, nature and the market. Rust, insects, drought, floods and other natural phenomena brought partial crop failures, while the bumper crops of some years brought disappointingly low prices set by supply and demand in a worldwide market. Large operators made big profits now and again, but their real money probably came from sales of both wild and improved land to small farmers. The latter was nothing new. Large, medium-sized, and even small farmers had been doing the same thing for a long time. Capital gains from the sale of improved real estate have contributed substantially to agricultural wealth throughout American history.

A more general capital gain yielded up by the Red River Valley took the form of knowledge—of the usefulness of new horse-drawn equipment. Farmers who witnessed or read in the *Prairie Farmer* or other farm journals about the highly mechanized operations of the bonanza farms were encouraged to acquire such postwar horse-drawn innovations or improvements as the gang plow, sulky, disc harrow, self-bind reaper, twine binder, and "combine" reaper-thresher. One index of the extent to which they did so is supplied by a rise in the number of farm horses from 7.1 million in 1870 to 16.9 million in 1900. Another is the rise in the annual value of American-made agricultural implements from $21 million in 1860 to $101 million in 1900, a nearly fivefold increase in total annual sales despite declining prices for many of these implements.

Mechanization was the main direct source of an increase of 56 percent in farm worker productivity in the output of wheat, corn, and oats that took place between 1840 and 1910. The other principal source was the Western movement itself, for this entailed an expansion of agriculture onto millions of acres of newly opened fertile land. The new machines, especially the reaper and thresher, enabled the farmer to place more acres under cultivation and thresh many more bushels of grain than had previously been possible with hand implements. This was especially true in the West, on whose great expanse of level land machinery could most successfully be employed in the operations of plowing, harrowing, and planting. Furthermore, since lands of the Prairies and Plains were relatively treeless, they could be placed in production at far less labor cost than elsewhere. Between 1870 and 1910 the number of man-years devoted to the clearing of land in the five Prairie states (North and South Dakota, Iowa, Nebraska, and Kansas) amounted to no more than 2 percent of the national total.

The rise of the Western livestock and agricultural industries was not without still other economic consequences. One of the more important was the steady continuity of the challenge to subsistence agriculture made by commercialization. Another was an increase in the amount of specialization in particular crops, not only by individual farmers but by geographic regions. Except for the South, which continued its antebellum specialization in cotton, regions tended to shift with migration to the West and accompanying transport and market development. On the eve of the Civil War, Illinois, Indiana, Wisconsin, and Ohio had led the nation in wheat production, but by the end of the century these states had given way to Minnesota, North and South Dakota, and Ohio. With the exception of Illinois, the leading corn producer in both 1859 and 1899, the corn belt also moved west, with Ohio, Missouri, and Indiana being displaced by Iowa, Kansas, and Nebraska. And except for Iowa, which had more beef cattle than any of the Great Plains states in 1899, the center of beef production moved to the realm of the Cattle Kingdom.

Older areas, once dominant, lost the comparative advantages they had once enjoyed. Upper New York State, the leading producer of wheat earlier in the century, turned to the truck gardening and orchard industries, producing potatoes, cabbage, spinach, and numerous other vegetables and fruits for the tables of urban New Yorkers and other nearby cities whose backyard gardens were rapidly disappearing. By the end of the century the value of New York's truck and small fruits sold in the East was nearly twice that of its nearest competitor, New Jersey. It held a similar predominance over Pennsylvania in the value of orchard fruits sold or consumed in the North. Farmers of northern New England adjusted in similar ways, concentrating on products that were effectively isolated from Western competition. Those of New Hampshire, for example, raised hay for city horses and vegetables, dairy, and forest products for local and regional markets protected by lower transport costs.

The fortunes of cities and farms have almost always been

intertwined in American history. Farm workers displaced by urban-made machinery and equipment, together with some of the sons and sometimes some of the daughters of farm families, have moved to the cities and found jobs, not only in New England but also in the Midwest and elsewhere. These linkages are displayed with particular clarity in the Prairie states after the Civil War. From the edge of the Prairies near Chicago, railroads ran out to the Mississippi River, bent northward to the Missouri and pushed west to the Great Plains and beyond. With ready access to the rapidly developing agricultural West, factories making the bulk of the machines for Western farms sought the locational advantages of Chicago and other cities along the southwestern shore of Lake Michigan and on the middle stretches of the Mississippi River.

Second only to Chicago in the manufacture of agricultural implements was the industrial center of Rock Island and Moline in Illinois and Davenport in Iowa, located on the upper Mississippi. Already by 1860 three great trunk lines, the Erie, the Pennsylvania, and the Baltimore & Ohio connected Chicago with the East Coast. Chicago was also the natural geographical center for the stockyards which, following the construction of the transcontinental railroads and the invention of the refrigerator car in the 1880s, fed the products of that city's meat packing industry to major urban markets throughout the country. Local slaughterhouse monopolies bitterly resisted the competition and temporarily had their own way when the Supreme Court, in an effort to restore the federal balance after its disruption by the growing power of the national government during the Civil War, ruled in the Slaughterhouse Cases in 1873 that Louisiana's grant of exclusive slaughtering rights to a privileged local group in New Orleans lay within the bounds of the police powers of the state. But, as we shall see later in more detail, when Minnesota and other states enacted a law in 1889 requiring the inspection of livestock by the state within twenty-four hours before slaughter, a requirement clearly designed to protect local packing interests rather than the health of local consumers, the Supreme Court in *Minnesota* v. *Barber* (1890) held that the law represented an unconstitutional regulation of interstate commerce. Here, as in other instances to be observed, the high Court kept open the channels in which commodities of all kinds might flow throughout the national market.

No commodity in that flow was more important than wheat, and two cities of the Prairie states emerged as world capitals because of the nature of their relation to that grain. Minneapolis became the capital of the flour milling industry and Chicago of the internal grain trade. Annually, railroads, which penetrated the grain fields of the West, brought to Chicago tens of thousands of carloads of three to four hundred bushels each, but since the city itself was never a great consuming center, almost all of the wheat was shipped on to the East via lake navigation and railroad. Shipments more than doubled between 1870 and 1890, rising from 77,105,740 to 150,515,761 bushels. Elevators were necessary adjuncts of railroads, which built many of them, for they enabled cars from the West to unload, and carriers from the East to obtain loads without delay. As late as 1880, 80 percent of the wheat received from the West went into storage, but after that the rapid development of through service reduced the proportion to 54 percent by 1890. In 1888, the storage space provided by Chicago's elevators totaled 30 million bushels, the amount having doubled in each of three preceding decades.

Elevators were huge skyscraper warehouses holding from 500,000 to 5 million bushels each. Long, slender, perpendicular bins enabled cars and boats to be loaded by gravity. Grain was carried from the bottom to the top of the building and delivered to the proper bin by a long, endless, power-driven belt equipped with buckets. Each bin held grain of a designated grade, with the grain being mixed accordingly instead of separated by ownership. The owner or his agent was given a warehouse receipt entitling the bearer to withdraw a designated portion of a specified grade of grain. The development of standard grading and of warehouse receipts enabled trading in grain to proceed rapidly and easily on an exchange, merely by the transfer of receipts. By about 1880 Chicago grades had become standard throughout the commercial world.

Chicago's vast store of grain functioned like a gold reserve, for the huge issues of warehouse receipts based thereon served as collateral for advances from local banks, Eastern investors, and grain merchants, the resulting credit being used to buy more grain and Eastern goods, and even to build railroads. Thus the grain trade served as a prime source for Middle Western growth. Grading and warehouse receipts, together with the durability and constantly flowing supply of grain facilitated by the elevator system, also enabled futures trading to develop at Chicago. In the absence of these preconditions, extensive short selling, i.e., operations in which a dealer seeks to profit by selling for future delivery at one price and by making delivery with grain bought later at a lower price, could not have occurred. Despite the almost universal condemnation of grain speculators, futures trading reduced many of the risks inherent in a free market. "By protecting millers, dealers, and exporters from losses, they helped narrow the difference between the average price paid to farmers and the average price charged to the ultimate consumer."

The production of American wheat and flour was responsive not alone to domestic demand but to the stimulus of foreign markets as well, especially that of England, whose dependence upon American breadstuffs increased markedly in the decades following the repeal of the British Corn Laws in 1846. Between 1870 and the turn of the century, Britain purchased about half of her annual imports from the United States. Indeed, by the 1870s "the American supplies had come to be regarded as the principal factor in the international wheat trade." The American trade became so highly developed and tightly organized, its techniques of assembling, handling, financing, and transporting grain so vastly superior to those of any other nation, that other countries, hoping to emulate the efficiency of American operations, sent numerous missions to the United States to study the technology involved, especially Chicago's grain elevators and its systems of grading and inspection. In the main, however, they failed to appreciate the role of futures trading, which was of fundamental importance to the whole system.

Britain's dependence on American wheat was so substantial before the 1880s that the volume and price of American exports was primarily influenced by the size and condition of British harvests. Other countries, however, especially Argentina, Australia, and Canada were also beginning to emerge as major producers and exporters. Increasingly, therefore, the export price of American wheat was determined in the international market centered in England by total world supply and demand. American farmers accustomed by poor British yields to count on good prices for their own crops now found prices unexpectedly lower because of bumper crops in distant parts of the world. While it is true that this was not the first time in American history that the expectations of farmers were disappointed by distant factors of demand or supply beyond their control, it is nevertheless reasonable to believe that the consequences of the development of the international wheat market played some part in the growth of agrarian protest organizations and political movements, especially their espousal of Populism in the early 1890s. But the organization of postwar farm protest began in the late 1860s and early 1870s and multiplied for many reasons that historians are far from fully understanding.

Before roughly the end of the second World War, historians tended to echo the protests of Midwest farmers themselves against what they regarded as unfair treatment by railroads, moneylenders, manufacturers and retailers of farm equipment, banks, and other "middlemen," "who by virtue of monopolistic position and undue influence on government policy were able to deprive the farmer of what should have been his share in rising American income." More explicitly, farmers accused railroads of bribing legislators and subsidizing the press, of charging more for a short haul than for a long one, of discriminating against some persons and places in favor of others, and, along with other elevator owners or managers, of cheating them by grading their wheat falsely, charging too much for storage, and practicing other abuses. It was difficult to distinguish between railroads and warehousemen in these respects, for the former built their own elevators (warehouses) or leased land on their right-of-way to warehousemen with whom they worked very closely.

Livestock shippers had their own set of complaints, accusing the railroads of taking poor care of their cattle, of putting them in inadequate cars crowded with animals improperly fed and watered, cars in which they were sometimes trampled and killed, and often bruised, with the consequence that the survivors brought lower prices. Banks, mortgage associations, and other moneylenders, both East and West, were accused of demanding extortionate interest rates on mortgages.

Historians depicted farmers as bowed beneath burdens of debt, emphasizing that the rapid expansion of agriculture into the Plains states in the 1870s and 1880s and the resulting heavy capital requirements for establishing new farms and financing railroads led to a large burden of debt and taxation. They also pointed to the long secular decline in the level of farm prices between 1869 and 1896. They therefore defended agrarian support of the Greenback Party's opposition to further withdrawal of greenbacks from an already too scarce money supply, and subsequent support by farmers of the silverite demand that free coinage of silver dollars be resumed by the United States Treasury. Finally, historians charged that short-term loans needed for carrying on farm operations were hindered by inadequate banking facilities. It is for these principal reasons, then, that farmers are said to have engaged in various forms of collective action during the period: from the organization of the Grange in 1867 and Farmers Alliances in the 1870s and the 1880s, numerous cooperative organizations for the marketing of wheat, dairy products, livestock, and fruits, and of mutual insurance companies, to political action, particularly in support of the Greenback and Populist parties, but also in the form of pressure on legislatures in Illinois, Iowa, Wisconsin, and Minnesota to place the railroads under closer public supervision.

More recent studies by economic historians cast doubt upon the validity of some of these views. For one thing, while it is true that the prices of farm commodities underwent a long-term decline between 1869 and 1896, the prices of the goods which farmers bought declined still more, if only slightly so. The farmer's real terms of trade, therefore—the quantity of goods which his output would buy—trended in his favor during the period. Additional support for this position, and a partial refutation of the charge of monopoly pricing of farm equipment, is provided by a study made long ago—in 1901—by the Department of Agriculture. This study shows that of fifteen "typical machines" used on farms, the prices of seven rose while those of eight declined or remained the same between 1895 and 1900. If 1880 is selected as the earlier of the two dates, none of the fifteen items is disclosed as having risen in price by 1900, two remaining the same and the other thirteen declining, some by more than half.

Recent scholarship also challenges other charges. One historian has shown that interest rates were falling rapidly with the secular deflation of the period and that credit was easily available. Another suggests that the short life of mortgages in the Midwest allowed rapid adjustment at lower rates of interest, and still others maintain that "the low average size of debt relative to equity indicates that most farmers in most regions of the country could not have experienced a heavy real burden of debt in the agricultural conditions of the late nineteenth century." As for freight rates, both earlier and later historians agree that railroad rates fell faster than farm product prices.

And that's not all. The most recent study of the relationship between economic conditions and farm protest movements denies the very existence of a general depression in agriculture in the last decades of the nineteenth century! On the contrary, it finds that agricultural gross product per worker rose in every one of the thirty states examined (New England and the Mountain states were excluded) over the course of the 1870–1890 period. However, rates of growth varied considerably from one region to another, increases being greatest in the Northwest Central states, especially in the Plains states, and least in the South, with the Eastern and Mid-Atlantic states holding intermediate positions. Agricultural depressions were not always general either. Although all states were hard hit in the early nineties, depression struck the Southern states with particular severity in the early 1870s. Interstate differences in agrarian protest movements and those in support of Greenback and Populist Party candidates partially reflected interstate and interregional variations in degrees of economic decline. And they partially reflected the broad social and political impact of industrialization, urbanization, and the expansion of a complex market system into previously semiselfsufficient and frontier areas. For developments of these kinds altered the relative political power and status of different social groups.

These modern studies enrich our understanding of the economic and social forces behind movements of protest in the later nineteenth century, but they by no means reduce to irrelevancy the specific counts on the indictment drawn up by farmers and other small businessmen at the time. Take for example the complaint that the railroads charged more for a short haul than for a long one, even when the goods being shipped were traveling the same line and going in the same direction. The classic case is one which played a key part in the Supreme Court's decision in *Wabash, St. Louis & Pacific Railway Company* v. *Illinois* (1886). Gilman, Illinois, was eighty-six miles closer to New York City than was Peoria, Illinois, yet the Wabash charged more for shipments from Gilman. In 1877, to cite another instance, freight rates on the

Burlington Railroad west of the Missouri River were almost four times as high as those east of the river, and half as high down to 1900. In general, rates were lower between Chicago and the East Coast than from comparable mileages west to Chicago.

Farmers and other local producers rightly believed that their interests mattered less to the railroads than broad regional concerns. It had not always been so. Before the 1840s, especially the 1850s, the early railroads had been financed in the main by local businessmen, usually with supplemental aid from state or local governments in the form of bond subscriptions or other loans. Their objective was improved access to markets, with all its attendant advantages—for example, increases in population and in real estate values, economic diversification, and an enlarged tax base. The identity between the interests of the owners of the railroad and the businessmen and producers of a given area had been close.

This close relationship began to change as railroads came to be viewed as worthwhile investments in themselves, as outside investors bought into strategically located companies for speculative purposes. The value of railway properties became measured more and more by their ability to produce dividends. Without the infusion of outside capital most American railroads, particularly those in the West, would not have been completed. But the growth of absentee ownership led to a sharp division between the interests of the new proprietors and those of local businessmen and governments. Frequently, the former sought to develop regional transportation and marketing systems and in doing so they were not inhibited by state boundaries or by local concerns.

Operating as they did in broad regional markets, the railroads were naturally sensitive to the existence or absence of competition from other carriers. The Northern Pacific Railroad charged almost twice the rate on wheat shipments from Fargo to Duluth as from Minneapolis to Chicago, although the latter distance was twice the former. Why? Minneapolis shippers had a choice of railroads on which to ship while shippers in Fargo did not. And why were freights cheaper east of Chicago than west? Because of the competition provided by the water route—the Great Lakes, the Erie Canal, and the Hudson. There is also another point to be made. Once a shipment of freight was loaded, the cost of transporting it 100 miles was only a little less than carrying it several times that far. If long-distance traffic had to be carried at the same rates as those charged for short hauls, many bulky products like corn and wheat, whose value is low in proportion to their weight, could not have paid the freight charges.

The economic discrimination in favor of long hauls, however clear and defensible, could hardly appease farmers and other local interests injured by it. Nor could smaller producers be expected to sympathize with the economic leverage of big shippers or their ability to obtain volume discounts from a particular line in return for their patronage. Wheat growers in the Northwest, for example, complained that the James J. Hill railroads would haul no grain from elevators of less than 30,000 bushel capacity.

Rate wars between competing railroads in the sixties, seventies, and eighties were no less unsettling, and small businessmen as well as farmers complained about the fluctuating and uncertain departures from established rates. When asked whether the railroads had given lower rates to any of his competitors, Gideon Holmes, treasurer of the Plymouth Cordage Company, replied: "We do not know that they have, but there is a feeling of unrest when we have to run around to see whether we can get any special advantages, and sometimes succeed." Holmes added: "All that we ask for is at all times to know that none of our competitors get a lower rate of freight than we are getting. We should be better satisfied if we knew that every one of our competitors had to pay the same rate of freight; whether it is 20 cents or 50 cents, we do not care." Vacillating and uncertain rates challenged a quest for certainty and calculability that marks the business mind of the era.

Finally, the complaint that the charges levied by the grain

elevators of Chicago were too high, that railroads and warehouse-men cheated on weights and tampered with grain in store, keeping the best for themselves, and that warehouse receipts were not accurate and reliable, is clearly sustained by the evidence. In the 1860s and 1870s, during the almost continuous fight of merchants and farmers for cheaper transportation, it was a powerful Chicago elevator ring that seemed the logical point of attack. As one historian has expressed it, "It is quite certain that the Chicago elevator industry of the 1860's and 1870's was a virtual, if not a virtuous monopoly." In 1869–1870 a whirlwind of discontent gathered force. Backed by farm sentiment—but also by outraged grain dealers, other businessmen, and people concerned for the reputation of the city—the constitutional convention of 1870 inserted articles in the constitution not only prescribing governance of grain elevators but also directing the legislature to "pass laws to correct abuses and to prevent unjust discrimination and extortion in the rates of freight and passenger tariffs on the different railroads in this state." The following year the legislature set maximum passenger fares, stipulated that freight charges should be based entirely on distance traversed, and established a board of railroad and warehouse commissioners to enforce the laws.

Illinois was not alone. Three other Midwestern states—Minnesota, Wisconsin, and Iowa—also enacted so-called Granger laws in the early 1870s. The railroads fought back, either by obeying them in such a way as to make them appear obnoxious to the public, or by lodging lawsuits in state courts. On and on dragged the suits, in appeal after appeal. Finally, they were settled—for the time being—by the Supreme Court. In *Munn* v. *Illinois* (1877) the Court found in favor of the state regulatory laws. In the words of Chief Justice Waite: "When private property is devoted to a public use, it is subject to public regulation." More prophetic of the future was the dissenting opinion of Justice Stephen Field. "Of what avail," Field asked, "is the constitutional provision [the 14th Amendment] that no state shall deprive any person of his property except by due process of law, if the State can, by fixing the compensation which he may receive for its use, take from him all that is valuable in the property?" Historically, "due process of law" had referred to procedural safeguards—to the right of the accused to be confronted in court by his accuser, for example. Field converted procedural into substantive, arguing that the very substance of a state law, its specification of a maximum rate chargeable for the provision of a service, deprived a company of its property without due process of law.

In *Chicago, Milwaukee and St. Paul Railway Company v. Minnesota* (1890) the Court majority adopted Field's position, declaring, furthermore, that the reasonableness of rates was a matter for the courts to decide, rather than the legislature. In essence, the Court overturned *Munn*. But we need not follow the course of the law into the nooks and crannies of judicial interpretation of the 14th Amendment. More arresting is the reflection that, a century before, agrarian pressures on the legal system in Massachusetts and other New England states had brought forth stay laws, moratoria on debt collection, commodity payment laws, and other provisions designed by the states to relieve the distress of farmers. Such laws had helped generate the contract clause of the Constitution, which Chief Justice John Marshall soon thereafter employed to protect property rights from assault by state legislatures. A century later, the Court in which Justice Field was a member was to do the same thing, this time employing the new doctrine of substantive due process to protect property rights in railway and grain elevator investment from such laws as those of Illinois, Iowa, Wisconsin, and Minnesota, laws which, by prescribing maximum rates (or by authorizing commissions to do so) were so low in the eyes of the companies concerned as to deprive them of their property without due process. Thus had history come full circle. The causes of agrarian discontent were multiple in the 1780s and no less so one hundred years later. How important was each count on the agrarian indictment? Who can say?

The Supreme Court's disallowance of state efforts to regulate commerce whose origin or destination lay beyond the state's boundaries—including even that part of the transportation lying entirely within the state and despite the absence of federal action—meant that railroads would not be regulated at all unless the Congress acted. In view of the acute grievances we have discussed, this was a step Congress could not avoid taking. It did so when it passed the Act to Regulate Commerce—more familiarly known as the Interstate Commerce Act—in 1887. The Act prohibited discrimination between persons, commodities, or localities, prohibited pooling, forbade charging more for a short haul than a long haul, and set up a five-man commission to enforce the law.

Support for the legislation was widespread among farmers and businessmen. It is even possible that some railroad executives also applauded the Act, preferring federal authority to the unpredictable threat of control by the various states. As Charles E. Perkins, president of the Chicago, Burlington & Quincy Railroad remarked in 1886, "The only point with the people is that in the State Courts the railroads cannot get justice, and therefore they want to put us there." Did they expect the Court, in this heyday of laissez-faire at the federal level, to pull the Act's teeth? The Court was indeed soon to do exactly that—and soon to do the same to the second piece of major federal regulatory legislation passed in this era, the Sherman Antitrust Act of 1890. We do not know what railroad executives expected of the courts, but they did want protection from their competitors and from large shippers demanding expensive rebates. They had been seeking protection by consolidating their lines and forming pools, especially in efforts to avoid the losses incurred in competitively cutthroat rate wars—as we shall see in the next chapter. Pools were illegal at common law, and many executives favored a law that would legalize them. But the act forbade them, and the presidents of most of the nation's railroads opposed it, indeed worked for its defeat by exerting pressure on Senators and Representatives.

Not till 1903, when Congress tightened the ban against rebating and personal discrimination by passing the Elkins Act, and especially not till 1906, when the Hepburn Act amended the original law, did it become clear that the railroads were going to be subjected to effective federal control. The Hepburn Act expressly delegated to the Interstate Commerce Commission (ICC) the power to determine and prescribe just and reasonable maximum rates. In addition, it authorized new procedures to insure prompt enforcement of the commission's orders. Still other deficiencies in the commission's authority were remedied by the Mann-Elkins Act of 1910. Finally, the Supreme Court itself contributed to the revitalization of the commission by shifting its position to one which attributed to ICC's findings a greater measure of finality than it had previously been willing to vouchsafe.

Armed after 1906 with the authority essential to effective regulation, the members of the commission proceeded to react negatively to railroad requests for general increases in rates. In the light of railroad history and the unfavorable climate of public opinion which that history had engendered, it would have been difficult for them to have done otherwise. Nevertheless, the fact is regrettable. Times had changed. Most of the abuses of the past, especially rebating and the various forms of discrimination—in favor of particular persons and places, and in favor of long hauls over short ones—were products of the rate wars of the 1860s, 1870s, and 1880s, products of bitter, cutthroat competition. In the nineties railroads, as well as manufacturing concerns, were combining their interests in various ways to lower the costs of competition.

The Congressional reaction was to forbid combination, to insist on the economic and other benefits of competition, and while this was a valid stance with respect to manufacturing, its application to railroads, especially to the interstate lines, is questionable. Essentially, railroads were public utilities. Their construction had been subsidized in part by government money or land, and be-

cause they were public utilities, government was right in requiring them to be regulated in the public interest. The fundamental
problem was that the ICC, overreacting to the historical events
which had led to its creation, was unable to see clearly what the
public interest was.

That interest lay in an expanded, modernized, and technologically improved system rather than the spindly legged product of
competitive, overrapid nineteenth-century construction. Nearly
everything required improvement and enlargement: motive
power, rolling stock, signal systems, terminals, and other aspects
of railroading, including regrading and bridging, right down to the
tracks themselves. The railroads were certainly making an effort
to meet the huge needs of a new century. "During the enormous
development of the last four years," President Edward H. Harriman of the Union Pacific Railroad wrote to President Theodore
Roosevelt in 1904, "the railroads have found it very difficult to
keep pace with the requirements imposed upon them, and the
so-called surplus earnings, as well as additional capital, have been
devoted to providing additional facilities. . . . This work . . . must
go on [and] during the next decade every single-track railroad in
the country will have to be double-tracked, and provide enlarged
terminal and other facilities."

Modernization, as Harriman made plain, cost money, and
since the federal government was not itself disposed to nationalize
the roads and provide the necessary capital via public appropriations, the need had to be met by private investors. Until 1907,
from the ending in 1898 of the severe four-year depression of that
decade, annual investment in railroad plant kept pace with the
economy's growing demands upon the system. After that it faltered, turning downward almost as consistently, as investors lost
interest with the advent of the ICC's repressive denials of general
rate increases. The profitability of railroad operations collapsed
after 1911, and by the outbreak of World War I in 1914, the system
was showing "unmistakable signs of distress owing to capital un-

dernourishment." In another two years it nearly collapsed under the weight of wartime demands, and was at last taken over by the government. Entrepreneurial and managerial ability followed the flight of capital to more attractive growing sectors of the economy.

For the railroads the story is a sad one. For the public too. And not least for the farmers, producers, and shippers whose very real grievances had so much to do with the writing of the story in the first place. The grievances of factory workers were real too, as we shall see, but they were not unalloyed with material benefits and opportunities opened up by the more rapid industrialization of the economy.

V

Completing the Industrial Revolution

Between the Civil War and World War I the United States emerged as the leading industrial nation in the world. And as industry advanced, agriculture retreated, shifts in relative position traced everywhere by economies undergoing processes of modernization. Calculations of the value added by the two sectors show manufacturing rising from 43 percent to 65 percent between 1870 and 1900 and agriculture falling from 57 percent to 35 percent. Changing shares in commodity output measure the same phenomenon, that of manufacturing increasing from 33 percent to 53 percent and that of agriculture declining in exactly reverse proportions, i.e., from 53 percent to 33 percent. Finally, between 1870 and 1910 workers in agriculture fell from 52.5 percent to 31.4 percent of the labor force—from more than half to less than a third—while those in manufacturing rose from 19.1 percent to 22.2 percent.

Behind these changes lay a number of other necessary developments. For one thing, a diminished labor force in agriculture could not possibly have supplied the needs of a growing population without itself undergoing a technological revolution. Machines and other capital goods were replacing that diminished labor force. These goods were produced by the industrial sector, which of course also had to produce the industrial capital goods necessary to the production of capital goods for agriculture! The two sectors thus enjoyed a mutually interdependent, reciprocal relationship. Yet capital goods by no means exhausted the demands made upon industry. This is where that near tripling of incomes per capita comes in. It would have been virtually impossible to spend the added income on foodstuffs alone, particularly in a country where average levels of living were as high as they were in America. Increased savings and an increased demand for the products of industry were natural consequences. Yet without certain institutional developments that we shall sketch, these savings would have been less in amount and not available at places of need. And that's not all. Still other developments converted these higher incomes into the mass demand of a national urban market.

It is often said that the national market was created by the railroads, but in fact they could not have done so all by themselves. After all, if a national market consists only of noncontiguous settlements linked by a means of transportation, then the American colonies constituted such a market in the seventeenth and eighteenth centuries: All were within fifty miles of the coast and joined together by the Atlantic Ocean. True, after independence the Western movement disrupted this early national market, but the turnpikes, canals, and railroads built by the movement for "internal improvements" restored it between the 1820s and 1840s. And when the discovery of gold in California in the late 1840s disrupted the market once again, by stimulating a mass movement to the Pacific Coast, the transcontinental railroads restored it in the 1860s. But more than geographical linkages are implied by the term "national market." Above all, it denotes a free trade area, a national domain within which goods and services are free to move from place to place without cumbersome burdens imposed on them by states seeking to protect their local business interests from outside competition. In short, not only geographical but legal links were necessary if a national market was to become a common market. In its role as guardian of that market, the Supreme Court kept in repair the foundations of the country's economic development which the Constitution of the United States had originally put in place.

These preconditions identified, we are back to the main point: Mass demand called for mass production and distribution, and the economy responded. Mass production held out the promise of economies of scale, of reduced unit costs over a wide range of output, and mass distribution promised a reduction in unit transaction costs. To achieve production and distribution in high volume, however, required substantially enlarged investment in plant and equipment, in producers' durables, and in branch offices and other facilities. In sum, what was needed was massive capital deepening. But not of physical capital alone. Knowledge and experience were also required.

Economists refer to the acquisition of knowledge and experience as human capital formation. But we may usefully distinguish the kind that results in technical improvement in machinery and equipment (together with skill in their use on the part of the labor force) from the kind that enables the business firm to improve its control over the uses of the factors of production. The latter include not only spatial realignment of productive processes, and time-and-motion studies of those processes, but also organizational and administrative changes and developments in accounting, which improve the flows of information on which business decisions are based. Innovations of these kinds are comparable to the imbedding of knowledge in management and are deserving of recognition as business capital formation. We cannot assume, however, that firms of all sizes and degrees of entrepreneurial perceptivity will at all times be equally motivated to invest in business capital. We shall see that Big Business had other priorities for a generation after its rise at the turn of the century.

What made possible the required deepening of physical capital was a marked rise in the rate at which Americans were saving—diverting current income from expenditure on consumer goods, or, expressed in "real" terms, diverting current product from consumption to capital formation. Even before the Civil War, it is true, Americans had devoted a substantial portion of their output, from 14 percent to 16 percent, to capital formation. But the postwar shares were higher in every decade, amounting to 24 percent by the 1870s and to 28 percent by the 1880s.

In all probability, the transfer of funds from the East to the West, from a region of relative capital surplus and inelastic investment demand to one in which the opposite of these conditions obtained, was also an important factor in shifting the saving rate upward in the postwar years. Nor can we overlook the contribution to income inequality made by the debt management policies of the government during and after the Civil War. (For one thing, the use of excise taxes to finance debt payments after the war transferred income to savers and investors.) Finally, the simple fact that there were more people and workers provided every inducement to accumulate more capital to supply workers with tools, households with residences, businesses with buildings, and society as a whole with more hospitals, inventories, improved transport and communication facilities, and other "infrastructure."

There was indeed every inducement to accumulate capital. Yet had it not been for the development of a number of financial institutions whose function it was to mediate between saving and investment capital, accumulation would have been much more modest. It is true that surpluses of capital existed in the maturer economies of Western Europe, where returns were less attractive than in such areas of capital deficit as the developing American economy. In consequence, net capital flows into the United States, set in motion primarily by English investors, amounted to $1.5 billion between 1870 and 1895. Most of the investment went into municipal and other local bonds, and into railroads and public utilities, although a few manufacturing firms were also among the beneficiaries. Domestic savings far outstripped foreign investment. Even when we select the low rate of 25 percent to represent the portion of Gross National Product (GNP) saved, total savings by governments, businesses, and households amount to $8.5 billion during the decades between 1870 and 1900. It was just for this reason that domestic financial institutions are so important. If we add to this scenario the fact that interest rates during these years were declining substantially, it becomes even more clear that financial considerations posed no obstacle to rapid development.

Long-term capital needs were supplied in part by such financial intermediaries as mutual savings banks, building and loan associations, life insurance companies, and mortgage companies, all of which grew rapidly and played significant roles in the mobilization and transfer of long-term capital from surplus to deficit areas. In part, too, they were supplied by the rapid growth of an open market for funds in the late nineteenth and early twentieth centuries, especially by the New York stock and bond markets, and by the rise of investment banking. In contrast to the variety of institutions instrumental in developing the long-term capital market, the market for short-term capital (i.e., loans and investments running less than a year) was primarily the province of the commercial banking system.

There was a widely held view that commercial banks ought to make only short-term self-liquidating loans, loans that would bridge the gap between the shipment and receipt of goods, between seedtime and harvest, or between the purchase of raw materials and the sale of finished goods—transactions which, when completed, would yield the revenues out of which the loans could be repaid. Despite this view, substantial numbers of commercial banks did not confine themselves to short-term lending. To a considerable extent commercial loans were made to meet needs for working capital rather than to finance self-liquidating operations. Nearly half of all unsecured loans made in a large city were renewed at maturity, a procedure that converted an estimated 20 percent of short-term loans into a means of financing fixed capital.

The supply of short—and potentially long—term capital went up, and its cost to borrowers went down because of a large increase in the number of commercial banks incorporated by the states in the second half of the nineteenth century. Despite the passage of the National Bank Act in 1863, with its invitation to bankers to take out federal charters, national banks operated under restrictions—for example, the prohibition of real estate loans—to which state banks were not subject. The resulting multiplication and spread of the latter, especially in the South and in the Midwestern, Western, and Pacific states, eroded the power of local monopolies to charge for loans what the market would bear, and interest rates declined.

Nevertheless, sharp differences in rates between regions would have continued to exist had it not been for the development of institutions facilitating transfers of capital funds. Such differences were natural: In areas of early settlement which have already developed a diversity of economic enterprise, interest rates tend to be relatively low and new investment opportunities more scarce than they are on developing frontiers. These situations call for the innovation of ways to transfer funds from the one area to the other. In the colonial period, the bill of exchange, in use in Europe since the fourteenth century, permitted transfers of funds from England to America. In the second half of the nineteenth century, the development of two newer instrumentalities accomplished a similar purpose, viz., the correspondent banking system and the commercial paper house.

The deposit of funds by banks of Region A in correspondent banks of Region B not only earned interest for Region A banks but permitted them to draw on the funds when their customers needed means of payment in distant places. The maintenance of accounts with correspondent banks also facilitated other services, the most important being the obtaining of loans. The National Bank Act required its member banks to maintain reserves against their liabilities but permitted a portion of the reserves to be kept on deposit in banks in other cities—the exception being national banks located in New York City, which were required to keep their reserves in their own vaults. The more numerous state banks and private banks and trust companies did the same thing, sending their idle balances to New York, Boston, and other cities. Especially to New York: There was a constant flow of goods and funds between New York and the interior, so that most interior bankers found it convenient to keep funds on deposit in that great American city of the nineteenth century. In short, the correspondent banking system provided an effective channel for the transfer of short-term funds from the West to the East via deposits of required reserves and idle balances, and for a return flow from East to West and South via interbank borrowing.

The commercial paper market offered another important channel for the interregional flow of funds. This market expanded rapidly in the late nineteenth and early twentieth centuries as business firms, seeking to escape the monopoly power and high interest charges of banks in their own locality, chose to offer their paper, including their own promissory notes, to houses which specialized in purchasing such paper and then reselling it to commercial banks and other investors in other parts of the country. Business firms had still another reason for looking outside their own communities for financing. With the growth of large-scale industry after the Civil War, they often could not obtain locally the amounts needed because of limitations on loans which a national bank was permitted by law to make to a single borrower. The commercial paper house was certainly interregional and probably national in scope—a list of offerings of a Boston house as early as 1873, for example, included paper from firms in Cincinnati, Oshkosh, Memphis, and St. Louis as well as the East Coast—and the opportunity to secure financing far broader. Together with the correspondent banking system, the commercial paper house gradually created a national market for short-term capital. Interregional differences in interest rates narrowed, those in New England and the North Central states being virtually equal by 1900. While differentials still remained farther West, decreases in rates were dramatic.

While they did not dominate the commercial paper market in the way they did the flows of the correspondent banking system, New York banks did play a role in the development of the market for long-term capital. In essence, their call loans—loans to stock brokers that were subject to call without notice—converted short-term into long-term capital. These loans permitted brokers to make loans in turn to the purchasers of stocks, thus financing capital expenditures by firms in the rapidly industrializing Midwest as well as elsewhere. However, before 1885 an investor interested in industrial issues would have been more likely to turn to Boston than to the New York market, and even there the market was thin. Throughout much of the nineteenth century, securities markets had aided the interregional mobilization of funds for the public sector and for the transportation industries, but they had made only a small contribution to manufacturing. In 1885, however, the New York Stock Exchange organized a department for unlisted securities, and this enabled a number of distant manufacturing companies to reach the Big Board. Even then it was their preferred stock rather than their common that was offered for sale. Not till a decade later did the endorsement of J. P. Morgan, the prestigious investment banker, make it possible to raise large sums through the sale of common stock. Only Morgan's firm, and possibly Kuhn Loeb, could have marketed successfully a major industrial issue in 1900. By the 1920s, however, several others were able to do so.

Despite the limitations of stock exchanges, some industrial firms were able to raise capital by selling their securities to insurance companies. Insurance firms emerged after the Civil War as the most important nonbank intermediaries for the mobilization and interregional transfer of capital. Indeed, their assets increased more than twentyfold between 1869 and 1914, rising in the final quarter of the century from $403 million to $1.7 billion. Collecting premiums from savers in many parts of the country, they proceeded to invest their funds in out-of-state mortgages and corporate securities. Their contribution to transport development and to intraregional industrialization was an important one. For example, by 1890 more than half of the loans made by the Massachusetts Hospital Life Insurance Company went to textile companies in Massachusetts, New Hampshire, and Maine—companies whose capital represented more than one fourth of the textile capital of those states.

In sum, the mobilization and transfer of capital was facilitated by the development of a number of institutions in the later decades of the nineteenth century. What proportion of the nearly $7 billion in deposits created in 1900 by some 12,000 commercial banks (commercial banks made loans by creating deposits subject to withdrawal by check) represented finance extended to agriculture, transportation, and manufacturing seems impossible to know. But of this we can be sure: Institutional innovation enabled American capital markets to respond to the huge demands engendered by the massive growth and structural change of the postbellum economy. And the primary source of the increased supplies of capital, once more, was a remarkable rise in the saving rate.

Increased supplies of capital had the effect of shifting the relative prices of the factors of production, the price of capital declining relative to that of labor and land (natural resources). This shift reinforced the intrinsic bias of late nineteenth-century technological change toward capital and created incentives for adopting labor-saving techniques. It also facilitated a heavier use of resources, such as iron ore and coal, which capital-intensive methods of production often required. The amount of capital invested in plant and machinery rose dramatically between 1870 and 1900. Investments increased nearly fivefold in iron and steel plants, more than sixfold in those manufacturing electrical machinery,

and twelvefold in those producing agricultural implements. Together with investments in railroads and the growing requirements of cities for transit lines, road systems, water and sewage
systems, lighting systems, and bridges and buildings, they are in-
dicative of the massive capital deepening that took place. The
average worker was provided with additional capital to work with,
and this enabled him to increase his output per man-hour.

The rising stock of physical capital per worker was the main
source of the productivity gains generating higher per capita incomes. But it was not the only source. The quality of the labor
force also went up. Workers were healthier, more fit, longer-lived,
and hence better able to adapt to the changing industrial order.
We have already seen how measures leading to the decline of
infectious diseases improved the health of the American population. Formal education also improved their skills. Increasingly, the
children of urban workers, if to a far lesser extent the parents
themselves, benefited from widening support of common schools
and public secondary education by local communities. But the
process was a slow one. Many, many families, almost universally
those living in rural areas, continued to depend on the labor of
their children, and over the period 1870–1910 children ten to
fifteen years old represented 6 percent of the labor force. As late
as 1900 almost a fifth of the youths in that age group worked
instead of attending school. In part, rising incomes lessened the
need for children to work, but the main reason for growing enrollment rates after 1900 was the enactment of compulsory education
and child-labor legislation by the states.

By 1910 public elementary school enrollment had risen from
about 12.5 million in 1900 to about 16 million, with the average
number of days spent in school climbing from 86.3 to 113 per
semester. Yet it was not enough to get the child out of the factory.
Ways had to be found to keep him in school. For the expansion in
school population was offset by a high dropout rate. Contemporaries estimated that only from 40 percent to 50 percent of the

children finished the eight grades of elementary school and that only from 8 percent to 10 percent finished high school. Between the ages of thirteen and fifteen more than half dropped out, most of them in sixth and seventh grades. Agreeing that the curriculum was not meeting either the interests or needs of children, urban settlement workers, rural publicists, businessmen's associations, labor unions, and avant-garde pedagogues joined in advocating programs of vocational training, and in less than two generations the character of the American school was transformed. By 1910, twenty-nine states had made provisions for some form of industrial education.

Manual training in the elementary grades and high school instruction in such areas as carpentry, wood turning, forge work, brazing and soldering, and bench and machine work in metals coincided nicely with the needs and interests of the world's foremost industrial nation. The new industrial order required that a new-style army, an industrial army of semiskilled workers, be recruited and trained. The function of the public schools was to provide the training for the privates, to supply an education with a vocational bias, one that would predispose the children to enter the factories and manual trades, impress upon them the dignity of labor and equip them with "industrial intelligence"—ability to handle tools and machines, sufficient literacy to read and understand directions, and enough discipline to enable them to conform to the requirements of large-scale rationalized factory routine. All this fit well with the "real needs" of children of "the masses." As the foremost educational philosopher of the age, John Dewey, explained, "In the great majority of human beings the distinctively intellectual interest is not dominant. They have the so-called practical impulse and disposition." These were not the proudest years of the great American democracy.

Meanwhile, advocates of vocational aid looked to the nation's professional schools of engineering, science, and business to recruit the officer corps of the industrial army. Professional schools were increasing in number and vitality as the professions them-selves—engineering, for example—split into a number of subdisci-plines, each with its own organization, elite, and body of knowl-edge. The era was one of rapidly growing specialized knowledge, of new colleges and universities, of new departments manned by specialists, of new professional organizations and scholarly jour-nals. Scholars organized national associations of their peers, for example, in law, history, economics, philology and education. In the 1870s at least seventy-nine learned societies were founded and in the 1880s 121. The explosion of knowledge was particularly marked in science and technology.

One major consequence was a radical change in the nature of inventive activity. Throughout most of the nineteenth century, although decreasingly so toward its end, inventions were the prod-uct of a crude empiricism, of a trial-and-error use of problem-solving skills that were heavily concentrated in metallurgy, ma-chine tools, steam power, and engineering. With the dramatic growth of the chemistry-based, electrical- and electronics-based, and biology-based industries of the twentieth century, technologi-cal change has become increasingly dependent upon the exploita-tion of complex bodies of scientific knowledge. Important, even epoch-making innovations were sometimes achieved by empirical methods, although at the cost of a wasteful, inefficient search pro-cess. For example, a long series of attempts by British ironmasters to smelt iron with a mineral fuel instead of charcoal preceded Abraham Darby's successful substitution of coke for charcoal in his Shropshire blast furnace in 1709. The advance of metallurgical technique ahead of scientific understanding culminated in 1856 when Sir Henry Bessemer reported on his successful attempts to control the quantity of carbon in molten pig iron by blowing air through the iron and thus turning it into steel. Bessemer had conducted his experiments with Swedish charcoal iron, which was free of phosphorus. Only later did he and his emulators discover to their dismay that his technique would not work with ores that contained even slight traces of phosphorus. It was these failures that led to systematic study of the chemical processes involved in the production of iron and steel, to the beginning of modern metallurgical science. The "basic process" developed in 1878 by the chemists Thomas and Gilchrist was a direct outcome of systematic study and so too was the advent of the Siemens-Martin or open hearth process—which soon followed—of avoiding brittleness of steel by removing nitrogen from molten iron.

Yet it was the introduction of the Bessemer process which transformed the pre–Civil War iron industry into the postwar iron and steel industry in the United States. The output of steel grew spectacularly in the 1870s and 1880s, rising from less than 70,000 gross tons in 1870 to 1.247 million tons ten years later. And associated with the growth was a large increase in the size of plants. Early in the century iron had been made deep in the Appalachian forest in small charcoal furnaces and forges. By 1900 blast furnaces 100 feet high were integrated with the giant steel mills that rose above the Monongahela, Lake Erie, and Lake Michigan.

Before 1880 almost all Bessemer steel was used for rails, but the demand for other iron and steel products rose even more rapidly thereafter. Especially prominent was the demand for steel plates, sheets, and structural shapes to build heavy machinery, transport facilities of all kinds, and the steel skeletons of the new skyscrapers. In 1890 steel production rose to 4.277 million tons, in 1900 to 10.188 million tons, and in 1910 to 26.095 million tons. Until 1890, Bessemer steel accounted for at least 85 percent of total annual output, but with the passing of the peak demand for rails, its relative importance declined. By 1910, its proportion of output had fallen to 36 percent, and the primacy of the open hearth process was firmly established. Unlike the Bessemer process, the open hearth technique could utilize a wide spectrum of the abundant phosphoric ores in the United States. In 1910 the open hearth proportion of output stood at 63 percent. In triumphing over crude empiricism, scientific inquiry thus imparted an economic value to materials which had lain useless in the earth for centuries. Not surprisingly, chemists and engineers, only 0.14 percent of the labor force in 1890, increased in number to 1.08 percent by 1950, a more than sevenfold gain.

The economic impact of technological change in the production of iron and steel was delivered in the main to industries using its products, and of these by far the most important were those making producers' goods. On the eve of the Civil War the three largest industries in terms of the value added to raw materials by manufacturing processes made goods for consumers, viz., cotton goods, lumber, boots and shoes. By 1910, the top three were making producers' goods, goods for the producers of consumer products, and of these machinery ranked first. In industry after industry machines were becoming larger and more complex. At the beginning of the century a skilled weaver made one pick (throw of the shuttle) per second with his hand loom, but by 1900 a factory worker could look after twenty Northrop automatic looms that together made sixty picks a second. And these were looms that lowered labor requirements by permitting an automatic replacement of empty bobbins and automatic stoppage of the loom when threads broke.

In the cotton industry, the ring spindle, adapted to coarse rather than fine yarns, to ordinary rather than quality goods, gradually replaced the mule spindle. Together with the use of higher-speed sewing machines and cutting machines able to slice through several thicknesses of cloth, the ring spindle and automatic loom made possible the rise and expansion of a clothing industry mass-producing standardized garments. As Adam Smith observed, it is mass demand which leads to specialization, the high degree of which in the shoemaking industry in the years just after the Civil War is amusingly illustrated by the case of a shoemaker of Marblehead, Massachusetts, who went from shoemaking to the study of law and then, following the outbreak of the depression of 1873, back to shoes. Such was the advance in the division of labor in the interim that he found himself one of sixty-four men working on successive phases of the production of a single shoe. Not surprisingly, he described himself as "one 64th of a shoemaker." By the end of the century a variety of machines had assumed nearly all of the basic tasks of shoe production.

And so it went in field after field. And the more machines replaced men, the greater the demand for metal-shaping machine tools—lathes, planers, boring machines, milling machines, precision grinders—to make those machines. The machine tool industry played a role of fundamental importance in the process of industrialization. The production of goods by machines requires great skill and highly specialized knowledge of the technical problems involved. Solution of these problems enables machine tools to be developed that are capable of making the goods-producing machines. How quickly an economy becomes industrialized depends to no little extent upon the speed with which this technical knowledge is diffused from its point of origin in one industry to other industries.

Technical knowledge originated in successful efforts by machine-making firms to meet the needs of specific customers. At first, in the early decades of the nineteenth century, these firms did not specialize in making machines. They were either firms which, because they made metal or wooden products, also possessed the skills and facilities necessary to make machines, or they were companies like those that owned the early New England textile mills, which set up their own shops to make the machinery needed for textile manufacturing. The more successful of these shops proceeded not only to manufacture textile machinery for sale to other firms but also to produce a range of other kinds of machines as well, for example, steam engines, mill machinery, and machine tools. Simply by expanding their output, then, producers at this early stage transferred to other industries skills acquired in the production of one kind of machine.

With the growth of the market for a widening array of specialized machines, machine tool production emerged as a separate industry. Most of its member firms specialized on a narrow range of products, often making only one type of machine tool, although in different sizes or with auxiliary attachments or components. Responding to the machinery needs of a succession of industries—textiles, railroads, firearms, sewing machines, bicycles and, in the early decades of the twentieth century, automobiles—the machine tool industry served not only as the point of origin of technical knowledge and skill but as a means for diffusing that knowledge throughout the machine-using sector of the economy. It could do this because the technical skills acquired in the industry of origin had direct applications to production in other industries.

The use of machinery to cut metal into precise shapes involves a relatively small number of operations and therefore of machine types. Among these operations are turning, boring, drilling, planing, grinding, and polishing. Machines performing the operations confront similar technical problems, for example, power transmission (gearing, belting, shafting), control devices, feed mechanisms, and friction reduction. These were problems common to the production of a wide range of commodities, e.g., firearms, sewing machines, and bicycles. In sum, the machine tool industry could serve as a conveyor belt for technical knowledge precisely because nineteenth-century industrialization involved the application of a relatively small number of broadly similar productive processes to a large number of industries. And because nineteenth-century industrialization also involved the growing adoption of a metal-shaping technology that relied more and more on decentralized sources of power.

Those sources changed dramatically in both quantity and kind during these years. Primary power capacity in manufacturing—the work done by such prime movers at the waterwheel, steam engine, steam turbine, internal combustion engine, and electric motor to convert the energy of nature directly into the energy of motion—expanded substantially over the course of the later nineteenth and early twentieth centuries, rising from 2.346 million horsepower in 1869 to 29.41 million in 1919. Water continued to be the major source of power well past the middle of the nineteenth century, but thereafter the relative position of steam improved at water's expense. By 1899 steam accounted for over four fifths of the total. The dominance of steam was precarious, however, and by 1919 it was being challenged by electricity.

It is not alone the increasing quantity but also the changing industrial distribution of power that testifies to the essential nature of the industrialization process in these years. In 1859 the lumber and food group of industries had almost 60 percent of total capacity. By 1919 their combined share had fallen to 22 percent while the primary metals group, continuously increasing its share after 1869, emerged as the group with the largest capacity. The group was dominated by iron and steel.

Except for New England, which was much slower than other regions to reduce its dependence on waterpower, coal was the energy source that powered the machines of the late nineteenth century. It was coal, specifically the opening up of the anthracite fields in Pennsylvania, that permitted the beginnings of factory production in industries other than textiles. Coal in quantities essential for industrial purposes became available in the mid-1830s. Before then, almost all production was carried on in small shops or at home. By 1880, the manufacture of goods by machinery was concentrated in factories. According to the compiler of the census for the year, Carrol D. Wright, "of the nearly three millions of people employed in the mechanical industries of this country at least four-fifths are working under the factory system." Yet the availability of coal and machines alone does not explain why the factory system expanded as rapidly as it did. Far more important was the reliability and speed made possible by the advent of the railroad and telegraph. It would have been difficult for manufacturers to maintain a permanent work force or to keep in profitable operation expensive machinery in the absence of a steady, all-weather flow of goods into and out of their factories.

In an increasing number of industries, manufacturers were making use of two techniques of production essential to output in high volume: use of standardized interchangeable parts and continuous processing. Both innovations antedate by many years periods of rapid industrialization, but as in the case of skills honed in the machine tool industry, it is not so much the initial appearance of an innovation as its diffusion that increases productivity and economic growth.

Interchangeability is "a method of producing mechanisms possessing closely fitting and interacting components in such a way that a given component of any of the mechanisms [will fit] and perform equally well, *with no adjustment*, in any of the other mechanisms." The method requires a high degree of standardization and precision manufacture of component parts, features that greatly facilitate mass production at lower unit costs—by eliminating or substantially reducing costly fitting activities—and at the same time results in products far easier to maintain and repair than products requiring high degrees of craftsmanship. Originating in firearms production, interchangeability came to dominate the light metal-working industries, and then in the nineteenth and twentieth centuries spread to a wider range of products: to clocks and watches, sewing machines, agricultural implements, bicycles, and automobiles.

Continuous process manufacturing, or the handling of material by mechanical means with minimal human intervention, had its origins in a flour mill built by Oliver Evans of Philadelphia in 1782. From beginning to end, the entire process, once commenced, proceeded automatically, the grain being moved horizontally from one machine to another by a conveyor and vertically from floor to floor, much as automobile bodies were to be moved in Henry Ford's plant of 1914. The next major advance in mechanical materials handling was taken at least by 1860 if not before, and not inappropriately for a country still primarily agricultural, it also facilitated the processing of food.

> In the slaughterhouses of Cincinnati the "disassembly" of pigs was carried out by a technique involving workmen at fixed stations while a system of overhead rails suspended from the ceiling moved the carcass, hanging from a hook, at a carefully predetermined rate, from one phase to the next. Each man performed a single operation: one split the animal, the next removed its entrails, another removed specific organs—heart, liver, etc.—and the last man washed down the carcass with a hose. Although it was impossible to eliminate the reliance upon the human eye and human skill in the slaughter-house, the skillful handling of materials, the rationalized positioning of the workers, the elimination of time loss between operations, the minimization of energy expended by the workers in handling heavy carcasses, and the minute sub-division of labor brought about very substantial increases in the productivity of labor.

Similar productivity-enhancing principles were implicit in the post–Civil War application of continuous-process machinery and nearly continuous-process factories to the production of tobacco, grain products, soap, film, and canned foodstuffs. By the mid-1880s continuous-line canning operations included the preparation of the product, washing, peeling, grading, filling, cooking, cooling, and warehousing. Such methods greatly raised the volume of output while at the same time sharply decreasing the labor force required in processing. We shall see how, after the turn of the century, Henry Ford integrated the principle of manufacture by the use of interchangeable parts with that of the assembly line. The combining of the two principles was to become the most distinguishing feature of American methods of mass production in the twentieth century.

Rationalization of the work process helped quicken what some contemporaries called the throughput, or flow of materials through the plant or system of plants. The economic significance of speeding up the velocity of the throughput is deserving of emphasis. Large increases in the daily use of equipment and personnel raised the volume of output and created economies of scale. Essentially, the increased intensity of use represented additional inputs of capital and labor, and since the former was undoubtedly the greater of the two, the consequence, even without technological change, was an even larger increase in output per unit of labor input. These economies of speed depended, however, on the development of new machinery, better raw materials, and more intense applications of energy, as well as upon the creation of organizational designs and procedures to coordinate high-volume flows through the several processes of production.

The major seed bed for modern factory technology and organization came to be located in the metal-working industries. Declining demand and unused capacity, attributable to the prolonged depression of the 1870s, forced manufacturers to seek ways to reduce costs. In addresses before annual meetings of the recently formed American Society of Mechanical Engineers, business executives emphasized the need for better shop management and accounting practices, the former to improve coordination and to control the flow of work, the latter to make possible a more precise determination of the relationship between time and wages, and of various costs and expenses. Herein lay the beginnings of what came to be known as "scientific factory management," a phase indelibly associated with the name of Frederick W. Taylor.

Engineer, industrial manager, publicist, and inventor, Taylor is generally regarded as father of the movement. As chief engineer of the Midvale Steel Company in the 1880s, he standardized belting, maintenance, and other procedures and introduced stopwatch time study and an incentive wage plan, which he hoped would induce workers to meet his "scientifically" determined production standards. In the nineties Taylor introduced improvements in accounting, especially standardized forms and procedures, and a monthly balance of accounts, and in the first decade of the twentieth century he devoted much attention in his popular writings to systematic motion study. By the time of his death in 1915 his ideas were widely diffused among manufacturers and engineers. He had published his *Principles of Scientific Management* in 1911, a Taylor Society had formed, and his disciples were giving not only Taylor's ideas but also their own improvements on them wide currency. After Louis D. Brandeis popularized the new method in the Eastern Rate case of 1910–1911, an efficiency craze hit the United States.

There was much talk indeed. Less impressive is the record of adoption. Between 1901 and 1917 at least forty-six industrial firms and two governmental manufacturing plants introduced scientific management, but these were small and middle-sized companies rather than large ones. Before the 1920s large corporations were mainly preoccupied with problems of administrative consolidation and with efforts to stabilize their companies' positions in their respective markets. The limited diffusion of productivity-enhancing practices goes a long way to explain why average annual rates of change in total factor productivity (output per unit of labor and capital combined) in the manufacturing sector were relatively unimpressive. Between 1899 and 1909 the rate was 0.7 percent and between 1909 and 1919 it fell to 0.3 percent. In contrast, the pre-1988 rate was 1.4 percent. Evidently the initial impact of Big Business on the country's economic growth was not a favorable one.

Big Business was the product of a vast merger wave that swept over the manufacturing sector between 1897 and 1903. Before then most firms in most industries were relatively small, although they increased their capitalization to accommodate the need for larger individual plants. In some industries, however— for example, in meat packing and oil, in transportation and in the electrical industry—a few corporate giants had carved out secure economic positions. Seminal studies by Alfred D. Chandler, Jr., show how they did so. Some, particularly firms whose product tended to be somewhat new in kind and especially fitted for the urban market, followed the path of vertical integration taken by the Swift Brothers in meat packing, who first built their own nationwide marketing organization and then created one for purchasing as well.

Aware that Boston, New York, Philadelphia, and other cities were outrunning local sources of meat supply, while at the same time great herds of cattle were gathering on the Western plains, Gustavus F. Swift saw the possibility of using the refrigerated railroad car to connect the new supply and the growing demand. In 1878 he formed a partnership with his brother Edwin for that purpose. During the eighties the Swifts created a nationwide distributing organization built around a network of branch houses. Each house had its own storage plant and marketing organization, the latter including outlets in major towns and cities, often managed by the Swifts' own salaried representatives.

The growing distributing organization soon required an increase in supply, especially after the partners began to market lamb, mutton, and pork as well as beef. So the Swifts set up meatpacking establishments in Kansas City, Omaha, and St. Louis and, after the depression of the late 1890s, also in St. Joseph, St. Paul, and Fort Worth. Before the end of the late 1890s, they had established a great, vertically integrated organization, with major departments for marketing, processing, purchasing, and accounting tightly controlled from their central office in Chicago. The techniques proved so successful that other leading meat packers had to build up similar integrated organizations in order to compete effectively. Before long the Big Four among them would contest yet another effort on the part of local interests to find shelter from the competition of national firms behind walls erected by state legislation. The Big Four were Swift, Armour, Cudahy, and Schwarzschild & Sulzberger.

From the beginning the Swifts had had to contend with prejudice against eating meat killed more than a thousand miles away and many weeks earlier. They did so by advertising. They also had to combat boycotts of local butchers and the concerted efforts of the National Butchers' Protective Association to prevent the sale of their meat in local markets. The association was confident it could do this by inducing various state legislatures to pass a law prohibiting the sale of dressed beef, mutton, or pork unless it had been inspected by state officials twenty-four hours before slaughter. The requirement would effectively banish the Big Four from all but the Chicago market.

In 1889 the association persuaded lawmakers in Minnesota, Indiana, and Colorado to enact such a law, and within a year the leading case of *Minnesota* v. *Barber* (1890) was on the docket of the Supreme Court. Counsel for the association argued that the states had long used inspection laws to improve the competitive position of their producers and that these laws were also essential if the health of their citizens was to be protected. Counsel for the defendant, an Armour agent, countered with the argument that if such laws were upheld as constitutional, the idea of a national free trade unit would be sacrificed at the altar of plenary state inspection power. A unanimous Court agreed, exhibiting once again its determination to strike down state laws inhibiting the flow of goods throughout the national market area.

The resulting competition between large distant and small local producers induced many of the latter, especially firms making established staple items, to take a second path leading to bigness, viz., that of horizontal combination. In the 1880s and early nineties, firms did so in the petroleum, leather, rubber boot and glove, linseed and cotton oil, distilling and other corn products, sugar and salt, biscuit, and fertilizer industries. At one end, capital costs per unit of output were rising with the adoption of new technologies; at the other, price competition was cutting into revenues. To make matters worse, these were years punctuated by repeated periods of stagnant demand. In terms of real output the depression of 1873–1879 was mild; yet it was the longest on record, in monetary statistics second in severity only to the contraction of 1929–1933 among post–Civil War business cycles, and marked by numerous bankruptcies, with their attendant impact on business confidence.

The effect of these periodic setbacks was to compound for businessmen a major problem set in motion by the new national competition and by technological change, viz., how to cope with declining prices. The competitive tactic of lowering prices to expand sales made sense in the short run because of the nature of the cost structure of manufacturing and transportation firms during a period of capital-intensive technological change. Their fixed or overhead costs, in the form of interest on bonds issued to finance the purchase of plant and machinery, for example, had to be met regardless of how much or how little they produced. Their direct or variable costs—expenditures for wages and materials— naturally varied with the volume of production. These were by far the larger part of total costs, and firms could reduce them by curtailing production—and stop them altogether by stopping production. But even if they did, their overhead costs would continue. Andrew Carnegie spoke for many industrialists when he commented in 1889:

> As manufacturing is carried on today, in enormous establishments with five or ten millions of dollars of capital invested and with thousands of workers, it costs the manufacturer much less to run at a loss per ton or per yard than to check his production. Stoppage would be serious indeed. The condition of cheap manufacture is running full. Twenty sources of expense are fixed charges, many of which stoppage would only increase. . . . While continuing to produce may be costly, the manufacturer knows too well that stoppage would be ruin.

The higher the ratio between a firm's investment in fixed assets and its output—the greater its capital–output ratio—the more severe the pressure it was under to expand its sales by cutting its prices. In this way, its overhead costs could be spread over a larger volume, its capital–output ratio lowered. As long as the revenue received more than covered the direct costs of production, at least some part of the overhead costs could be met. Obviously, no firm could continue to price its goods in this way indefinitely, could sell its output at prices below its long-run average total costs. In would become bankrupt if it did, or forced to sell out to a competitor. In sum, price-cutting might work as a short-run tactic, but as a long-run strategy it courted disaster. It was a situation well calculated to induce businessmen to look for some way to put an end to their bitter and costly price competition. "Combinations, syndicates, trusts—" Carnegie frankly admitted. "They are willing to try anything. The manufacturers are in the position of patients that have tried in vain every doctor of the regular school for years, and are now liable to become the victim of any quack that appears."

Initially, business managers sought to dull the blade of competition by loose, informal arrangements, such as the "gentleman's agreement" and the pool. In the main, the former was a verbal pact to set and maintain prices, and its principal disadvantage was the early discovery that not everyone was a gentleman. Pools fared somewhat better. In the 1880s and 1890s they were widely used, mainly as a device to restrict output, by makers of meat products, explosives, whiskey, salt, steel rails, structural steel, cast-iron pipe, and tobacco products. Here, too, there were disadvantages. To the degree that they were effective in maintaining prices they encouraged new entrants into a business. And when they broke down because of some participant's unwillingness in a time of business decline to adhere to his agreement not to encroach on the sales territory of some other member of the pool, or not to exceed his assigned output limits, there was nothing that could be done about it. Under the English common law, enforceable in every American state except Louisiana, the pool was regarded as an illegal, and hence unenforceable, restraint of trade. To achieve the ends they sought, devices were obviously required to ensure tight managerial controls over the centrifugal tendencies of independent firms, and a number of firms soon turned to more closely knit arrangements.

The first and most famous of these—the trust—was the brainchild of S. C. T. Dodd, a lawyer attached to John D. Rockefeller's Standard Oil Company. Trusteeship is an ancient fiduciary device for managing property in the interest of another. In the depression-ridden years of the 1870s Dodd thought of a new use for it. Employing ruthlessly competitive business practices, Rockefeller and his associates had succeeded during that decade in gaining control of over 90 percent of the oil-refining capacity of the country. In 1882, three years after the formation of the Standard Oil trust under the laws of Ohio, they induced the stockholders of forty oil companies to turn their shares over to nine trustees. The latter thus acquired voting control of the forty companies. (This is why the trust, as a technical form of business organization, is sometimes called a voting trust, to distinguish it from the generic name "trust" that was popularly applied during the period to all big businesses.) In place of stock, the former owners received "trust certificates" entitling them to dividends. So profitable did the device prove to be, and so successful as a means of centralizing control of an entire industry, that it was soon widely imitated. During the 1880s trusts were formed to control production in the tobacco, sugar, whiskey, cotton oil, linseed oil, and lead industries.

The fatal defect of the trust form of combination was that it was a matter of public record. And since an agreement to restrain trade or an attempt to gain a monopoly was illegal in the eyes of the common law, trusts were soon attacked in the state courts. In consequence of one such suit, the supreme court of Ohio ordered the Standard Oil Company to withdraw from the trust on the ground that it was attempting to create a monopoly. Clearly, some other form of combination would have to be used in place of the trust, and the solution to the problem became the holding company.

Holding companies do not make or sell anything. Their sole function is to manage operating companies that do these things, and this they do by purchasing and holding the securities of one or more subsidiary companies. The device is thus one that enables a corporation, formed for that purpose alone, to bring under unified control a number of previously independent firms. Some states had created holding companies by special acts of incorporation. What is new about the period of consolidation in American business is New Jersey's revision of its general incorporation laws in 1888–89 in such a way as to allow corporations to purchase and hold the securities of other corporations. It proved unnecessary even to consult nonvoting preferred stockholders or bondholders. Indeed, the common stock itself was often so widely distributed that it was possible to exercise effective control by purchasing less than 50 percent of it. New Jersey's Holding Company act proved so successful in bolstering that state's finances with revenues from incorporation fees that other states soon "liberalized" their corporation laws in an effort to induce businesses to seek charters from them. The word "liberalized" is deliberately placed in quotes. Most state corporation laws were highly conservative at that time. Few of them required corporations to divulge significant information to the investing public. It was only after much mulcting of unprotected investors, stock watering, and other abuses by large corporations that the states, at about the turn of the century, abandoned their excessively liberal attitudes and began requiring increased publicity.

The holding company played the principal role in a giant merger wave that rolled over American industry between 1895 and 1904, figuring in 86 percent of the mergers. The holding company was incorporated, it should be said again for the sake of clarity, for the sole purpose of consolidating a number of previously independent firms, firms which, after the consolidation, retained their firm names as the operating parts of the corporate structure. As a rule, a holding company was created when the size of the companies to be consolidated was large, for then a large capital sum was required to purchase control of their stock. Where firms were small, a company already in existence acquired control of other firms, which disappeared into the merger and lost their firm titles. "Acquisition," as distinguished from "consolidation," figured in 14 percent of the mergers of the 1895–1904 period.

Mergers took place in all major manufacturing and mining industries, but most were concentrated in eight of the latter: primary metals, food products, petroleum products, chemicals, transportation equipment, fabricated metal products, machinery, and bituminous coal. The wave gathered strength slowly, merely five consolidations being effected in both 1895 and 1896. Suddenly, in 1897, that number doubled, then rose to twenty-six in 1898. The next year it soared to 106 before beginning an irregular tapering off to forty-two in 1900, fifty-three in 1901, forty-eight in 1902, fifteen in 1903, and nine in 1904. Altogether, between 1895 and 1904, 319 consolidations took place, with 1898–1902 the five peak years. The total capitalization involved was $6.3 billion, with 40 percent of that total accounted for by only twenty-nine of the 319 consolidations. Each of the twenty-nine had an authorized capitalization of $50 million or more. One, U.S. Steel, had a capitalization of $1.370 billion—the first billion-dollar corporation in history (it alone accounted for 23 percent of the total).

While the number of consolidations taking place affords one view of the great wave, another is presented by a count of the number of firms disappearing into mergers. In the period 1895–1904 the average annual number was 301. In the five peak years of 1898–1904, however, merger activity reached heights never exceeded in our history, with 1,028 firms disappearing in the year 1899 alone. The huge turn-of-the-century wave produced U.S. Steel, American Tobacco, International Harvester, Du Pont, Corn Products, Anaconda Copper, and American Smelting and Refining, to name only a few of the well-known firms of the twentieth century. Of the largest corporations in the country in 1955, twenty were born during the period 1895–1904. The effect of the merger wave on American industry was therefore widespread and enduring.

According to a conservative estimate, by 1904, 318 firms had come into possession of 40 percent of all manufacturing assets. The absolute size of many of the new companies was a disturbing feature to many contemporary critics. But it was not the only one. More disturbing still was their size in relation to the markets they served. As a result of the merger wave between 1895 and 1904, a single firm came to account for 60 percent or more of total output in at least fifty industries. DuPont, General Electric, Westinghouse, Pullman, and American Tobacco were among sixteen companies controlling 85 percent or more of their respective markets. Surely the principal result, and probably also the principal purpose of the mergers, was the control of output and price. Only thus could cutthroat competition be brought to an end.

The same kind of competition had beset the nation's railroads, too, for while traffic increased consistently throughout the nineteenth century railroad mileage grew even faster. More and more virulent rate wars during the hectic years between the two great depressions of 1873 and 1893 drove down the revenues of even well-managed companies and forced others into bankruptcy. In the decade 1882–1891 no fewer than 279 railroad companies went into receivership, the bankruptcies involving nearly $2 billion in capital and 38,000 miles of track. The primary cause, says the early twentieth-century historian of railroad finance and organization, was "over-expansion or excessive competition."

Like the heads of manufacturing firms, railroad presidents also resorted to mergers. Their most distinctive, and also most important, technique for dulling the blade of competition was to form a "community of interest." One way to achieve this was for a railroad to purchase stock in other railroads, thereby gaining representation on their boards of directors. Such arrangements, which originated among Eastern railroads in the mid-1880s, accelerated rapidly following massive defaulting on bonds during the great shakeout brought on by the depression of 1893–1897. The president of the Pennsylvania Railroad Company, Alexander J. Cassatt, explained their advantages in an annual report to his stockholders:

> The only alternative [to indefinite cost reduction] is to arrest the reduction in revenue, which has been largely brought about by apparently uncontrollable conflicts between the railroad companies . . . to establish closer relations between the managers of the trunk lines, it seemed wise to your Board to acquire an interest in some of the railways reaching the seaboard and to unite with the other shareholders who control these properties in supporting a conservative policy.

By 1902 the Pennsylvania owned $52 million of B&O common stock, $26 million of Norfolk & Western, and $10 million of Chesapeake & Ohio, and President Cassatt reported that the community of interest was working well. Presumably it was also working well for the New York Central and other roads which had followed suit. By 1906 the greater part of the nation's railroad mileage and an even larger share of its traffic was accounted for by communities of interest. From a list containing merely thirty-nine names, it would have been possible to make up a majority on the board of directors of all the important railroads east of the Mississippi, railroads which controlled all access by land to the ports of New York, Philadelphia, and Boston.

One of these communities—by 1906 there were eight in all—was the Southeastern system of "Morgan roads." The group included eleven companies with almost 19,000 miles of track, besides a Morgan ownership interest in two other major groups, the Vanderbilt and Hill lines, which together amounted to nearly another 30,000 miles. The influence of John Pierpoint Morgan and his investment banking house was thus not confined to a single region of the country. The most outstanding private figure in the history of American finance, Morgan had assumed leadership of the forces attempting to stabilize American railroads since at least the 1880s, when he brought about harmony between the New York Central and the Pennsylvania.

Morgan had good reason for his concern that business relations among the railroads be orderly and harmonious, that the railroads abandon rate cutting and other competitive practices that threatened earnings, security values, and the financial stability of the industry. The railroads needed huge loans to upgrade their properties, and his banking house provided many of these loans by marketing their bonds. Indeed, Morgan & Company managed, comanaged, or participated in underwriting most of the major railroad loans of the Progressive Era. Morgan also sometimes gave his blessing to issues of common stock, which induced investors to buy what was then a relatively unfamiliar kind of security. To protect the interests of investors, Morgan men sat on the boards of corporations whose securities they issued. According to the 1912 report of the Pujo Committee, appointed by the Senate to investigate the activities of an alleged "money trust," Morgan or his partners held seventy-two directorships in 112 of the country's largest financial, transportation, industrial, and public utility companies. About half of the firm's total deposits of $162.5 million belonged to seventy-eight interstate corporations, and of these, thirty-two included one or more Morgan men on their board. Between 1902 and 1912 Morgan & Company's public security offerings reached a total of $1.95 billion.

In sum, Morgan & Company and other investment banking firms reorganized the nation's railroads in the 1890s. They rehabilitated numerous bankrupt or financially weak roads and then proceeded to regulate competition. They did so by restructuring and rationalizing the systems and managements of the troubled companies through consolidations and by arranging for rival lines to buy stock in each other's properties. Finally, Morgan & Company partners served on many railroad boards and finance committees for the purpose of influencing investment and vetoing unwise expenditures in the interests of corporate stability and profitability. One of those partners, George W. Perkins—he was also a vice president of the New York Life Insurance Company— unquestionably gave voice to the philosophy not only of Morgan but also of many of the nation's business leaders when he testified in 1905 before the Armstrong Commission of New York, charged with investigating the insurance industry of that state. "The old idea that we were raised under, that competition is the life of trade, is exploded. Competition is no longer the life of trade, it is cooperation. . . ."

To put an end to competition, however, was to do violence to one of the deepest of American traditions. Indeed, hatred of monopoly sinks its roots in English as well as American soil. The tradition has found expression in different ways at different times. At first it took the form of opposition to special legal privileges granted by the state—for example, those bestowed on early nineteenth-century corporations, including the First and Second Banks of the United States. Later, monopoly more often came to mean the exclusive control that a few persons achieved by their own efforts. Always, however, it meant unjustified power of one kind or another, especially when it got in the way of equality of opportunity.

As the latter implies, antimonopoly is something more than an economic tradition. It is also political, social, and moral. Nineteenth-century Americans were neither the first nor last to look upon the discipline of competition as a mechanism for the development of character. They also believed that there was a close connection between a competitive economy and the whole democratic way of life, and they looked to the legal system to block private accumulations of power that might threaten democratic government.

By the end of the 1880s public opposition to the "trusts," a term that soon came to stand for Big Business, was so strong that

Congress had no choice but to respond. As Senator John Sherman told the Senate in March 1890: "I did not originally intend to make any extended argument on this trust bill, because I supposed that the public facts upon which it is founded and the general necessity of some legislation were so manifest that no debate was necessary to bring those facts to the attention of the Senate."

Despite this acknowledgment of well-understood public facts, scholars remain uncertain why Congress cast a nearly unanimous vote—the Senate vote was 52 to 1, the House 242 to 0—in favor of the Sherman Antitrust Act of 1890. This was a conservative legislature, indeed one whose membership was so representative of the interests of Big Business as to have won the sobriquet "Billion-Dollar Congress." Yet the Stanfords, Platts, Paynes, Aldriches, and other members of that Congress condemned in sweeping language *every* contract or combination in restraint of interstate or foreign trade, and *every* person who should monopolize any part of that trade, or attempt to do so, or combine or conspire with any other person or persons to do so. Did they mean what they said? Intimately aware, as many unquestionably were, of the national market's imperative need for production in large volume by large firms—can they have meant to outlaw *every* combination by which size was achieved?

Big Business itself regarded the Act as impractical, unenforceable, and hence innocuous. Some members of the 51st Congress felt much the same way. If the Sherman Act were "strictly and literally enforced," said Senator Cullom of Illinois, "the business of the country would come to a standstill." Senator Platt of Connecticut accused his colleagues of playing politics: "The conduct of the Senate . . . has not been in the line of honest preparation of a bill to prohibit and punish trusts. It has been in the line of getting some bill with that title that we might go to the country with. The questions of whether the bill would be operative, of how it would operate, . . . have been whistled down the wind in this Senate as idle talk, and the whole effort has been to get some bill headed 'A

Bill to Punish Trusts' with which to go to the country." Mr. Dooley, the Will Rogers of his day, quietly observed that "what looks like a stone-wall to a lay man is a triumphal arch to a corporation lawyer."

Complex questions of motivation do not yield final answers; their solutions are judgment calls. In my view, there is something to be said for the suggestion that the main attention of the Congress during the years 1888–1890 was fixed on the tariff, that discussion of trusts was frequently intertwined with it, and that since some opponents of the tariff had raised the cry that the tariff was the "mother of the trusts," Congress enacted an antitrust bill to weaken opposition to the tariff. Yet the circumstance that talk about trusts was often intermixed with tariff talk does not mean that the latter was essential to the former. Such was the public concern over the trusts that political address of the question was probably inescapable. In the end it may be that the social and cultural context in which the law was enacted played a subtly significant role. If one commences with an awareness of the postbellum era as one of rapid and almost tumultuous change, as a period of unprecedented population increase and movement, of quickening urbanization and industrialization, it will not be difficult to appreciate the sense of uncertainty, of unsettlement, indeed of frustration and loss of identity that must have accompanied the impact of these changes on once-secure values. Viewed in these terms, monopoly takes on a symbolic significance, a significance not unlike that vested by the Age of Jackson in the Monster Bank. Antimonopoly becomes a cry of protest on the part of individuals increasingly depersonalized and lost in corporate anonymity, of small towns increasingly invaded by the railroad, of small business and small farmers increasingly menaced by large-scale and distant competition. It may well be that Congress heard this outcry and responded to it. If so, that response was not fraudulent, but one of moral affirmation. Viewed in this light, the Sherman Act becomes not so much law as Resolution. Speaking for the nation, Congress affirmed the validity of a traditional value—the belief in competition, a value closely linked with the political, social, and moral values of democratic government.

At the same time, one must not rule out the possibility that a conservative Congress passed the buck to the administration and to the federal courts in confident expectation that the Sherman Act would not be enforced or interpreted in ways hostile to the interests of Big Business. If so, the early history of the enforcement of the law justified the expectation. Even more conservative than the Congress, the Supreme Court ruled in the *E. C. Knight case* (1895) that even a virtual monopoly (98 percent) of the manufacture of refined sugar did not violate the Sherman Act—but labor unions did (*Loewe* v. *Lawlor,* 1908). This and other exuberances— e.g., the *Gompers Case* of 1911—led the Congress to assert in the Clayton Act (1914) that "Nothing contained in the antitrust laws should be construed to forbid the existence and operation of labor . . . organizations . . . nor shall such organizations, or the members thereof, be held or construed to be illegal combinations or conspiracies in restraint of trade, under the antitrust laws." Despite the decisive language of Congress, the Supreme Court soon rendered it a nullity in the case of *Duplex Printing Press Co.* v. *Deering* (1921) and, a few weeks later, *American Steel Foundries* v. *Tri-City Central Trade Council.* It did the same with Congress' effort to compel employers of child labor to observe specified standards, declaring the law unconstitutional (*Hammer* v. *Dagenhart,* 1918). Not till the 1930s was labor to receive the benefit of a new deal, from the judiciary as well as Congress and the executive branch of government.

By present standards, the age of America's first industrial revolution must be regarded as callous in its relative indifference to the welfare and safety of workers. The unemployed worker was cast adrift. As a rule, there was no such thing as public relief, and private charity was either insufficient or offered only on demeaning terms. The risks of injury or death on the job were grievously high. The United States had one of the highest industrial accident rates in the Western world. From 1880 to 1900, 35,000 workers were killed each year and another 536,000 injured. According to estimates made by the Bureau of Labor Statistics in 1921, 2.5 million industrial accidents occurred each year in the United States. Of these, more than 21,000 were fatal, with 105,000 resulting in permanent partial disability. Roughly 227 million man-days a year were lost, at a cost exceeding $1 billion in lost wages. By then, fortunately, numerous workers were covered by workmen's compensation laws. Railroad workers were so covered after 1909, and after 1914 a number of states enacted even broader legislation that was acceptable to the courts. Before then, however, workers suffering injury on the job could expect no compensation. Few could afford insurance, and the common law continued, as in the early nineteenth century, to reflect the needs of a developing economy for capital formation.

It did so by effectively exonerating the employer from responsibility for injuries—or death—incurred by his workers. In the 1842 case of *Farwell* v. *The Boston & Worcester Railroad Corporation,* Chief Justice Lemuel Shaw of the Massachusetts Supreme Judicial Court laid down a principle of common law which was to hold during most of the remainder of the century. An employee could not sue his employer for injuries caused by the negligence of another employee (the "fellow servant" rule). Adopting a contractarian view of the relationship between employer and employee, Shaw held that a worker entered into an implied contract to assume the "natural and ordinary risks and perils incident to the performance of [his] services" and that these were perils which he was "as likely to know, and against which he [could] as effectually guard, as the master." Indeed, his wages included a premium for the risks he assumed. To be sure, he could sue his employer, provided his injuries were caused by the personal misconduct of the employer himself. But the factory system and corporate ownership of industry made this right virtually meaningless. In all likelihood, the owner of a factory was a soulless legal entity, and even if the owner was an individual proprietor, the chances were that he did not have anything to do with the operation of machinery and equipment. If an employee was injured, then, legal fault would be ascribed to a fellow worker, if anyone. And fellow workers were men without wealth or insurance. Thus, the fellow servant rule, by relieving employers from nearly all legal consequences of injuries, encouraged investment in industrial enterprises.

This same Chief Justice Shaw, it must also be said, held labor unions to be legal, rather than conspiracies in restraint of trade. But his was a voice sounding in a wilderness. The bias of the federal courts leaned heavily against workers and their unions for the most part. From the late 1880s on, strikes, picket lines, and boycotts were easily broken up by the use of the labor injunction. Judges usually issued these restraining orders on request, many of them believing economic coercion by unions to be illegal. It was not till 1895 that the Supreme Court, for the first time in its history, passed on the scope and validity of an injunction in a labor dispute. Not surprisingly, it ordered the leaders of the American Railway Union to end their strike against a number of railroads *(In re Debs)*. Thus was the famous Pullman Strike of 1894 brought to an end, in the words of Eugene v. Debs, "simply and solely by the action of the United States Courts in restraining us from discharging our duties as officers and representatives of the employees."

The interests of workers generally fared better at the hands of state legislatures and courts. Labor was strongest in the industrial Northeast and Great Lakes regions, and states in those areas enacted an increasing volume of protective laws. Some forbade the blacklist, some outlawed the yellow-dog contract (which exacted from workers as a condition for employment their promise not to join a union), some required employers to pay their workers in cash instead of in goods at the country store, or to pay them weekly or biweekly, and some even punished infringement of the union label. While the fate of such laws varied from state to state, they were generally upheld. Indeed, most were never even questioned.

Few unions, however, were able to organize nationally and endure. Among those which succumbed to depression in the 1870s were the Sons of Vulcan (iron and steel workers), the Knights of St. Crispin (shoemakers), and the Workingman's Benevolent Association (miners). The Knights of Labor, a chaotic mixture of unions of skilled craftsmen and of semiskilled and unskilled workers, lasted longer (originating in 1869 among Philadelphia garment cutters, it was all but dead by 1900), but fell victim to poor leadership on the part of its officers, especially Terence V. Powderly, who was part idealist, part politician, and part mountebank. The "pure and simple unionism" of Samuel Gompers, head of the American Federation of Labor from the time of its organization until his death in 1924, proved far more successful. (Once, when asked what the goals of the AFL were, he is said to have replied simply, "More.") An amalgam of national unions of skilled craftsmen, the AFL boasted a membership of over 2 million by the eve of World War I.

Even so, not even 8 percent of the American labor force was unionized at any time before 1914. The ethnic heterogeneity of the urban work force militated against labor unity. To a large extent occupation was determined by nationality. The most highly skilled workers—railroad engineers and printers, for instance— were predominantly American-born. The older immigrants, Irish and German, dominated the building trades, and the Germans were established in cigar making, brewing, and furniture work. The lake seamen of Chicago were Scandinavian, the apartment janitors Flemish. The Czechs, Poles, and Italians crowded into the big cities were mainly unskilled—and available as strike breakers. Feelings of class solidarity permitted urban workers to unite for brief periods, but ethnic rivalries soon asserted themselves.

Gains in wages and hours achieved during these years were owing not to the labor movement but to increases in productivity stemming from heavy inputs of capital, both physical and human. In general, almost all workers in manufacturing benefited from a reduction in the number of hours worked per week—from about sixty-five hours in 1860 to sixty in 1890 and to 56.6 in 1910. Essentially, the average worker took part of his income in the form of leisure. When he worked, he also took home more pay. Between 1860 and 1890, the average daily money wage, annual money earnings, and the net rise in real wages all amounted to approximately 50 percent in manufacturing. Average hourly earnings changed very little in money terms between 1890 and 1899, but they went up substantially from 1900 to 1914. Real wages rose 37 percent throughout the period 1890–1914.

Increases in wage rates, needless to say, bring more take-home pay only to the employed. Unhappily, unemployment, sometimes prolonged, punctuated these years. Continuous depression marked the years 1873–1879; by 1879 at least 2 million workers in manufacturing were unemployed. This was 13 percent of the labor force. A lesser rate of perhaps 7.5 percent characterized the depression year 1885, but the depression of the 1890s was one of the severest before the 1930s, with an estimated 3.305 million, or 13.4 percent of the labor force unemployed at the end of 1893. The percentage rose to 18.4 percent the next year.

The wage gains of the employed, however, failed to keep pace with advances in productivity. The most reasonable explanation of the lag is that immigration increased the supply of workers, and that this, at a given level of demand, tended to drive down the wage rate of industrial workers in general, native as well as immigrant. But this does not mean that employers discriminated in favor of native workers and paid them more than immigrants. On the contrary, there is strong evidence that variations in earnings between native Americans and immigrants were significantly related to the length of time workers had lived in the United

States. As length of residence increased, so too did the worker's mastery of the English language, level of literacy, and probably other skills as well. Variations in these linguistic factors go far to explain differences in wage payments not only between natives and immigrants but also between ethnic groups among the latter.

Had some employers discriminated by offering immigrants a wage lower than the value of their services to the firm, other employers could have increased their profits by hiring them at a slightly higher wage. Soon the competition for workers would push up the wage to a level at which it equalled the worker's value. In industries marked by a high degree of concentration, however, the competitive blade was undoubtedly dulled. And other forms of discrimination probably occurred. Foreign-born workers faced discrimination in employment security: They were the first to be fired in periods of reduced industrial activity. In addition, their real earnings were probably reduced by price discrimination—for example, in the form of rents paid by new immigrants.

Women and children were also discriminated against. To be sure, most gainful workers ten years of age or older were white males, their numbers increasing from 12.505 million in 1870 to 38.167 million in 1910. But the number of immigrant and native women joining the labor force also rose smartly during these years, from 1,836,300 to 8,075,800. The mechanization of industrial processes gradually diluted the skills required for employment and created new opportunities for the unskilled of both sexes—in food processing and canning, for example, or in the manufacture of paper and cardboard boxes, or the production of irons, heaters, and other products in the new electrical industry. Job opportunities for women as salesclerks in department stores and as clerks, typists, stenographers, and bookkeepers in growing numbers of bureaucratized corporations also expanded rapidly. But while women do not appear to have been paid less than men where both did the same work, they rarely did. As a rule, they worked in a narrower range of occupations and in less skilled positions than men. In sum, the labor market was segmented by sex. The labor force had two separate work and wage tracks, one for men and one for women, with men more than twice as likely as women to land jobs as professionals, managers, foremen, or skilled laborers. To be sure, the great majority of native American women workers were young single girls who withdrew from the labor force after marriage. But it is also true that the number of working wives continually expanded, rising from 14 percent of the female labor force in 1890 to 25 percent twenty years later.

The labor of children was nothing new to an economy long dominated by agriculture and a scarcity of workers. Farmers had always trained their children to do the milking, haying, plowing, planting, hauling, and other chores, and throughout the period of our present concern, agriculture continued to be the greatest field of their employment. Children had also been employed in large numbers in industry, notably in the early New England textile mills. By 1820, about 45 percent of the cotton mill workers in Massachusetts were children; in Rhode Island the figure was 55 percent. Nevertheless, child labor never became a really substantial source of labor in America, not even in agriculture or in cotton textiles. While children between ten and thirteen still constituted 13 percent of the wage earners in the latter industry in 1900, their employment everywhere in manufacturing was on the wane. This was more true of the children of native than of immigrant parents, however, for one out of every four working children that year fell into the latter category. In contrast, only one in ten was a child of natives.

In retrospect, the row was longer and the hoeing more difficult for immigrants. They came in on the lower rungs of the economic ladder, like other groups of immigrants before them, but as they learned English and acquired other skills, their earnings rose. Each group followed in the footsteps of those who had preceded them, and ethnic discrimination had little or no impact on wage levels. But their own impact on American economic growth was undoubtedly substantial. Two out of every three immigrants fell within the prime working ages of fifteen to forty, and although a large proportion had no industrial skills, this was not true of all newcomers. We can say, about those who did possess skills, that much of the cost of this human capital formation—the cost of training them—was borne by Europe, while the benefits were reaped in America—benefits that took the form of capital inputs to production processes. As for the far deeper pool of unskilled labor, the least we can say is that Europeans bore the cost of nurturing to maturity a host of willing workers whose ability is attested to by the long list of industries that came to depend on them. Finally, increases in capital resulting from the higher labor force participation rate of immigrants—a larger proportion of immigrants than of natives joined the labor force—are calculated to have generated economies of scale that raised the per capita income of the native-born population by nearly one fourth over the century ending in 1920.

VI

Between the Wars

T HE interim between the two great wars of the twentieth century is one of vivid contrasts. It would be difficult to select two other decades of our history in which the economy fell so unexpectedly from a peak of prosperity into a deep trough of depression. The stock market provided one index of that prosperity and in the judgment of a respected Yale University economist, Irving Fisher, it reached a "permanently high plateau" on October 2, 1929. Only three days later stocks lost 12 percent of their value, the biggest percentage drop in our history, before or since. By March 1933, one out of every four workers was looking for a job in vain. As late as 1939 unemployment stood at 17 percent of the labor force. What caused the Great Depression and why did it last so long?

Now, of course, not everybody was poor in the thirties and rich in the twenties. Not every industry, occupation, or area of the country shared equally in prosperity or distress. And the market values of stocks are only one of many indices of an economy's health. To determine how vigorous or weak the economy was in either decade, we have to look at the principal sectors that make it up. We need to go down on the farm and into the city and ask how the real economic actors were doing. The values of securities influence managerial decisions about raising capital but a lot of other things do too. And these include not only interest rates and tax policies but, above all, judgments about the future.

Probably the future looked bright to most people most of the time in the twenties. After steep declines in output and incomes in 1920–1921, businessmen regained their confidence and invested sharply in production facilities of many kinds. New manufacturing plants made possible a huge expansion in the output of durable goods, of automobiles, refrigerators, and radios, furniture and vacuum cleaners. Continued growth in central power production and distribution facilities added to the capital available to the American people. So did the construction industries. The twenties witnessed a housing boom, in city apartments as well as single family residences in the suburbs. States raised their expenditures on highway construction from $70 million in 1918 to $750 million in 1930. Together with city governments, they floated bonds to finance the building of schools. In a word, what economists called a process of "capital deepening" took place in the 1920s.

A similar deepening process had been going on at least since the closing decades of the preceding century. Manufacturing plants were built up, hand and animal work in agriculture gave way to mechanization, and railroad leaders double-tracked much of the country. What differentiated the twenties from all this was the quality of the capital put in place. It was better capital, technologically superior, and this made possible a larger amount of output for every dollar invested. A major wave of capital-improving innovations broke over the manufacturing sector in the twenties and raised productivity in petroleum refining, and in the paper, chemical, and other industries. More and more, technological progress was reflecting the progress of science itself. Less and less was it dependent on the trial-and-error methods of most of the nineteenth century. Finally, the technology consisted not only of "hardware" but also of "software" in the form of better organization and management of business firms. And the capital inputs into the production process were human as well as physical, a consequence of society's greater attention to the importance of education.

More and better capital to work with raised the efficiency of the labor force and made possible increases in wages. Real income per worker went up from $629 a year between 1909 and 1918 to $738 a year between 1919 and 1928. The increase per capita of the whole population (which is how economic growth is measured) was from $517 to $612. In sum, investment in new and better plants raised productivity and incomes which, when spent, not only repaid the cost of the investment but encouraged more of it. But people did not restrict their spending to the amount of cash they had. They also bought "on time." Finance companies specialized in providing installment credit, and the amount of it rose remarkably, from $1.375 billion in 1925 to $3 billion only four years later. Buyers made wide use of the technique to purchase cars, furniture, radios, and other electrical equipment for the home.

However financed, the twenties witnessed what can only be called a consumer-durables revolution. According to a popular but astute writer on economic subjects during those years, Stuart Chase, the estimated 27 million American homes had durable articles in the following numbers in 1928:

15.3 million	electric flat irons
6.828 million	vacuum cleaners
5 million	washing machines
4.9 million	electric fans
4.54 million	electric toasters
2.6 million	electric heaters
755,000	electric refrigerators
348,000	ironing machines

In 1920, Chase added, there were sixty-one telephones per 1,000 city people. In 1928 there were ninety-five per 1,000. In the same interval the number of radios rose from just about zero to 10 million. While Chase doubted that the home of the average American was as comfortable as it had been in 1890, he acknowledged that it nevertheless had running water, a bathtub, electric lights, and probably a radio and telephone—"which makes it a cleaner, better lighted, more strenuous and far noisier home."

A consumer durable parked outside the home was noisy too, especially when the "UHOOGAH" of its concerted horns blared to protest the traffic jams. But it transformed personal and social relations, and changed patterns of settlement and mobility. The automobile promised romance, adventure, and escape from monotony: "North America lies in the hollow of our hands!" Chase exulted. "Mountains, canyon, pass and glacier; mighty rivers, roaring cataracts, the glint of the sea—jump in, step on it, all are yours." The automobile "fired the blood like wine."

It fired the economy too. To Chase, the automobile, the production of which rose 255 percent in the twenties (passenger car registration increased from 9.3 million to 23.1 million between 1921 and 1929) provided the fundamental explanation of the prosperity of the decade. The booming car industry interlocked at one end with large increases in the production of gasoline and oil, rubber products, plate glass, metals, and other inputs, and at the other end with highways, residential and commercial construction, and the cement, lumber, and still other industries. Even with these linkages in mind, it remains true that no single industry can account for more than a small fraction of the economy's total output. Nevertheless, automobiles were the leading growth industry of the twenties. What made it so were the efficiencies achieved by its techniques of mass production. These cheapened the cost of automobiles and made it possible for millions of people to afford them.

Henry Ford did not invent the moving assembly line, but he did encourage his assistants in experiments which culminated in mass production at unprecedented speed and on a scale never seen before. Instead of workmen bringing parts to the point of assembly and putting them together, an assembly belt moved the chassis frame, axles, motor, and other major components past stations at speeds perfectly timed to enable workmen to perform their assigned operations. The work moved to the worker. Ford himself described the process in *My Life and Work:*

> In the chassis assembly are forty-five separate operations or stations. The first men fasten four mudguard brackets to the chassis frame; the motor arrives on the tenth operation. . . . Some men do only one or two small operations, others do more. The man who places a part does not fasten it—the part may not be fully in place until after several operations later. The man who puts in the bolt does not put on the nut; the man who puts on the nut does not tighten it. On operation number thirty-four the budding motor gets its gasoline; it has previously received lubrication; on operation number forty-four the radiator is filled with water, and on operation forty-five the car drives out. . . .

As a rule, one drove out of the Ford factory about every forty-five seconds. Up to 1926, when Ford discontinued production of his famous Model T, he had sold 15 million cars, half of the nation's entire output of new cars, more than double that of his nearest competitor, General Motors. In 1923 alone Ford had made and sold nearly 1.7 million. The introduction and perfection of the moving assembly line had enabled him to increase his annual output more than 150 times and to lower production costs and the sales prices of his cars.

Famous as Ford became (he may have been more widely known than any other American in the early 1920s), his automobiles didn't sell themselves, certainly not at first. Ralph Waldo Emerson said that the world would beat a path to the door of the man who invented a better mousetrap. But he was wrong: The inventor would have to advertise. And Ford did too. Announcing his intended product in 1909 he told the public:

I will build a motor car for the great multitude. It will be large enough for the family but small enough for the individual to run and care for. It will be constructed of the best materials, by the best men to be hired, after the simplest designs that modern engineering can devise. But it will be so low in price that no man making a good salary will be unable to own one—and enjoy with his family the blessing of hours of pleasure in God's great open spaces.

Not only automobiles had to be advertised. Manufacturers of other products also sought to differentiate their wares from those of their competitors. The twenties saw the birth of modern advertising, of advertising as an important part of America's secular culture. Not that only secular subjects were grist for its mills. In *The Man That Nobody Knows,* a best-seller in the midtwenties, Bruce Barton portrayed Jesus as a supersalesman, the parables as "the most powerful advertisements of all time." Jesus was a top-notch businessman: "He picked up twelve men from the bottom ranks of business and forged them into an organization that conquered the world." Anyone doubting that business was His main concern had only to read the Bible. Hadn't Jesus Himself said, "Wist ye not that I must be about my father's business?" If even Jesus had to be advertised, who or what was immune?

What a difference a few decades had made! In the late nineteenth century the warning "No Beggars, Peddlers, or Advertising Men" had appeared on signs affixed to many a shop and office door. Advertising was widely regarded as on the fringe of legitimate business activity. Media advertising revenue in 1865 was on the order of $7.5 million, but by 1921 revenue amounted to ninety times that sum. By 1929 expenditures on advertising reached a total of $3.4 billion, more than 3 percent of the Gross National Product.

In sum, the prosperity of the twenties rode a rising wave of incomes that crested in installment credit and then flowed into channels marked off by salesmen and advertisers. These higher incomes were themselves products of gains realized in the efficiency of production. But not all production was efficient and not all industries did well. If they had, there would have been no Great Depression. The lumber industry first overexpanded in response to the construction boom and then followed the decline of the latter in the later twenties. The value of forest products fell sharply from $311 million in 1928 to $173.2 million in 1929. Lumbering, like coal mining, also suffered from depleted resources in various parts of the country, most notably in the northern portions of the Great Lakes states. The railroad industry was hurt by severe competition from newer forms of transit. Trucks deprived them of some of their freight, and buses and private automobiles of some of their passengers. Railroad passenger-miles declined from 47 million in 1920 to 34 million in 1927. (The return on railroad investment exceeded 5 percent in only one year, 1926, when it reached 5.2 percent.) Above all, agriculture was afflicted. Mainly because of the difficulties experienced in agriculture and in lumbering and mining, per capita income growth in the West North Central states and those of the Mountain West and South lagged behind gains achieved in other regions.

The farmer was the "sick man" in the economy of the twenties. His basic problem was the same as it is today: He produced too much. For one thing, he put under cultivation more land than was justified by the demand for agricultural products. Demand had been high during the first World War when the needs of the Allies had to be added to those of a growing urban population in this country. To meet those needs, farmers had placed under cultivation an additional 40 million acres. While all of these acres by no means remained in production in the postwar world, the land supply received another upward jolt in the twenties. Tractors replaced horses and mules, and this released for the production of salable crops some 24 million acres, which before had been used to produce oats and hay for the draft animals.

It wasn't just that farmers were working more land than was needed. They were also working it more efficiently. Except in the

South, the number of tractors on farms rose spectacularly, from 85,000 in 1918 to 827,000 in 1929. That meant substantial growth in numbers of tractor-driven grain combines and corn pickers. The increased use of still other mechanical equipment, and of more motor trucks and automobiles, raised the productivity of the farm worker. Neither foreign nor domestic demand could keep up with the oversupply. The postwar restoration of European agriculture, together with the adoption of protective tariffs by a number of foreign governments, reduced demand from that quarter. And although urban incomes were rising here, demand for meats, grains, and most of the major farm products was inelastic with respect to both income and price. (Increases in urban incomes or reductions in the prices of farm products brought about a less than proportionate increase in demand for those products.)

Slumping demand and growing efficiency meant that fewer people were needed down on the farm. In most years during the twenties, the net movement from farms exceeded the natural increase of the farm population. With fewer people in farming, demand for farmland declined, and with it its price. That made it hard on farmers, for most of them had not fully paid for their land. They had made a small down payment and signed a promissory note for the balance, a note that was backed by one or more mortgages on the land. As long as land values were rising, banks and insurance companies were willing to renew the notes. But when values fell, they faced a loss of equity and foreclosed. The value of farmland fell throughout the twenties, and the widespread foreclosures on mortgages that followed carried many rural banks into insolvency. They got the land, but in a declining market they couldn't sell it at a price that would have enabled them to recover the amount of the loan. No wonder income from farming represented a declining share of national income. Between 1919 and 1928, that share fell in half, from 18.5 percent to 9.5 percent.

Compounding these general agricultural problems were special ones faced by farmers in various regions of the country. Some of the worst mortgage trouble spots were in areas of recent settlement by people unacquainted with the physical limitations of those places. Inexperienced settlers from farther east, where rainfall was plentiful, located on farms in the Great Plains that were too small for a semiarid region. Introducing crop farming into areas that in the long run were unsuited to it, they found themselves in trouble. Similar mistakes were made by settlers in the cut-over areas of the Lake states. Soils there were relatively unproductive and normally capable of supporting little more than subsistence agriculture. Farm mortgage distress in the region, especially in northern and central Minnesota, upper Michigan, and a large part of Wisconsin, was of major proportions. Foreclosure rates were also very high in the Corn Belt, but the highest rates occurred in such poor soil regions as southern and northwestern Iowa, northern Missouri, and southern Indiana. Unquestionably, a number of regions were overpopulated in relation to their supply of natural resources. People would have been better off if they had migrated from areas of stunted opportunities to others where life chances were superior. Most stayed put. Perhaps they were unwilling to admit defeat.

To make matters worse, farmers in some regions had expenses that others could avoid. Where drought was a problem, as in the Great Plains, Mountain states, and parts of the Northwest, they had to pay taxes to cover the costs of operating and maintaining irrigation districts. Hot winds, hail, and frost added to their problems by reducing crop yields. And while insect pests, noxious weeds, and plant and animal diseases reduced production in some cases, in others their costs took the form of cash outlays for control measures. In Louisiana, the mosaic disease almost wiped out the sugar industry, before it was conquered in the late twenties and early thirties by the introduction of new varieties of cane. Making its appearance in the cotton states of the Southeast in the late teens, the boll weevil blanketed the cotton South by 1923. In Georgia, the pest reduced yields by 45 percent in 1921, 44 percent in 1922, and 37 percent in 1923. In South Carolina, the greatest reduction, 40 percent, occurred in 1922.

In both the twenties and thirties, the South was a chronic trouble area. The basic cause was the farmer's nearly total dependence on cotton. Cotton prices hit lows in 1921–1922 and then recovered, in part because of poor yields in the eastern cotton belt. The explanation for this apparent anomaly is simple. Technological innovation in the chemical industries, especially the development of rayon and nylon as substitutes for natural fibers, was somewhat reducing the demand for cotton and exerting downward pressure on its price. Reduced supplies of cotton helped counteract this pressure. But cotton farmers everywhere had high costs, and these lowered their income. Those in the eastern cotton belt had to pay relatively high debt service charges. Those in the Mississippi delta—Arkansas, Mississippi, and Louisiana—had not only to pay drainage taxes but also additional imposts for levee districts, road districts, and sometimes even fence districts.

Behind the cotton farmer's monocultural predicament lay a host of social and demographic problems as well as economic ones. In short, what lay behind it was Southern history. The relative failure of industry to develop left the South still 67.9 percent rural even in 1930, with 42.8 percent of its labor force still working on farms and earning a per capita income of $189, in contrast with $484 for nonfarm occupations. The rural scene was the old and familiar one of a patient Negro driving a mule, walking endlessly behind a plow in search of an elusive freedom from economic slavery. For blacks, poverty, ignorance, illiteracy, and superstition remained bitter by-products of racial oppression and parsimonious expenditures on public education. But these characteristics experienced little difficulty in crossing the color line. Application of an effective insecticide, calcium arsenate, to the weevil scourge was frequently resisted by farmers, who insisted that the weevil represented a judgment of God. Similarly, obstinate folkways hampered the war on the cattle tick, bearer of Texas fever.

Some farmers did better than others, of course, and the same is true of factory workers. Men and women with skills made more money than those who lacked them. The skilled proportion probably rose in the twenties. One reason for believing so is that public expenditures on education doubled between 1920 and 1928. A good deal of the increase went into secondary education, and the number of seventeen-year-olds graduating from high school went up by 10 percent. The number of men and women graduating from college rose even more impressively, the former doubling, the latter nearly tripling. In 1928 a quarter of the American population was enrolled in school. That was a higher percentage than for any country in Europe.

A second reason for believing that the proportion of skilled workers rose is that restrictions on immigration reduced the numbers of unskilled. After passage of the National Origins Act in 1924, the annual flow of immigrants fell to less than a fourth of what it had been before the war. Immigrants had accounted for 73 percent of the growth of the labor force between 1900 and 1914, but between the latter date and 1930 the percentage fell to 40 percent. The resulting decline in the numbers of unskilled foreign workers tended to raise the wages of the native unskilled and to narrow the gap between those wages and the earnings of the skilled.

Not only were the average incomes of factory workers higher than before the war: Inflation did not erode the purchasing power of the dollars they earned. Prices were essentially stable from the end of the 1920–1921 depression to the end of the decade. Not least among their advantages was the abundant availability of consumer goods on which workers could spend their money. In the late twentieth century, the rare Soviet worker who can afford a car has to wait six months or more for delivery. Workers in Japan save as much as they do not only because of government incentives but also because of a severe housing shortage.

American industrial workers in the twenties were well off in other ways as well. The factory, especially the large one, was a safer, cleaner, and more spacious place in which to work. It was better lighted, heated, and ventilated. Machines and equipment were engineered for safe use and plants laid out to avoid hazards. In consequence, the industrial safety record dramatically improved. Employees also worked fewer hours: By 1929 workers in manufacturing enjoyed close to a forty-hour week. Unemployment was low, too, averaging only 5.1 percent of the labor force between 1923 and 1929.

One additional improvement in the lives of workers should be noted. They didn't have to bribe a foreman to get a job. Under the notorious "drive" system of the late nineteenth century, factory foremen rather than employers generally did the hiring, made job assignments, set piece-wage rates, maintained discipline, and decided whom to promote and whom to fire. It was a system marked by fear, profanity, and abuse. But it began to crack under the pounding of craft unions. At least skilled workers could be protected from the power of foremen by rules governing methods of shop organization and by output quotas saving them from overexertion. But the unskilled had no alternative except to quit, and the resulting labor turnover and social unrest became a matter of concern to employers as well as reformers. Many therefore decided to establish personnel management departments in their firms and to set up standardized procedures for handling labor relations. More and more, the capriciousness of the older system became a thing of the past.

Employers also took other steps to increase the loyalty of their workers. Many not only provided housing but also opened and operated schools, libraries, restaurants, stores, parks, and other recreational facilities, gardens and greenhouses, moving picture houses and bathhouses. United States Steel even established a company morgue! Profit sharing, stock ownership plans, group insurance, pensions, and paid vacations began to supplement older, more paternalistic practices. The twenties, in short, were the heyday of "welfare capitalism."

One of the major purposes of welfare capitalism was to weaken the power of independent unions. The tactic proved highly successful: Company unions flourished while membership in the independents fell off severely. Numbering 5 million workers in 1920, membership never rose above 3.7 million after 1923, despite substantial growth in the labor force. Company unions were incapable of coordinating their acts with similar organizations in other firms, could not strike, and, had they been authorized to do so, could not have financed a stoppage.

The weakness of labor fit well the mood of the twenties. The use of injunctions in labor disputes and of yellow dog contracts was widespread and upheld by the courts. The Clayton Act (1914) had solemnly declared that "the labor of a human being is not a commodity or article of commerce" but in *Adkins* v. *Children's Hospital* (1923) Associate Justice George Sutherland could find "no difference between the case of selling labor and the case of selling goods."

While the roots of the Great Depression do not descend to the weakness of unions, labor's enfeebled bargaining power proved incapable of pushing average wage levels as high as they might have gone without risking inflation. Wages rose, but they failed to keep pace with productivity gains. Despite the lag, however, in the boom year before the stock market Crash, American consumers continued to purchase durable goods on installment credit and to take out mortgages to buy homes. Indeed, household liabilities thus incurred increased by 20 percent that year, in contrast with a rise of only 12 percent the previous year. As a result of the Crash, however, the value of such financial assets as stocks, bonds, and life insurance policies fell by 4 percent in 1929–1930, by 6 percent in 1930–1931, and by 8 percent in 1931–1932. The effect of this price deflation was to increase the real burden of indebtedness. In consequence, spending by consumers declined drastically, by $3 billion in 1929–1930.

The decline in spending on capital goods by producers—that is to say, investment—was more gradual but, because investment sustains employment, even more fundamental. Private construction activity peaked as early as 1926 and fell by $2 billion between then and 1929. Commercial construction was off, too, as was investment in the textile industries and automobiles. The former had been suffering from overcapacity for some time, and by mid-1929 it was clear that the automobile market had been oversold. The production of cars reached a peak of 622,000 in March 1929 and fell to 416,000 in September—with attendant impact on the demand for tires and other inputs. In sum, investment opportunities were increasingly restricted simply because they had been so thoroughly exploited in the earlier 1920s.

Declining aggregate demand turned what might otherwise have been a mild recession into a major depression. The economy was in a sense set up—highly vulnerable to the psychological effects of the stock market Crash. Experience had led businessmen to expect that signs of a resumption in activity would follow closely after a decline. But as the autumn of 1930 wore on and these failed to appear, the effects of the decline spread throughout the economy, and businessmen lost the confidence that underlies private investment. The Great Crash was thus more a symptom of the Great Depression than a cause. At best, it provided a spark to underlying dry timber. Without that timber, there would have been either no fire at all or one small enough to have been contained and stamped out.

To contemporaries, though, it appeared to be a major conflagration. During the 1920s probably far fewer than a million people were actively involved in purchasing and selling securities, but the number of players does not accurately reflect the amount of public interest in the market. Like batting averages, gyrations in the values of stock appealed to the statistical heart of the country. And what gyrations there were! Stock prices began to rise in the last six months of 1924 and continued to do so through the next year. The market suffered something of a setback in 1926, resumed its upward course in 1927 and then, after the winter of 1928, took off in great vaulting leaps. Radio, the speculative symbol of the time, gained 18 points on March 12, 1928, and on the following day opened 22 points above its previous close. During the year as a whole it went from 85 to 420. Numerous other issues also did well that year. DuPont rose from 310 to 525, Montgomery Ward from 117 to 440, and Wright Aeronautic from 69 to 289. At the top of the boom, in September 1929, Radio, adjusted for stock splits, reached 505.

Fueling the speculative mania was a vast volume of credit provided in the main by commercial banks and other corporations and by wealthy individuals, both foreign and domestic. Attracted by interest rates that rose from around 5 percent at the beginning of 1928 to 12 percent the final week of that year, these lenders poured funds into the call money market. The funds, subject to call without notice, enabled brokers to finance their customers' purchases of stock "on margin"—at some percentage, usually a low one, of the price of the stock. Standard Oil of New Jersey invested a daily average of $69 million in the call money market in 1929. Electric Bond and Share averaged over $100 million. A few corporations even went so far as to sell their own securities and to lend the proceeds to brokers. As much as $3 billion of corporate funds may have gone into brokers' loans in the late twenties. In 1929 loans by commercial banks to brokers, dealers, and individual speculators reached $8.3 billion. In the early twenties the volume of brokers' loans ranged between $1 billion and $1.5 billion a year. During the summer of 1929 they increased by about $400 million a month and by the end of that summer totaled more than $7 billion.

The fault for not braking down the engine of speculation must, to some extent, be laid at the door of the Federal Reserve

Board. It may justly be said to have set the stage for speculation in 1927, when, in an effort to help Britain remain on the gold standard, it lowered the discount rate—the interest rate charged by the thirteen Federal Reserve Banks to the commercial banks which make up the membership of the system—from 4 percent to 3.5 percent. The Board also purchased government securities in considerable volume, which automatically increased the reserves of "high power money" of the member banks. These actions enabled banks to expand the volume of loans to speculators and others. The board also refused—at least till August 1929 when it may have been too late—to allow the New York Federal Reserve Bank to raise its discount rate to deter overborrowing by member banks making loans to speculators. The board did not want to restrict the flow of credit to legitimate borrowers needing money for productive purposes, so it relied instead on moral suasion.

Bolder policy on the part of "the Fed" would certainly have helped. But the river of money on which speculation floated was far too wide for the board to control. It could moderate the behavior of member banks, but not of corporations and wealthy individuals making funds available on the call money market.

And so the reckoning came. In the fall of 1929 the whole mad structure began to fall apart. In September the industrial averages stood at 452. Two months later they were half that. By July 1932, they had sunk to 58. Between September 1929 and July 1932, the market value of all listed securities fell from $89,668 billion to $15,663 billion. In the same interval GM fell from 73 to 8, U.S. Steel from 262 to 22, Montgomery Ward from 138 to 4. And that wasn't all. Between 1929 and 1933 the net national product, measured in current prices, fell by more than half, in constant prices by over a third. Monthly wholesale prices, too, were down by more than a third. As of 1932–1933 industrial production was down by more than half, gross private domestic investment by nearly 90 percent (in constant prices), and farm prices by more than 60 percent. In March 1933 unemployment stood at 25 percent of the labor force. The nation had plunged into a catastrophic depression, the most severe in its history, before or since.

Within a year of the Crash, banks began to fail in the agricultural areas of the South and Midwest, then in the Far West. In four years' time, from 1930 through 1933, more than 9,000 banks suspended operations, imposing losses of $2.5 billion on stockholders, depositors, and other creditors. Attributing the failures to bad management or speculative excesses, the Federal Reserve Board drifted indecisively, not knowing what to do to help the situation. Depression settled into the land. The only highs were bankruptcies and unemployment. Everything else was in decline—all the broad indicators, for example, production, wholesale prices, and personal income.

What to do? The President of the United States thought he knew. Fearing the consequences of coercive government, Herbert Hoover believed that private and public organizations must work together to achieve national objectives. One of Hoover's first acts as President was to summon Henry Ford, Pierre DuPont, Julius Rosenwald, and other leading industrialists to a conference in the White House. Warning that the depression must last for some time and that no one could measure the destructive forces to be met, Hoover urged the industrialists not to lay off workers and not to cut wages. Reductions in wages would only deepen the depression by reducing purchasing power and inviting industrial strife. Let the first shock fall on profits instead. Maintain your planned construction programs, he urged, and spread the available work among all employees by shortening the work week. If labor will go along, so will we, replied the industrialists. That same afternoon William Green, William L. Hutcheson, John L. Lewis, and other labor leaders gathered at the White House and accepted the proposals worked out in the morning.

The very next day Hoover called a conference of leaders in the building and construction industries in an effort to maintain investment and output, and the day after that he telegraphed a

request to governors and mayors throughout the country to coop-
erate with the federal government by expanding public works in
every practical direction. And so it went. Conference after conference, address after address ("I am convinced with unity of effort
we shall recover," he told the Chamber of Commerce in May
1930). The President seemed to be everywhere, talking to bankers, public utility magnates, workers, and federal officials, admon-
ishing, cajoling, trying to stimulate positive responses to the disaster, creating a number of new agencies in a continuing effort, all
through 1930 and 1931 and into 1932, to obtain cooperative action
without resorting to governmental coercion. His objective, once
more, was to win agreements to maintain wage rates and industrial peace and to enlarge private investment and governmental
expenditures for public works. "Mr. Hoover's concern with the
problem [of unemployment]," wrote the famed journalist and social philosopher Walter Lippmann in May 1932, "has been quite
as sincere and his efforts to deal with it quite as persistent as those
of any man living."

Those efforts took many forms. In December 1929 he called
upon Congress to reduce income tax rates. Lower rates, he believed, would encourage consumers to spend and businessmen to
invest, increasing the demand for labor. Congress responded by
reducing rates one percentage point on 1929 incomes. The nation's governors and mayors also responded to his appeal to increase the amount of spending on public works. State and local
expenditures went up by $336 million between 1929 and 1930,
the federal government's rising more modestly by $54 million.
Altogether, government spending on construction projects rose
from $2.468 billion to $2.858 billion. Unhappily, the public sector's
increase was swamped by a decline in private construction. Despite the President's plea, private nonresidential construction fell
from $5 billion to $4 billion and residential construction from $4
billion to $2.3 billion.

The scale of the administration's efforts rose markedly in

1932. With the passage of the Emergency and Relief Construction Act in July of that year, $2 billion became available for federal public works and another $300 million for loans to the states. The latter, Hoover said, were "to be used in furnishing relief and work relief to needy and distressed people in relieving the hardships resulting from unemployment." He was against direct federal relief to the unemployed because he was afraid it would break down the "sense of responsibility of individual generosity," discourage "mutual self-help in the country in times of national difficulty," and "strike at the roots of self-government."

Loans to the states for work relief were only a palliative, though. Far more promising would be loans to endangered business enterprises, for almost all employment depended on the survival and health of the private sector. At the insistence of the President, Congress in January 1932 created the Reconstruction Finance Corporation (RFC). The Treasury purchased the corporation's capital stock of $500 million and during fiscal 1932 and 1933 lent it an additional $1.5 billion. Wholly financed by the federal government, RFC had as its essential purpose the making of loans to banks, insurance companies, building and loan associations, railroads and other businesses to enable them to meet their obligations and remain afloat during the depression. In addition, RFC loans established Agricultural Credit Banks, helped finance public works, and aided states with inadequate resources "to extend full relief to distress and to prevent any hunger and cold in the United States." In the fiscal year 1932 the Department of Agriculture made available to more than 500,000 farmers RFC loans totaling $64 million.

Federal Land Banks were another source of loans to farmers. Created by federal law in January 1932, the banks were allotted a capital of $125 million to relieve pressure on farm mortgages. If farm prices improved, however, that pressure need not develop in the first place. Hoover believed that government should encourage them to improve. As he expressed it in accepting the presidential nomination in 1928, "A nation which is spending ninety billion a year can well afford an expenditure of a few hundred million for a workable program that will give to one third of its population their fair share of the nation's prosperity." He proceeded to sponsor a plan to promote orderly, cooperative marketing of farm products and in June 1929 signed into law the Agricultural Marketing Act.

The Act set up a Federal Farm Board, allotted it a revolving fund of $500 million, and instructed it to build up, as Hoover expressed it, "farmer-owned, farmer-controlled marketing organizations" that would enable farmers to obtain better prices for their products. The Board proceeded to make loans to cooperatives organized to stabilize prices by purchasing surplus cotton, wheat, and other products. It was with evident satisfaction that Hoover reported in his annual message to Congress in December 1931 that the Board had enabled "farm cooperatives to cushion the fall of prices of farm products in 1930 and 1931." They had thereby secured "higher prices than would have been obtained otherwise" and averted "the failure of a large number of farmers and country banks." Unhappily, when it became evident that the Board was losing money on such purchases without achieving price stabilization, the Board decided, with Hoover's approval, to abandon the effort. Ultimately, the board lost approximately $345 million, mainly because of the depression, which began less than six months after the passage of the act creating it.

Hoover also made a strong effort to prevent people from losing their homes. He considered it "one of the tragedies of this depression" that there had occurred "literally thousands of heartbreaking instances of inability of working people to attain renewal of existing mortgages on favorable terms, and the consequent loss of their homes." After his repeated plea that it do so, Congress finally passed the Home Loan Bank Bill in July 1932. Under the Act home owners were able to obtain long-term loans payable in installments, thus saving existing homes from foreclosure and encouraging the building of new ones. The latter, of course, gave a shot in the arm to employment. Twelve Home Loan Banks were established in various parts of the country, each with a minimum capital of $5 million. Building and loan associations, savings banks, and insurance companies were invited to borrow from the banks, the loans to be secured by mortgages on homes. It was Hoover's hope that the banks could be expanded into a general mortgage discount system, owned cooperatively by banks and mortgage companies. What he wanted was a governmental institution that would parallel in the field of long-term credit the short-term credit provided by the Federal Reserve System. Just two weeks before leaving office, he urged Congress to look into the possibility.

Finally, Hoover was by no means indifferent to the cause of labor. It was he who signed into law the Norris-LaGuardia Act of 1932, a landmark piece of labor legislation, which forbade both yellow dog contracts and the use of injunctions in labor disputes. In 1931 he had signed the Bacon-Davis Act, which provided a basic eight-hour day on public construction projects and the payment of "prevailing wages," which meant, essentially, union wages.

Needless to say, the President's efforts on these many fronts did not lift the nation out of the Great Depression. But neither did the even greater efforts of his successor in office, Franklin Delano Roosevelt. Hoover's failure, then, must be viewed as a relative one. He has been unjustly maligned, both in his own time and by at least one generation of historians, as a man inhibited by a "doctrinaire adherence to inherited principles." Certainly, a belief in laissez-faire was not among them. As he noted in his presidential address before the Federation of American Engineering Societies, long before he moved up to a larger presidency, governmental regulation of public utilities alone was "proof of the abandonment of the unrestricted capitalism of Adam Smith."

Soon after the inauguration of Roosevelt, Hoover commented somewhat bitterly to a friend that "the Brain Trust and their superiors are now announcing to the world that the social thesis of laissez-faire died on March 4. I wish they would add a professor of history to the Brain Trust." Presumably the professor would let Roosevelt's associates know that history had overwhelmed the thesis "half a century ago," that the "visible proof" of this was the enactment of the Sherman Antitrust Act, the Federal Reserve System, and the 18th Amendment, among other laws. Even more recent were the institutions created by Hoover's own administration, not least among them Home Loan Banks and the Reconstruction Finance Corporation.

More recent evaluations of Hoover's policies differ markedly from earlier ones. The succession of Roosevelt to Hoover, one historian writes, did not represent a shift from laissez-faire to a managed economy "but rather from one attempt at management, that through informal business-government cooperation, to another more formal and coercive attempt." For all we know, Hoover's advocacy of close voluntary cooperation among government, labor, and business enterprise, while ineffective in the thirties, may yet prove a useful model for the renewal of American economic leadership and the preservation of American living standards in the closing years of the twentieth century and beyond. If so, Hoover's place among our Presidents will continue to be reassessed. For the shifting judgment of history views a person not only in the context of his own present but also in relation to currents of change which bring the future into being.

When Franklin Delano Roosevelt assumed the presidency in March 1933, the nation's economy had all but collapsed. Thirteen million workers, more than a quarter of the labor force, were unemployed. Millions more had only part-time jobs. Joblessness varied from one industry and community to another. Automobiles were hard hit and so were the cities in which they were manufactured. Employment at the Ford Motor Company, which dominated Detroit, plummeted from 128,142 persons in March 1929 to 37,000 in August 1931. Things were no better for Willys-Overland in Toledo or for auto firms in Pontiac and Flint. By the end of 1930 almost every other mill hand in New England's textile industry was out of a job. Even in the cities boasting diversified industry, like Philadelphia, Buffalo, and Cincinnati, employment was off sharply. With little or no work to be had and relief for most families inadequate where it existed at all, a pall of poverty hung like an evil mist over much of the land. A Philadelphia storekeeper told a reporter about a family he was trying to keep going on credit: "Eleven children in that house. They've got no shoes, no pants. In the house, no chairs. My God, you go in there, you cry, that's all."

It was an economy moving at a snail's pace which generated conditions like these. In March 1933 the nation's factories, farms, mines, and service industries were producing one third less than in 1929. Debt default or delinquency was widespread, embracing the obligations of state and local governments, business firms, homeowners, and farmers. The financial system was virtually prostrate: Almost every bank in the country had either closed its doors or severely restricted its operations. The securities markets were shut down, the international gold standard gone, international capital movements at a standstill, and international trade on its knees, beat down by a drastic decline in world incomes and by protective tariffs, exchange controls, and other restrictions.

Something had to be done. Hoover had certainly tried, but for all the surprising activism of this Republican President, he had relied fundamentally on the self-regenerative powers of the private sector, and it had failed to respond. By the fall of 1932 an aroused electorate was demanding that government mount a bolder and more far-reaching assault on the grinding forces of deflation. Elected by a landslide, polling 472 electoral votes to Hoover's 59, Roosevelt was in a commanding position to undertake measures that would have been generally disapproved just a few years before. Even the Chamber of Commerce was solidly behind him. "In Franklin D. Roosevelt," declared Henry I. Harriman, the chamber's president, "business greets a leader of courage, resourcefulness, and trustworthiness. It glows in the audacious pioneering spirit in which he is tackling our common problems."

That was in June 1933, three months after the inauguration of the new President. Roosevelt had acted audaciously, indeed. Only two days in office, he had issued an executive order temporarily suspending banking activities throughout the country. No bank could reopen for business till examination of its condition by government officials and certification of its soundness. Over 2,000 banks were either liquidated or consolidated with other banks to make them stronger.

Next, the new President tackled the problem of the hungry and needy by establishing the Federal Emergency Relief Administration. Set up in May 1933, FERA funneled a half-billion dollars to states and cities. The latter then made direct grants of cash to people on the relief rolls. This wasn't enough in the eyes of Harry Hopkins, a former social worker whom Roosevelt appointed to head up the new agency. Anticipating a harsh winter in 1933–1934, Hopkins persuaded his boss to create a second agency to provide work for the unemployed. Men hired at minimum wages by the Civil Works Administration proceeded to build or improve some 500,000 miles of roads, 40,000 schools, 3,500 playgrounds and athletic fields, and 1,000 airports before succumbing to conservative criticism in the spring of 1934. It was replaced the next year by a more permanent work relief program. Also headed by Hopkins, the Works Progress Administration not only built or improved some 2,500 hospitals, 5,900 school buildings, and 1,000 airport landing fields, it also funded the Federal Theatre Project, the Federal Writers Project, the Federal Art Project and the National Youth Administration. An early casualty of the Second World War, WPA eventually spent $10 billion for the relief of 3.5 million desperate blue-collar, white-collar, and professional people.

The banks needed relief too if they were to be able to provide loans to the private businesses on whose health employment depended. The Reconstruction Finance Corporation (RFC) sprang to the rescue. Under the administration of Jesse Jones it not only lent more than $2 billion to some 8,500 endangered banks, it also invested more than $1 billion in the capital stock of over 6,000 banks—a sum representing a third of the total capital of the nation's banks in 1933. Expanding its reach to ailing businesses themselves, the RFC became in effect the world's largest and most powerful bank. Originally created by Hoover, it became Roosevelt's greatest engine of relief during the Great Depression, lending over $1 billion to eighty-nine railroads, $90 million to 133 insurance companies, and $1.5 billion to farmers. In addition, it created a number of new agencies, including the Export and Import Banks, the Rural Electrification Administration, and the Disaster Loan Corporation, and in doing so extended its aid to cities, cooperatives, and individuals. Thus, RFC relief, as Jesse Jones claimed, "spread out like a rippling wave in a quiet pond."

Relief was essential, but it wasn't enough. Some of the nation's institutions and business practices cried out for reform as well. The banking system in particular was in need of repair if the circulating medium was to be protected and the interests of depositors and investors safeguarded. Small commercial banks were highly vulnerable in times of depressed business conditions. The overwhelming majority of the banks that suspended in the 1920s were small: four out of ten had begun business with less than $24,000 in capital; nine out of ten had assets under $1 million. The overwhelming majority—nearly 9 out of 10—were located in small rural communities, where agriculture was depressed. Unable to diversify credit risks or draw upon more than the local supply of management talent, these small banks also found themselves unable to raise additional cash when faced with liquidity problems. That is because most of them (85 percent) did not belong to the Federal Reserve System, one of whose essential functions is to act as lender of last resort. Most continued to remain outside the System, but thanks to a provision of the Glass-Steagall Banking Act of 1933, which established the Federal Deposit Insurance Corporation, the deposits of even nonmembers might be insured if approved by the corporation. The upshot was that within six months of the date when insurance first became effective—January 1, 1934—some 97 percent of all commercial bank deposits were covered. Ever since then there has been a dramatic decline both in commercial bank failures and in losses borne by depositors in banks that did fail.

Many of the larger commercial banks encountered problems of quite another kind. Attracted by the profits to be won from transactions in securities, they organized investment affiliates. For example, Charles E. Mitchell was chairman of the board of both the National City Bank and its investment affiliate, the National City Corporation. The former was the world's second largest commercial bank, the latter the country's largest investment banking house. It was therefore possible to use funds deposited in the commercial half of the enterprise for speculative ventures in the investment half—and thus to jeopardize their safety. Unimpeachable testimony and documentary evidence presented in 1933 to a Senate investigating committee, under the direction of its able counsel, Ferdinand Pecora, disclosed investment affiliates speculating on the stock exchange and taking part in pooling agreements that earned large profits for the participants. Executives of the affiliates also traded heavily in the stocks of their allied commercial banks, the demand for which they were able to increase by advising depositors therein to buy the stock of the bank. And not only that stock, but also dubious foreign bonds and the stocks of corporations on whose boards some of them sat as directors.

Other abuses consisted of transferring losses on loans from the books of the bank to those of the investment affiliate without informing the latter's stockholders, and of huge annual bonuses voted by top executives for themselves and not reported in annual statements. Probes into the affairs of such private banking houses as J. P. Morgan and Kuhn Loeb disclosed none of the gross violations that disfigured the records of such incorporated firms as Mitchell's National City Company and Albert H. Wiggins' Chase Securities Corporation. However, the revelation that not a single Morgan partner owed any income taxes for the years 1931 and 1932 aroused widespread public indignation.

Not surprisingly, therefore, the Glass-Steagall Banking Act of 1933 required banks belonging to the Federal Reserve System to divorce themselves from their security affiliates, compelled private banks to choose between deposit and investment banking, prohibited partners or executives of security firms from serving as directors or officers of commercial banks that were members of the Federal Reserve System, increased the authority of the twelve Federal Reserve District Banks to supervise and control the amount of credit extended to their members, and empowered the Federal Reserve Board to regulate bank loans secured by the collateral of stocks and bonds. In addition, the law prohibited their payment of interest on demand deposits, in order to discourage outlying banks from sending large sums to metropolitan centers, especially New York, where they might feed speculation by being re-lent on the call loan market. A second by-product of the Pecora investigation, the Securities Exchange Act of 1934, prohibits various kinds of manipulations and trading abuses and requires companies whose securities are traded on the exchange to provide full and accurate financial data for the guidance of investors.

The New Deal also achieved historic reform in the field of labor law. In July 1935, the National Labor Relations Act (Wagner Act) was passed, enabling independent unions to bargain collectively with employers over wages, hours, and working conditions. For business firms to support or encourage the formation of a company union was declared to be an unfair labor practice, and a National Labor Relations Board was established to enforce compliance. Three years later Congress also enacted the Fair Labor

Standards Act. The legislation established a standard work week of forty-four hours—reduced to forty after two years—with time-and-a-half pay for overtime. It also set minimum rates of hourly pay and generally prohibited child labor below the age of sixteen, as well as sweatshop industrial labor at home. These minimum rates were minimal indeed, merely 40 cents an hour. Furthermore, the law allowed numerous exemptions from its requirements. Imperfect though it was, the law nevertheless laid foundations on which future Congresses could build. It must be remembered that in 1937, 12 million workers in industries affected by interstate commerce were making *less* than 40 cents an hour.

Other reforms addressed the financial needs of the elderly, the unemployed, the blind, and fatherless children. The Tennessee Valley Authority, a public corporation which produced and sold hydroelectric power and fertilizer in competition with the private sector, alienated many businessmen, but nevertheless TVA rectified a dismal situation by bringing electric power to an entire region of the South. (In 1932, only one Mississippi farm in a hundred enjoyed the uses of electric power.) The Rural Electrification Administration also wrought startling change. When it was created in May 1935, nine out of ten American farms had no electricity. By 1950 only one out of ten still lacked it.

President Roosevelt also sought in other ways to obtain a more fair share of the good life for the nation's farmers. The worldwide depression had fallen with cruel force on agriculture, continuing the downturn in the fortunes of the farmer so evident in the 1920s. Stagnant industrial production brought down domestic demand for fibers and raw materials, and falling incomes reduced consumption of food products. Exports also declined in volume and in price. In 1919 the estimated farm value of exports had constituted 15.8 percent of gross income from farm production. By 1932 that percentage was down to 6.5 percent. Prices behaved accordingly. Between 1929 and 1932 leading commodities were down 50 percent or more. Wheat, for example, fell from $1.04 a bushel to 38 cents, corn from 80 cents to 32 cents, oats from 42 cents to 16 cents, and barley from 54 cents to 22 cents. Livestock fell too: beef steers from $13.43 per cwt to $6.70, hogs from $10.16 to $3.83. Cotton was down from about 17 cents a pound to 6 ½ cents. Taxes, interest charges, rent, wages, and operating expenses, on the other hand, underwent only moderate declines, so that net income from farming shrank even more severely. In 1932 the average net income of farm operators from farming was less than a third of what it had been in 1929.

These drastic declines resulted in a wave of foreclosures and other distress transfers of farms. For example, the fall in cotton, the principal cash crop of the South, led during 1931–1933 to more than twice the annual number of transfers of the preceding six years. In general, however, farm mortgage distress was especially acute in areas that had escaped the ravages of the twenties, such as the eastern Great Plains and Mountain region. Other troubles fell on parts of the West, too. Prolonged droughts in some areas, for example, in the Red River Valley of the North, produced severe damage in the form of wheat rust, while many parts of the Dust Bowl area of western Kansas and eastern Colorado became uninhabitable, leading to a mass exodus of population. Natural calamities like these intensified the distress of the farm families experiencing them.

Prices of farm products were generally at their lowest and farm distress at its worst during the summer, fall, and winter before Roosevelt was sworn in as President on March 4, 1933. Farmers began taking matters into their own hands. During the winter grim mobs gathered to stop foreclosures, while pickets manned the highways to prevent the movement of produce to town. Edward A. O'Neal, the head of the Farm Bureau Federation, warned a Senate committee in January 1933: "Unless something is done for the American farmer, we will have revolution in the countryside within less than twelve months."

What Roosevelt did was to instruct his supporters in Congress to give priority to agricultural legislation. The upshot was the passage of the Agricultural Adjustment Act of May 1933. Underlying this law was the belief, expressed in the Act itself, that the "acute economic emergency" was partly due to "a severe and increasing disparity between the prices of agricultural and other commodities, which disparity has largely destroyed the purchasing power of farmers for industrial products. . . ." Since "disparity" implied "parity," Congress defined the latter by declaring it to be the policy of the government:

> To establish and maintain such balance between the production and consumption of agricultural commodities, and such marketing conditions therefore, as will re-establish prices to farmers at a level that will give agricultural commodities a purchasing power with respect to articles that farmers buy, equivalent to the purchasing power of agricultural commodities in the base period. The base period in the case of all agricultural commodities except tobacco shall be the prewar period, August 1909–July 1914. In the case of tobacco, the base period shall be the post-war period, August 1919–July 1929.

The fundamental assumption on which the Act rested was that the prices of "basic" agricultural commodities could be induced to rise by restricting the acreage devoted to their production to a level one-third lower than in the previous three years. The Act designated as "basic" wheat, cotton, field corn, hogs, rice, tobacco, and milk and its products. Farmers were to be encouraged to comply voluntarily with this "domestic allotment" program by being offered contracts in which they agreed to limit their acreage plantings (or, in the case of hogs, to limit their marketings) in return for benefit payments. These payments were to be financed by taxes levied on the sale of the products to processors. Before the first year was over, however, the Agricultural Adjustment Program departed from its voluntary character with respect to cotton and tobacco and also added price-supporting

loans. Loans on cotton and corn made by the Secretary of Agriculture in the fall of 1933 were made at levels in excess of current
market prices—marking the beginning of present-day government price-support loan operations. In the event the market price
failed to rise to the level of the loan rate, it was agreed that the
producer might deliver his crop to the government in full repay-
ment of this "nonrecourse" loan.

After the Supreme Court in 1936 declared it unconstitutional
to collect processing taxes to finance the program, new legislation
(1938) was framed on the basis of the interstate commerce clause.
The Act directed the Secretary of Agriculture to make nonrecourse loans available to producers of the major storable crops
within a range of 52 percent to 75 percent of parity. The law also
authorized the Secretary of Agriculture "to invoke marketing
quotas upon the approval of two-thirds of the producers if supplies
reached certain levels in relation to normal marketings." The
Court upheld the constitutionality of the new law in Mulford v.
Smith (1939), and in the interim since then it has not been successfully challenged.

The impact of the adjustment program on agricultural
prices and farm incomes is almost impossible to determine. Consider, for example, the first year of the program. Prices of basic
commodities were substantially higher than they had been; between 1932 and 1933 wheat rose from 38 to 74 cents, corn from
32 to 52 cents, oats from 16 to 34 cents, barley from 22 to 43
cents, cotton from 6 ½ to over 10 cents. But Mother Nature
brought forth adverse weather that year and therefore had a
hand in the production of short crops. In addition, a substantial
measure of increased business activity and consumer purchasing
power must also be credited to some extent, as must purchases of
food for purposes of relief. Finally, the depreciation of the dollar
in terms of gold and the foreign exchanges directly helped raise
prices of such crops as cotton, wheat, and tobacco, of which
there were substantial exports or imports. Even at the end of the

thirties, it is safe to say, the goal of "price parity" was far from being achieved, for in no year during that decade did the farmer's average net income from his farm operations reach the level it had attained in 1929. Although the legislation probably did help raise farm incomes from their low point in 1932, it seems to have done so not by generating increases in national income but by redistributing existing income—from consumers, who were obliged to pay higher prices for food products, to farmers. The total impact of the program on purchasing power may therefore have been negative, for farmers were a declining sector of the American economy, both in numbers and in their contribution to aggregate output.

Nevertheless, the policies of the Agricultural Adjustment Acts of the 1930s profoundly altered the structure of the labor markets of the plantation South, and in so doing helped prepare that long-beleaguered area for the modernization that came after the Second World War. Ever since Reconstruction days cotton plantations had been divided into smaller farms operated by sharecroppers and tenants. These institutional arrangements guaranteed a supply of labor throughout the annual cotton cycle, from ground breaking, planting, and cultivation (especially weed control), to the harvesting of the crop, the time of peak labor demand. The reason why the plantation South was an exception to the rule of widespread adoption of the tractor in the 1920s was not only that the tenant plots were too small to justify this partial mechanization, but also, and more importantly, because it would have displaced workers. Workers were needed to pick the cotton at harvest time, and Southern economic development did not generate an adequate supply of casual workers who might have been paid wages to do the picking. Consequently the agricultural labor supply had to be retained year round—placed on hold, so to speak—so that it would be available for the harvest. Opportunities for nonagricultural employment in the plantation areas during the off-season were insufficient and this generated a fear that unless a worker had an annual interest in the crop he would not be available when needed most.

The Agricultural Adjustment Acts from 1933 to 1939 altered this situation by providing incentives to displace tenants: the payment of government subsidies to take cotton land out of production, plus the expectation of a cotton price stabilized by government, lump sum cash payments for the purchase of tractors and trucks, and a supply of agricultural labor sufficiently abundant—not least because of the stagnation created by the depression—to meet spurts in demand. These new factors reduced the cost of testing the old arrangements, and small plots were consolidated into large enough farms to make the use of tractors economically feasible. Moreover the demand for labor during the Second World War led to a massive migration of erstwhile farmers and agricultural workers to the industrial centers of the North and South. And the resulting labor shortage, together with the newfound disposition to mechanize, increased the cotton planter's receptivity to the mechanical cotton picker—an invention whose basic engineering principle had been patented in 1850 but which was not produced in commercial quantities till the late 1940s.

But we get ahead of our story. On and on dragged the heavy wheels of the Great Depression. Why? What had the President failed to do? What had he done that he should not have done? He had sought to address the major problems of every sector of the American economy—its banking institutions and financial markets, its industry, work force, and agriculture. The helping hand of the RFC had extended aid on a massive scale to foundering enterprises of many kinds. Yet the helping hand of government had not been able to put the ailing patient back on its feet. It is true that the most commonly accepted index of economic health, net national product in constant prices, rose at a spectacular annual average rate of 12 percent between 1933 and 1937, a rate of growth unmatched by any other four-year period from 1869, when recorded figures start, to 1960. But even at the top of the business cycle in 1937, nearly 8 million workers were still unemployed, a figure representing 14.3 percent of the civilian labor force. And output per capita was lower than it had been in 1929. To top things off, the years 1937–1938 witnessed one of the sharpest business contractions on record, a recession reminiscent of 1920–1921. Many scholars attribute the recession to the President's call for a balanced budget, to reduced federal expenditures and higher taxes. Belief that the budget should be balanced was widely shared, abroad as well as at home. But the timing of the call and of its supporting fiscal policy was devastating. Aggregate demand severely declined.

Federal expenditures had risen every year from 1932 to 1937 and had helped stimulate an economic rebound. But had they risen enough? Those who subscribed to the doctrines of the British economist John Maynard Keynes (they did not include the President) argued they had not. Unemployed men and resources, Keynesians believed, should be put back to work by increased federal spending and lowered taxes. Many in the private sector, however, believed that such a fiscal policy would not only lead to inflation but also raise the public level of competition with private enterprise. From their point of view, and with TVA in mind most especially, the government was spending too much rather than too little. And since it was coupling its policies with explicit denunciations of businessmen, notably by the Secretary of the Interior, Harold L. Ickes, the Secretary of Agriculture, Henry A. Wallace, the administrator of the Works Progress Administration, Harry Hopkins, and the President himself, businessmen became increasingly alienated and embittered. They resented being called "economic royalists," and they were disturbed by the President's penchant for military analogy to characterize both the economic crisis and the ways in which the government intended to deal with it. After all, this was a decade of dark dictatorship in Germany, Italy, and Japan. They distrusted "that man in the White House" and chose to confine their risks to short-term investments rather than risk the greater uncertainties of a more distant future.

There is surely some merit in the argument that reform impeded recovery. But this cannot be the whole story. Businessmen had no reason to be wary of Hoover's administration, but they were reluctant to invest then too. On February 11, 1933, before Roosevelt was even inaugurated, Hoover's Secretary of the Treasury, Ogden Mills, said in a speech to the Young Republican Club of Missouri, "What is holding us back is uncertainty and lack of confidence." "How," asks an analyst of the Hoover presidency, could Hoover and Mills "overcome that paralyzing compound of fear, timidity, and caution—that lack of confidence—on the part of the business community which had frustrated all of Hoover's previous efforts?"

How indeed? Roosevelt and Jesse Jones of the RFC faced a similar problem in the early palmy days of the New Deal. "There is no ally that President Roosevelt needs quite so much to achieve and maintain recovery," Jones told the New York State Bankers Association in February 1934, "as the banker." Yet the "common cry almost everywhere," he added, "is that the banks are not lending." In part, the explanation is the same then as during the latter days of Hoover. The trauma of the depression made bankers fearful and timid. But other businessmen were also fearful, and in consequence the demand for loans was thin.

Banker and business assessment of market risk must therefore be added to the explanation of inadequate investment in the 1930s. But the other factor, uncertainty born of reformist legislation and of administration rhetoric, is there too. As Jones remarked in 1938, "Bankers seldom like the way government is run." They especially disliked the way Roosevelt's government was run. "One characteristic of bankers," Jones declared, "is that probably 95 percent of them don't like the New Deal, and while they would not intentionally 'cut off their nose to spite their face' . . . they naturally pull back." He might have added that businessmen in general also held back, in all probability for the same reason.

Yet, costly as reforms may have been for the short-run prospects of economic recovery, who can doubt that they were necessary? Reform touched not only the nation's securities and financial markets, its labor relations practices, and its treatment of the aged, infirm, sick, and unemployed, but also the egregiously irresponsible, indeed, corrupt practices of some businessmen. One particular target of reform was the multilayered public utility companies, which were outlawed by the Public Utilities Holding Act of 1935 if more than twice removed from their operating companies.

Many business leaders were alienated in the 1930s, but the irony is that much of the reform brought about by the New Deal is now an institutionalized part of American life. So too is the relationship of government to the economy: The trauma of the Great Depression has probably ended forever the relatively minimal contact between the two sectors that characterized all of American history before the 1930s. Regulations of economic conduct would be introduced by future administrations, and there would be shifts in the degree to which government would intervene in the economy, and changes in the industrial cast of characters subject to intervention. Nevertheless, it was the depression that introduced fundamental reform.

The New Deal, once again, did not end the Great Depression. But the President's policies did save the American economic system. Moreover, they did much to prepare the major institutions of America's political economy for rapid technological innovation and social change.

Roosevelt was a bold experimenter and a compassionate man, yet one who lacked a coherent program for economic recovery. He would undoubtedly have been the first to acknowledge the absence of system in his policies. He believed in trying one thing and then turning to another if it failed to work. A man of immense warmth and magnetism, a superb public speaker and consummate politician, he roused hope and instilled confidence in a groping and badly shaken people. Himself aristocratic, if ever that un-American word may be applied to a figure in public life, he had genuine feeling for the common man, for the worker, and especially for the farmer. Unfortunately, he was less sensitive to the humanity of the businessman, to his need for confidence that public utterances and policies not discourage the indispensable role which he too must play in the American economic system. Events soon to unfold would reveal once again the importance of that role in war as well as in peace.

VII

Government and Economy in and after the Second World War

A DOLF HITLER, with an assist from Japanese militarists, finally ended the Great Depression. Behind that startling statement are, first, some bare facts about the influence of the German war machine on government expenditures in the United States. It took a surprisingly long time for that influence to make itself felt.

That is because the American people wanted to remain at peace. Hoping to avoid incidents which might lead to American involvement in European war, Congress in 1935 had made it unlawful to export arms, ammunition, or implements of war for the use of belligerents, and in 1937 it broadened the Neutrality Act to include materials and articles other than munitions, if shipped in American vessels. Just after the German occupation of the Polish Corridor in September 1939, the American Institute of Public Opinion took a poll. Asked "whether we should declare war on Germany at once," 88 percent of the American people replied in the negative.

Nevertheless, American sympathies were clearly on the side of the Allies, and in November of that year the Neutrality Act was further revised to permit the shipment of arms and munitions to belligerents once title to them had been transferred to the consignee. With the adoption of this "cash and carry" principle, the British and French took steps to enlarge and coordinate their purchasing operations in the United States. Their contracts resulted in the construction of facilities for the production of armaments and thus strengthened American defense capabilities as well. The latter would be strengthened still more after the sweep of German armies across western Europe in the spring and early summer of 1940 cleared the way for additional appropriations for national defense and enabled the President to give precedence to the production of military supplies. Even so, expenditures for national defense in 1940 totaled only $2.2 billion in a GNP of $100 billion. And the average rate of unemployment remained high at 14.6 percent of the labor force.

The unemployment rate fell to 10 percent in 1941, and in the fourth quarter of that year—the quarter of the Japanese attack on Pearl Harbor—the transition to a war economy shifted into high gear. Not because the British economist John Maynard Keynes had advocated it but rather because it had no choice, the federal government mounted a huge increase in deficit spending. The ratio of the federal deficit to the GNP was twice as high in 1941 as it had been in 1939. And in the final quarter of 1941 the level of military expenditures, merely 2.2 percent of GNP in 1940, vaulted upward to 16 percent. The Great Depression sank at last into history.

War exerted a significant impact on the American economy. In the manufacturing sector, big business got bigger and small business smaller. Both came close to having been inevitable in the context of the nation's war needs. As the commanding general of the Services of Supply, Brehon Somervell, said, "All the small plants of the country could not turn out one day's requirements of ammunition." Big business had the plant and the know-how to handle enormous orders for military materials, the executives and engineers able to manage new and technologically difficult programs. Despite the establishment by Congress of the Smaller War Plants Corporation (SWPC) in June 1942, to make loans to small businesses and otherwise help them obtain procurement orders, more than half the total of $175 billion in prime contracts awarded between June 1940 and September 1944 went to the top thirty-three corporations (with size measured by the value of the contracts received). Small enterprises fared no better as recipients of subcontracts from large firms. According to a 1943 survey by the SWPC, although a group of 252 of the largest contracting corporations did subcontract about one third of the value of their prime contracts, three fourths of that value went to other large (over 500 employees) concerns. The result was predictable. Between the end of 1939 and the end of 1944, the percentage of total manufacturing employment accounted for by firms with fewer than 100 workers fell from 26 percent to 19 percent. Companies with 10,-000 or more employees saw their percentage more than double, from 13 percent to over 30 percent. In sum, the war appears to have weakened the market position of small manufacturers.

Other kinds of small businesses fared even worse. Between 1940 and 1945, 324,000 firms went out of business. This was a significant 10 percent of the 1940 total. Exists were especially heavy in construction, retail trade, and service activities, all havens of small business. Both incorporated and unincorporated firms went under, in roughly equal proportions. But the survivors did well, especially in view of wartime constraints on profits (the Revenue Act of 1942, for example, raised the excess profits tax from 60 percent to 90 percent). The profits of both groups went up 60 percent during the five years of war. That was a good deal better than the larger manufacturers did. Despite a remark by the Secretary of War, Henry L. Stimson, that "If you are going to try to go to war, or to prepare for war, in a capitalist country, you have got to let business make money out of the process or business won't work," most industry groups had lower net profits after taxes in the years 1942–1945 than in 1941. The only exceptions were firms producing beverages and transportation equipment, and, in the case of the largest corporations (assets of $10 million or more), lumber.

War left its impress on the labor force as well as the industrial sector. The proportion of women factory workers had been rising steadily since 1900, and by 1940 one of every four workers was a female over fourteen years of age. Their numbers rose during the war from 11 million to 19.5 million but in view of historical trends perhaps as many as 1.5 million women would have been added to the labor force even if there had been no war. War did affect the age composition of the group, however. Three out of five new recruits were over thirty-five and not a few over forty-five. Perhaps 20 percent of the latter found employment only because of the existence of wartime labor shortages. Despite those shortages, however, racial prejudice proved costly to the nation as well as to its victims. While black women improved their lot by transferring from low-paid, low-status employment as domestics to jobs in factories, they never got some of the best-paying jobs—as welders, ship fitters and riveters, and in steel mills.

Black men also benefited from the opening of urban occupational opportunities, especially in the North but also in the South and West. During the war almost a million blacks migrated from Southern farms and rural communities to industrial centers, with black employment in manufacturing increasing by 600,000. Most moving out of agriculture in the South were laborers rather than operators. The prosperity of agriculture during the war arrested a decline in operators which had set in during the 1920s. It also advanced large numbers of black operators from tenants and part owners to full owners of farms. It was high time. In 1939 two out of every three farm families whose annual incomes were less than $1,000 were located in the South, and a high proportion of these were black.

Not only blacks but farmers generally benefited from the circumstance of war. Total net income of farm operators from farming rose from $4.482 million in 1940 to $12.312 million in 1945. In fact, farm operator incomes increased more rapidly than those of nonfarm businessmen and professionals. The farmer's share of a typical market basket of farm food products jumped from 40 percent to 53 percent, the number of mortgaged farms declined by 29 percent, and total farm indebtedness outstanding fell from $6.6 billion to $4.9 billion.

These favorable results would have been difficult to envisage from the vantage point of the depression period, for the outbreak of war in Europe found the country in possession of a two-years' supply of such major commodities as wheat, corn, and cotton. By the fall of 1942, however, Pacific sources of sugar, oil, fruit, and other foodstuffs had been cut off, and meat, fats, oils, dairy products, and canned foods were in short supply. Thereafter, the needs of the Allies and of American armed forces abroad for manufactured foods added their impact on agricultural production and food processing industries to that of domestic shortages.

Agriculture responded not so much by increasing the amount of land under crops (crop acreage harvested in 1945 was only 4 percent more than in 1940) as by raising output per acre. More capital rather than more labor enabled it to do so (total inputs of labor hours actually declined during these years). The capital took the form of fertilizer and liming materials and of mechanical power, including electricity and machinery. Between 1940 and 1945 the number of tractors on farms rose steadily from 1.567 million to 2.354 million, the number of motor trucks increased by 42 percent, grain combines by 97 percent, corn pickers by 53 percent, commercial fertilizer by 62 percent, and lime by 60 percent. In sum, wartime manpower shortages, in conjunction with rising demand for agricultural products, speeded up an historical process already well under way—the replacement of men by machines, the substitution of capital for labor. We shall see that this process has continued with even greater vigor in the postwar years and that one of its major consequences has been a concentration of production on farms of increasing size and diminishing numbers.

Capital raised the productivity of farming (it went up by 10 percent during the war) and also of industrial production (up by 27 percent between 1940 and 1944). Newly built and equipped facilities made the latter possible. At first it was touch and go how to provide the necessary capital. In the First World War, private business had financed 90 percent of the cost of expanded industrial facilities. The government had encouraged the investment by promising to allow businessmen to write off the cost of new facilities to the extent that they proved to have no value after the war. This would reduce their taxes, and ultimately owners of about one eighth of the $5 billion in private capital benefited. Subsequently, however, a Senate committee had challenged some of the settlements, and their recollection of this dulled the incentive effect of postwar tax advantages held out by Congress in October 1940.

Even after the country entered the "shooting war," businessmen continued to hesitate. Their memories of the recent prolonged depression were fresh. They were afraid that additions to plant and equipment would result in a postwar world of excess capacity, cutthroat competition, and flooded markets. Despite these early misgivings, however, the automobile industry converted to the production of military aircraft—in addition to its output of tanks, jeeps, and trucks, the industry became the largest single group of suppliers to the aircraft industry—the railroads increased the ton-mile volume of intercity traffic by 93 percent between 1940 and 1944, and oil and pipeline manufacturers raised their product by 125 percent during the same interval. Steel, too, expanded its ingot capacity during the war from 81.6 to 95.5 million tons, but in this case it was government financing that made the expansion possible. The same was true for magnesium, an item in critically short supply, and synthetic rubber. Japanese occupation of the Malay Peninsula and the Netherlands East Indies early in 1942 found the United States with a stockpile of natural rubber of only half a million tons. The government proceeded to finance and build the new capacity required for synthetic rubber. Leased to private operators for $1.00 a year, these plants increased their output from 8,383 long tons in 1941 to 753,111 in 1944.

Tax benefits did induce the private sector to invest $6.5 billion in new plant and equipment, but this was only 25 percent of the total so invested. Governmental agencies provided the rest. Most of the public investment went into the aircraft and closely related industries—magnesium, aluminum, and aviation gasoline—but large sums were also placed in pipeline transportation, the steel and chemical industries, and synthetic rubber. These evidences of the public economic presence are by no means the only ones to be seen. The government also controlled prices and wages, raw materials, machine tools, ships, freight cars, and other items in short supply, rationed scarce goods, and curtailed the right to choose an occupation or change jobs. In sum, governmental intervention in the economy was far more extensive than ever before in American history.

It did not long survive the war. Within days of the Japanese surrender in August 1945, President Harry S. Truman issued an executive order instructing federal agencies "to move as rapidly as possible without endangering the stability of the economy toward the removal of price, wage, production, and other controls and toward the restoration of collective bargaining and the free market." For the most part, controls were gone before the onset of winter. But although almost no one favored a continuation of controls, there was widespread concern that the end of the war would usher in heavy unemployment. Congress was flooded with proposals on how to deal with it and other anticipated postwar problems. Among them were proposals that reflected the bitter experience of the Great Depression. Some of the nation's economists in particular emphasized that it had taken massive expenditures by the government to bring the depression to an end. They had become converts to the countercyclical strategies of the British economist, John Maynard Keynes.

In the early postwar period, however, these strategies had not yet won over most Americans or their political leaders, a fact which is reflected in the Employment Act of 1946. An overwhelming majority of Congressmen were in agreement that keeping unemployment low should be an important national objective, and that the federal government had responsibilities to discharge if that goal were to be achieved. But they refused to go along with the statement that the government should promote "full employment." They feared this would lead to inflation if not accompanied by wage and price controls and that the latter would place in jeopardy the American system of private enterprise.

The upshot was compromise on a statement of policy which, for the time being, proved more symbolic than substantive. The undefinable objective of "full" employment was dropped in favor of "maximum employment, production, and purchasing power," and the government was called upon to use "all its plans, functions, and resources to achieve them." The Act also created a Council of Economic Advisers in the executive office of the President. Its function, in the language of one of its chairmen, was to "put at the President's disposal the best facts, appraisals, and forecasts that economic science, statistics, and surveys can produce." This information would presumably enable the President to discharge his responsibility under the Act to specify the levels of activity prevailing in the United States economy, the levels expected, and the levels needed to carry out the purposes of the law.

President Truman paid little heed to the council, at least up to the time of the Korean War. He was not at home with either abstract ideas or intellectuals. (He is reputed, probably apocryphally, to have remarked that, when he asked the council chairman for advice, he customarily received replies that began "On the one hand, this, but on the other hand that." To which he is said to have responded plaintively, "Can anybody get me a one-handed economist?") But neither the first chairman of the council, Edwin Nourse, nor his vice chairman and successor, Leon Keyserling, was greatly interested in fiscal policy. Indeed, Keyserling warned Congressional committees against preoccupation with overall conditions, like general inflation, or with overall measures of either fiscal or monetary policy. In what may prove to have been prescient advice, however, he acted as a leading advocate of a 1949 bill to empower the government to promote investment in specific industries, where it was clear that private investment was insufficient to generate balanced growth. American governments may yet decide to encourage the development of such industries that also have to compete in international markets with the government-subsidized industries of other countries.

Under Truman, fiscal policy was passive. Such was the President's preoccupation with the danger of inflation that it was not till the seventh month of a 1949 recession that he finally abandoned his effort to induce Congress to raise taxes in order to reduce the deficit. An active policy would have sought increased expenditures and lowered taxes to put more purchasing power in the hands of the public and encourage private investment. Fortunately, the passive policy of relying on the "built-in" response of tax revenues (which decline during recession) and such expenditures as unemployment compensation (which go up) worked out well. A budget surplus which had been running at an annual rate of $3.8 billion in the fourth quarter of 1948 turned into a deficit of $3.9 billion in the second quarter of 1949. Automatic declines in revenues and increases in expenditures account for almost all of this transformation. In a word, the fiscal response to the recession was "almost entirely automatic and unsought."

The election of Dwight D. Eisenhower as President in 1952 brought to Washington the first Republican administration in twenty years and raised the question whether it would accept the responsibility under the Employment Act to use the powers of government, including fiscal policy, to stabilize the economy and maintain high employment. The question was all the more important because of the fact that, just the year before, the Treasury and the Federal Reserve System had reached an accord which, by releasing the latter from its obligation to support the prices of government bonds, freed it to play the role of partner to fiscal policy. So far as the President's words were concerned, there was soon to be no doubt that he would. And to a limited degree he did. But the larger fact is that the new administration, like the one it had replaced, centered its policy on the public's fear of inflation and sought to balance the budget and avoid deficits.

These objectives called for opposition to tax cuts, even those strongly supported by Congressional spokesmen for the interests of the Chamber of Commerce and the National Association of Manufacturers. Almost at the beginning of his administration, Eisenhower had to confront pressures to allow an excess profits tax of 77 percent, imposed at the outbreak of the Korean War in 1950, to expire on its scheduled date of June 30, 1953. The President wanted the expiration date delayed for the sake of the federal revenues, and he had his way. Nevertheless, when the economy entered recession in the fall of 1953 with the decline of military expenditures, he made it clear that if conditions became worse, he would not be deterred by fear of deficits. In October 1953 he showed the flexibility of his attitude on balancing the budget:

> When it becomes clear that the Government has to step in, as far as I am concerned, the full power of Government, of Government credit, and of everything the Government has, will move in to see that there is no widespread unemployment and we never again have a repetition of conditions that so many of you here remember when we had unemployment.

The decline never reached the point where the administration thought that strong action was needed, so that it is not possible to say how far it would have gone to use the resources of government to combat it. According to the figures then available, unemployment was only 3 percent in December 1953; the Fed, moreover, was pursuing an expansive monetary policy. At the end of March 1954, however, Congress reduced excise taxes by about $1 billion a year, a move later characterized by Eisenhower's Economic Council chairman, Arthur R. Burns, as a cut made "for countercyclical reasons."

Recession came again in 1957–1958 and still again in 1960–1961, and in the first of these—in 1958—the country came closer than ever before to cutting taxes in order to encourage a general economic expansion. But it did not do so. Inflation continued to be viewed by the administration as the most important long-term problem, with recession representing merely a brief interlude. Moreover, the launching of the Soviet Sputnik in the fall of 1957 had called attention to American weakness in space exploration, missile capability, education, and economic growth, and raised the prospect of strongly rising expenditures—and even of tax increases to support them. If taxes were reduced instead, more would be threatened than the rising revenues required by these rising expenditures. So too would be the budget surplus needed to combat inflation after the economy returned to its "normal" condition. As it turned out, a slowing of the rate of economic decline in the spring of 1958 weakened the case for a tax cut to combat recession, and once again none was made.

Nor was one made in Eisenhower's last two years. This does not mean that the first Republican administration since Hoover was unsympathetic to business and its needs. Eisenhower realized full well that a prosperous, growing economy required a high rate of private investment, and in 1954 he had put the weight of his administration behind a tax reform program that permitted businesses to charge off their investment expenditures more rapidly, giving them more opportunity to balance losses of particular years against the gains of earlier or later years, and reduced the double taxation of dividends. These reforms sought to encourage private investment by raising its prospects of profitability. Four years later the rate of taxation of corporate income remained an elevated 52 percent, but profits had been high in 1955, 1956, and 1957, and many businessmen themselves believed that they were passing on the corporate tax in higher prices. While many continued to grumble over the failure to take further steps to reduce the double taxation of dividends or liberalize depreciation allowances, businessmen as a whole did not oppose Eisenhower's fiscal policy.

In the final two years of the administration, 1959–1960, the centerpiece of that policy continued to be the fight against inflation, with a large budget surplus its principal weapon. Eisenhower believed that a large surplus would not only help erode the inflationary psychology of the time but also promote economic growth. It needed promoting. In the late fifties the country awoke with a start from its dream that the American rate of increase of total output was not only satisfactory, but the marvel of the world. In fact, its average annual growth rate between 1948 and 1960 was only 2.9 percent—in comparison with Japan's 8.7 percent, Germany's 7.2 percent, Italy's 5.8 percent, France's 4.2 percent, Sweden's 3.7 percent, Canada's 3.6 percent, and Great Britain's 2.7 percent. As growth rather than mere stability rose in the scale of national objectives, Eisenhower believed his case for running a large budget surplus stronger than ever. Such a surplus would not only help contain inflation; it would also permit retirement of part of the national debt—almost $300 billion in January 1960—and thus reduce the interest burden on the debt. Eisenhower repeatedly referred to the debt in terms of a burden which would be passed on to our children and grandchildren, thus overlooking the fact that Americans then owned the debt as well as owed it.

A large surplus and the containment of inflation, finally, would strengthen international confidence in the dollar, and with it, America's prestige in the world. Ever since the end of the Second World War, the United States had been running almost continuously a deficit in its balance of payments, discharging its obligation either by exporting gold or placing dollar assets in the hands of foreigners in the form of United States government securities, or deposits in American banks. In the late fifties both American and foreign concern was mounting over the possibility that this loss of gold and increase in liabilities was weakening the United States reserve position. There was talk about loss of confidence in the dollar. In the opinion of many bankers and other financial experts, it was necessary that the United States should stop its inflation and its budget deficits. A balanced budget or surplus would help restrain inflation, increase the competitiveness of American exports, and improve the balance of payments. Clearly, a stabilization policy of combating recession and unemployment—nearly 8 percent in 1957–1958 and again in 1960–1961—by incurring deficits would have compromised these other objectives. Fiscal policy therefore remained essentially passive.

With the election of John F. Kennedy in 1960, the scenario dramatically changed. Called the first modern economist in the American Presidency, Kennedy late in 1960 urged a "return to the spirit as well as the letter of the Employment Act" in order "to deal not only with the state of the economy but with our goals for economic progress." In the main, the economists who exerted influence on his thinking were younger men than Eisenhower's advisers, weaned on the deficit spending and other compensatory doctrines of the brilliant British economist John Maynard Keynes, men who had come to believe that in a recession the government should spend more and tax less, and that in a boom the reverse of this compensatory policy was the appropriate one. In their eyes, the essential economic problem was full employment and economic growth rather than the curtailment of inflation. As for budget balancing—that was an irrelevancy. In general, they believed the free market worked well and should not be tampered with, yet they acknowledged that government intervention to influence the decisions of businesses and labor unions might be justified if high employment could not be achieved without inflation. As Walter Heller, Kennedy's chairman of the Council of Economic Advisers, later said: "It is hard to study the modern economics of relative prices, resource allocation, and distribution without developing a healthy respect for the market mechanisms. . . . But

I do not carry respect to the point of reverence." Enormously self-confident, the Kennedy economists believed that steady advances in fact gathering—together with their use of a wider statistical net, improved surveys of consumer and investment intentions, and more refined, computer-assisted methods—would enable them to make reliable forecasts of economic fluctuations, and to adopt the fiscal and monetary policy mix appropriate to goals of either stabilization or growth.

It was the latter, rather than the objective of averaging out cyclical periods of prosperity and recession, upon which the council fixed its focus. The rate of unemployment when Kennedy came into office was 6.7 percent, but the country, in the eyes of his advisers, was suffering from something even more fundamental. The basic problem was years of slack. The economy was running substantially below its full-employment potential—indeed, since early 1957 what came to be called the performance gap between actual and potential GNP had increased from about $10 billion to about $50 billion. The "old orthodoxy" had emphasized the importance of balancing the government's annual budget, but according to the "new economics," this had unbalanced the economy.

An expansive fiscal policy could take the form of increased expenditures or lowered taxes. The latter was more palatable politically, and Kennedy chose that option. In August 1962 he said he would ask the Congress the following January to approve approximately 20 percent reductions in both individual and corporate taxes. Tax reduction thus became the centerpiece of the administration's policy, but both Kennedy and his advisers saw the need for a period of gradual reeducation before Congress and the country, "accustomed to nearly sixteen years of White House homilies on the wickedness of government deficits, would approve of an administration deliberately and severely unbalancing the budget." The need for reeducation was real: By early 1963, with the deficit rising, expenditures rising, and the economy rising, accusations of fiscal irresponsibility reached their peak.

Kennedy did not live to see his major fiscal innovation become law. However, his successor, Lyndon Johnson, fully accepted the commitment to tax reduction and signed the measure into law in early 1964. Later, advocates of the policy hailed its impact on the economy as "almost exactly in accord with the economic analysis and projections on which it was founded." Evidence supporting the claim appeared impressive. By the first quarter of 1966 over 7 million additional jobs had been created, and the unemployment rate had fallen from nearly 7 percent to under 4 percent. Real per capita income, after taxes, was one fifth higher than it had been in the first quarter of 1961, and the realized growth rate of the economy had doubled, rising from 2.25 percent for the period 1953–1960 to 4.5 percent between 1960 and 1966. Corporate profits after taxes had also doubled, while the total real compensation of all employees was about 30 percent higher. In contrast with the preceding five-year period, when the weekly take-home pay of the average manufacturing worker had fallen 1 percent, pay rose 18 percent. Yet the rise in consumer prices for 1960–1965 amounted to only 1.3 percent a year (wholesale prices rose 2 percent). This record of wage-price moderation was assisted by the establishment of guideposts—an essentially educational process of "informing labor, management, and the public of the explicit ways in which wage and price decisions should be geared to productivity advances if they are to be noninflationary." Surely the record was a remarkable one—and the prestige of the economic advisers to the President rode high.

The bold activism of the Kennedy-Johnson tax cut—once again, made not to counter recession but to lift up a listless economy to a higher growth path—is the first indubitably clear instance in American history of the use of Keynesian fiscal medicine to cure an ailing patient. It worked. But it worked in a context of supportive monetary policy, and perhaps of psychological and unknown other elements conducive to success. Needless to say, if it were certain that, in all circumstances, some specific fiscal-monetary policy mix would single-handedly generate some specific quantum of growth, or degree of stabilization, the problem of economic management would be simple. Unhappily, economics is not an exact science. The claim that the economy expanded because of the Kennedy-Johnson tax cut is plausible, but it is not unquestionable.

Nevertheless, the expansion was real enough, and in the words of the economic report of the President in January 1969, it created a "prosperity without parallel in our history." Even though an upsurge in defense spending for the Vietnam War after mid-1965 generated strong inflationary pressures, the upward drift in prices from 1959 to 1969 was a moderate 2.32 percent per year in the Consumer Price Index (CPI). From 1962 to 1969 total civilian employment rose 2.24 percent, and hours of all persons in the nonfarm business sector 2.27 percent a year. And expenditures on research and development as a proportion of GNP were historically high.

Leading the growth in aggregate demand were two expenditure streams of approximately equal size (other than federal transfers), viz., those made by state and local governments and those made by businesses on nonresidential fixed investment. Between 1962 and 1969 the latter increased by nearly 95 percent, the former by 105 percent. Behind the increased spending by state and local governments were federal grants to those governments, which rose by about 155 percent in the interim. And behind the rise in business expenditures were several "supply-side" inducements, viz., an investment tax credit in 1962, a liberalization of tax depreciation guidelines, low long-term interest rates, a tax cut for corporations, and a reduction of the top tax rates from 91 percent to 70 percent. The role of government was thus a very important one. Indeed, some economists maintain that its role was fundamental in the prosperity of the sixties, with the rise in business fixed investment being primarily induced by governmental outlays at the federal as well as state and local levels.

Belief in fiscal activism reached its zenith in early 1968. "We now take for granted," proclaimed a buoyant chairman of President Johnson's Council of Economic Advisers, "that the government must step in to provide the essential stability at high levels of employment and growth that the market mechanism, left alone, cannot deliver." Soon, however, inflation began to accelerate far beyond the expectation of the fiscal activists. It did so between 1967 and 1969 and did not slow down even in the recession of 1969–1970. Here was a new phenomenon—stagflation—for in all earlier postwar recessions a drop in inflation had been recorded. Economists had confidently believed it possible to trade off a given amount of inflation for a given amount of unemployment, that the relationship between the two (as shown by the "Phillips curve") was stable, and that policymakers could select any combination of the two that seemed desirable. Now it appeared that there existed a "natural rate" of unemployment, and that if policy managed to push the rate below this point, inflation would continue to accelerate. In a word, the stage was set for the triumph of monetarism over fiscal activism.

It appeared to be well set, for the relationship between the money supply and national income had been quite close ever since 1959 (changes in the one being paralleled by changes in the other of roughly the same magnitude). Then with the acceleration of monetary growth in 1971, output expanded at a frenetic pace for more than a year. Throughout 1972, the country enjoyed the largest real growth (5.7 percent) since 1966 and the lowest rise in consumer prices (3.3 percent) since 1967. By the end of the year unemployment was down to 5.1 percent. The most remarkable aspect of the boom was the investment by consumers in durable goods and residential construction, expenditures which may have been partly due to optimism engendered by the wage and price control program set in place by the Nixon administration in 1971–1972. The importance of expenditures by state and local governments began to decline in comparison to consumer and business investment. After two decades of roughly 6 percent growth in real terms, spending by those levels of government increased at only

4 percent during 1967–73, and at 2.3 percent between early 1973 and 1978. After early 1973, however, the economy faltered, a victim of "supply shocks," especially those set in motion by OPEC, and with these events the influence of monetarism began to fade. The impact on inflation and output growth of higher energy and food prices seemed more relevant than alterations in the aggregate money supply. And besides, while advocates of monetarism had insisted on the need for a constant rate of monetary growth, it now appeared that the demand for money was a stable and predictable function of income and interest rates.

The remaining years of the seventies, and the early eighties as well, were marked by rising inflation and unemployment, and by booming growth followed by recession. At the beginning of 1973 the economy was humming near full capacity, but after the dropping of controls, farm prices exploded, followed by a general commodities boom, soaring inflation, tightened credit conditions, a jump in interest rates to record levels, and, at the end of the year, a fourfold increase in oil prices by OPEC. From an annual rate (CPI) of 3.3 percent in 1972, inflation surged to 11 percent in 1974. The confidence of businessmen and consumers turned to fright, and 1974 became the worst year for the American economy since the end of the Second World War, with real GNP falling by 2 percent.

By 1975 the country seemed well into a depression, but before the year was half over, a new boom began that was to continue through Jimmy Carter's election to the presidency in 1976 and to last until 1980. But like the Nixon boom, Carter's soon began to accumulate the "familiar symptoms of America's economic disorder: record inflation, huge trade deficits, a deteriorating dollar, abrupt and rigorous monetary restraint, bounding oil prices and finally a severe recession." The recession was destined to be the longest of the postwar period. Only in early 1983, halfway into the administration of Ronald Reagan, did the economy show signs of revival.

Whether or not "Reaganomics" or fortuitous factors were responsible for this—and also for a remarkably lower rate of inflation, together with mounting unemployment, which climbed to over 10 percent of the labor force in 1983—was for the future to decide. Certainly President Reagan had deliberately sought to dampen the long inflation, and to do so not by reducing demand but by increasing supply. In theory, rapid growth would then overwhelm inflationary pressures from the demand side. He and his advisers thus rejected the neo-Keynesian tactic of stimulating demand in favor of "supply side" tax cuts, especially on higher incomes. The hoped-for consequence was to be increased saving, investment, and growth. However, preliminary evidence seemed to cast doubt on the vigor of the investment response to increased saving, with rising consumer demand looked to, after all, as a prime source of economic revival. Credit for the lowered rate of inflation clearly belonged to the monetary restraints imposed adamantly by the Fed's chairman, Paul Volcker, although at the price of severe recession in 1981–83. For the future one thing seemed clear: Controlling the money supply alone would be insufficient without budgetary restraint, for the prime cause of inflation appeared to be the running of large fiscal deficits by the government and financing them with easy money.

In retrospect, government policies, especially since the sixties, had failed to achieve stability, had failed to tame the vicissitudes of the business cycle. Yet the sharpness of cyclical change would surely have been more keen without the built-in stabilizers that owe so much to the New Deal years. It would have been keener, too, in the absence of improvements made in the postwar years by the private business establishment, especially better inventory and cost control, less speculation, better matching of plant capacity to markets, and more restrained wage-price policies than in expansions before the sixties. Whether or not these changes will prove to be permanent remains to be seen.

VIII

Some Deeper Currents in the Recent Past

Ａs THE American people entered upon the closing years of the twentieth century, the vistas that opened before them were being shaped silently by two fundamental forces. One was demography, the other technology. As always, the two were closely connected. Technology in the form of medical research and improvements in health care was reducing mortality, lengthening the span of life, and increasing the proportion of the elderly in the population. Technology, especially in the form of lightning-quick flows of computerized information, was enriching the data bases upon which investment and other strategic business decisions were being made. It was these private decisions, the many-tongued voice of the market, which were determining the pace at which the economy was growing. And the latter was deeply influencing family formation, birth rates, and immigration.

Between 1950 and the end of 1986 the population rose by nearly 77 million people. More than half the increase, some 42 million, came between 1950 and 1965. This "baby boom" caught demographers by surprise. They had confidently predicted a postwar continuation of the declining trends of the 1930s. Although a steep decline in births set in after the crest of the boom was reached in the late 1960s, it was clear to demographers that the baby boomers of the postwar years would confront American society with grave problems in the early decades of the twenty-first century.

The percentage of the population older than sixty-five was expected to climb moderately from 11.3 percent to 13.1 percent between 1980 and 2000, but by 2030 it would exceed 21 percent. In consequence there would be heavy pressures to spend more money on both hospital and long-term care for a generation caught in the coils of degenerative illness. Chronic illness was one thing, acute illness another. Society was organized and financed to treat the latter—medical emergencies—but the sad truth was that chronic illnesses accounted for 80 percent of all deaths and 90 percent of all disabilities. A person suffering a heart attack might be sped to the nearest hospital. One with Alzheimer's disease was more likely to go broke gradually.

Baby boomers were not the only source of increase in the postwar population. Immigration from Asia and Latin America, especially from Mexico, was another. Its numbers may never be known, for much of it was illegal. Poverty and hopelessness at home sent tens of thousands of single men and families north to the farm fields of California and Texas, where they tried to melt into the native population. The influx reached its highest levels in the 1960s. In the seventies, legal and illegal immigration together accounted for perhaps one third the nation's estimated 15 million increase. To discourage illegality, Congress enacted legislation in 1986 conferring resident alien status on illegal immigrants already in the country. Proprietors of farms and other businesses attractive to immigrants would presumably be reluctant in the future to hire immigrants lacking documentary proof of the new status.

While the problems of many elderly even today are very real, more people are surviving to old age than did so in 1950. And in general the population is healthier. In 1980 death rates for both sexes were lower at all ages and for all races than they were thirty years before, with the decline greater for females than for males, and greater for nonwhites than for whites. The decrease in nonwhite death rates is the main explanation for the rise in the proportion of nonwhites in the population. Up to the mid-1950s, decline in mortality was owing in the main to the diffusion of a number of new antibiotic "wonder drugs." After leveling off, mortality rates once again began to fall in the late sixties, particularly for older men and women, reversing a historical tendency for improvement to have been most marked in younger age groups. Control of cardiovascular and cerebrovascular diseases, especially, and to some extent also infectious diseases, lay behind the drop in mortality at older ages, the decline in the former probably being due in part to new medical care developments permitting the identification as well as treatment of high risk cases. Tragically, violent death—accidents, homicide, suicide—is the chief killer of young adults, especially males, and for this group mortality has failed to decline. The economic as well as human cost of this loss of years of productive activity hardly requires comment.

The population has not only become larger, healthier, and longer-lived; it has also redistributed itself in significant ways over the American landscape. Historically, the story has been one of urban growth and rural depopulation in consequence of technological change in industry and agriculture. Since the midtwentieth century, however, the United States has been on the brink of still another memorable epoch in geographic settlement, viz., the repopulation of a number of previously rural areas. The first clue to this development appeared in the form of suburbanization in the earlier years of the century. Recently, however, population has been flowing to rural areas that do not border on major cities, and it has also been shifting to the Sunbelt. The latter is evident in net migration rates from the fifties through the seventies, with the South and West virtually tied as leaders in rates of population growth and net in-migration. In the eighties, however, both New England and the Midwest began to rebound, the former because of the movement of high-tech firms to an area abounding in educational resources. No less noteworthy was the fact that, in every region except the South, population growth in areas not bordering on major cities has been higher than in those areas which do.

What explains these shifts to the Sunbelt and to nonmetropolitan places? In part, the answer lies in the presence of such special factors as natural resource endowments or governmental decisions regarding the location of military, space, and educational activities. In the case of the South, for example, it appears that large military allocations and technological developments accompanying the Second World War provided the necessary external stimulus for the industrial and population growth long sought by the region's leaders. In the postwar decades, an increasing number of businessmen turned southward in response to lower operating costs, especially wages, promanagement state governments, and a growing regional market nurtured by increased federal expenditures. When the space industry boomed in the early 1960s, for example, Florida's population grew by nearly 3,000 persons a week. In the region as a whole, industrial development after the war first slowed population losses and then, between 1970 and 1976, spurred a net gain from in-migration of 2.9 million people.

But special circumstances do not explain longer-term developments. "Throughout the history of mankind residence decisions have been dominated by place of work." In long eras of the American past these decisions were governed by farming opportunities opened up by the vast extent of available land. Then with the advent of mechanized production in the nineteenth century, settlement patterns shifted in favor of urban locations. Unlike colonial shops, the new technology made possible important economies of scale; unlike shops, factories needed access to substantial markets for their products. Furthermore, the coal and iron ore required by industry were "much less ubiquitous than the agricultural and forest resources on which preindustrial technology was based." For this reason producers located at or near the sources of these new industrial inputs or at transport points that made them accessible at low cost.

In consequence, new business and job opportunities were opened up in urban centers, places which soon became key junctions in the railroad network. So-called agglomeration economies then accentuated the advantages of these centers as workers and consumers flocked to them. Rising per capita incomes then raised consumer demand for manufactured products, with the result that still more people were drawn to urban centers in search of job opportunities. The result was rural depopulation: In each of the two decades between 1940 and 1960, more than 3,100 American counties experienced absolute declines in their numbers of people.

Modern technology then proceeded to break the ties that bound the consumer's residence to his place of work. First, the horse-drawn trolley and electric streetcar, and then the automobile, made it possible for many urban Americans to exercise their preference for rural or semirural living places, a preference made possible also by the shortened workday brought about by modern economic growth. In addition, the transmission of electricity supplied the power essential for the operation of households in nonurban residential communities. Nor can the open-air recreational facilities of rural areas—camping, picnicking, and water sports—be ignored.

Business firms as well as consumers have been affected by the relative advantages of rural locations. They are no longer, as in the nineteenth century, tied to narrow resource requirements. Technological progress has diversified industrial materials, permitting a shift, for example, from ferrous to nonferrous metals and plastics, from coal to petroleum, natural gas, and other sources. Trucks have altered the rigid rail transport network. Above all, information essential to all business decisions is now transmitted by the telephone and the computer. Furthermore, former economies of agglomeration have turned into diseconomies as urban pollution and congestion have increased. All in all, in this century the location of business firms is far less bound than it has been in the past to a limited urban network. It is more responsive than ever before to consumer preferences, not least those of workers for more attractive locations in which to work.

Rural repopulation, in sum, represents a personal and business response to ways of living and working made possible by technological advance. It does not bespeak an increased demand for agricultural labor. Indeed, the opposite is true. Between 1945 and 1981 the farm population fell from 17.5 percent of the total to merely 2.6 percent, with farm employment down from 10 million to about one third of that. In 1947, more than one family in six lived on a farm, but by 1977 only one in twenty-six continued to do so. As late as 1929, payments for capital, labor, and natural resources by the agricultural, forestry, and fisheries sectors of the economy generated 10 percent of the national income, but by 1978 this percentage had fallen to 2.9 percent. Behind both of these developments in relation to agriculture lay major increases in productivity. The farm sector has shrunk by becoming more efficient. Crop output per hour quintupled between 1950–1979; output of livestock and livestock products rose sixfold. Meanwhile, hours of labor required on farms fell by more than two thirds.

Capital has displaced much of this labor. An index of farm inputs shows labor falling from 217 in 1950 to 65 in 1980. In part, mechanical power and machinery took its place, the index rising from 84 to 128. More importantly, the index for agricultural chemicals, including fertilizers, lime, and pesticides, jumped from 29 to 174 during the period. Unfortunately, there is no index for another important input, viz., intangible capital in the form of better management and knowledge of improved production techniques. Large public and private investments in education, in schools, colleges and research organizations, including those of the Department of Agriculture, have generated and spread this knowledge, stimulating new patterns of input use. Growing managerial efficiency and knowledge, then, as well as technology, help explain one of the truly amazing facts of American history:

In 1790, at the beginning of our existence as an independent nation, it required the labor of perhaps eighty-five out of every one hundred persons to provide for the agricultural needs of a population of 4 million, including needs that were met from the proceeds of modest exports. In 1981, in contrast, fewer than three persons out of every one hundred were required to feed and clothe a population swollen to over 230 million, and to generate, besides, huge surpluses. Surely this is a miracle of agricultural science.

Agriculture has become industrialized. Most farms are now firms; some are factories. Around the time of the Second World War an Agricultural Revolution, comparable in many ways to the earlier Industrial Revolution, began to take place in the United States. One similarity between the two was the tendency for production to become concentrated in fewer, larger units. In 1980 the number of "farms" in the United States was only a third of their total in 1920, but their average size had grown from 147 to 453 acres. Small farms of less than 100 acres still continued to represent 43.5 percent of all farms in 1978, but they harvested only 5 percent of the country's total cropland. They were essentially noncommercial farms. Their annual sales averaged less than $2,500. In contrast, farms ranging in size from 500 to more than 2,000 acres harvested 60 percent of the cropland. These larger units dominated American agriculture. Scarcely more than one farm in ten boasted annual sales of $100,000 or more, but these giants were responsible for 63 percent of the total sales. In many counties farm sales of leading commodities had become so concentrated on a few big farms by 1978 that the United States Department of Agriculture was prevented by disclosure laws from publishing the relevant figures in the agricultural census.

What brought about this result was not size alone but size together with heavy investments in capital, capital in the form of machinery and equipment, fertilizer, chemicals, and other inputs—in a word, mechanization. Widening mechanization, seeds with higher yields, improved breeds of livestock, and the use of herbicides, pesticides, and other products of agricultural chemistry, are to be found today in all major agricultural regions of the United States except the Great Plains.

Despite the technological innovations which are at the heart of this Agricultural Revolution, the American farmer has by no means enjoyed a record of unparalleled financial success. Nor has his banker, his suppliers, and those who service his equipment, processing, and transport needs—those, in short, who make up the complex of "agribusiness." "I've never seen a year like this," said Dean Jack, president of York State Bank in southeastern Nebraska in February 1985. "Half of our farmers are in good shape, about 25 percent are in trouble and about 25 percent are already broke." He added: "We have good water for irrigation, we have land that is as good as anybody's, and we raise as good crops as ever, and half our farmers still can't pay their debts." More broadly, in early 1985 one third of the nation's farms were encumbered by an average debt of $325,000. And when farms failed, they brought down the banks to which they were indebted. The year 1986 saw 138 bank failures, more than in any year since the establishment of the Federal Deposit Insurance Corporation in 1934. Most were located in farm- and energy-producing states, with Texas, Oklahoma, Kansas, Iowa, and Missouri heading the list.

The fundamental explanation of the financial predicament in which so many American farmers found themselves in the mid-1980s is simple: They responded incautiously to the price signals of the marketplace. The explanation itself, however, has to be explained, and that is anything but simple. The chronic farm problem in the United States has long been that of excess capacity, of an ability to produce more than domestic and foreign markets can absorb at remunerative prices, even with the aid of goods taken off the market by government support programs. In other words, in the aggregate, demand has been inelastic with respect to price. Ever since the days of the New Deal, government has tried to cope with this problem by mounting a host of programs—acreage allotments and marketing quotas, purchase agreements, soil banks, and others—designed to curtail supply by limiting production. And it has tried through commodity loans to farmers or to their cooperative marketing associations to provide floors under market prices. In addition, numerous programs have authorized payments to producers in the form of commodity price supports, or in return for adopting soil conservation measures. Analysts generally agree that average farm prices in the 1950s and 1960s would have been considerably lower if these programs had not been in existence, perhaps from 10 to 25 percent lower.

In the later 1960s prices, which with government support had held at reasonably constant levels from 1953 to 1967, began to move upward. And in 1973 they shot skyward to levels never before experienced except during wartime. What had happened? The explanation is that foreign demand rose massively in response to (a) the Nixon administration's approval of the sale of $750 million worth of wheat and feed grains to the Soviet Union in the summer of 1972—a sale which also sparked orders from elsewhere in Europe and from Japan—and (b) the Nixon administration's devaluation of the dollar in 1973, which cheapened American exports.

American farmers responded with enthusiasm to the prospect of upwardly spiraling demand, prices, and profits. Encouraged by their bankers to borrow, and by top officials in the Department of Agriculture to plant "from fence to fence," they increased the area under crops by 54 million acres between 1969 and 1981—and adopted improved production techniques besides to lower costs and raise output. Corn production, for example, went up from 5.6 million bushels in 1972 to 8.4 million in 1982. In the meantime, however, agricultural production abroad also expanded, and American surpluses soared.

Enter the value of the dollar. In contrast with the sixties and seventies, when the dollar was generally weak in relation to the currencies of Europe and Japan, the dollar of the earlier years of the 1980s developed phenomenal strength. Exports of manufactured goods as well as farm commodities were affected. Since they were priced in expensive dollars, they fell. In contrast, imports rose. Indeed, in 1986 the excess of imports over exports soared to an historically high deficit of $175 billion. The strong dollar reduced foreign demand for American goods, and this lessened foreign demand, which, in turn, increased quantities available for domestic sale. But although this lowered prices to consumers, it also lowered incomes for farmers. Falling incomes, in turn, made it difficult for farmers to repay their investments in equipment and supplies, with obvious economic consequences for manufacturers and tradesmen. Thus, as always since the rise of industry, the fortunes of the agricultural and manufacturing sectors of the economy were closely entwined.

In some ways, manufacturers had an even harder row to hoe. In contrast with the remarkable record of productivity growth encountered in the postwar history of American agriculture, manufacturing, once the pacesetting embodiment of the American System, as it was known and envied abroad, could boast no similar accomplishment in recent years. Just the opposite: The rate of increase in productivity has been slowing down. From an annual average of 3.4 percent between 1948 and 1966, the rate of increase fell to 2.3 percent during 1966–1973, to 1 percent during 1973–1977, and to 0.4 percent between 1977 and 1978. Then in 1979 and 1980 growth stopped altogether, and productivity actually declined.

Naturally enough, this strange unhistoric phenomenon aroused concern, and economists have been pondering its causes since the late sixties. Among the numerous factors cited were an increase in the proportion of youths and women in the work force ("Output per man-hour tends to be relatively low among women and among new entrants into the labor force"), relatively low rates of investment after 1973, a decrease in the proportion of the Gross

National Product devoted to research and development in the late sixties and early seventies, and the shift of national output away from goods and toward services, where possibilities of productivity growth are more limited. The litany goes on and on. Some suggest that the solution to the puzzle might begin with the dismantling of government policies that have raised costs and discouraged savings. Others emphasize the importance of retaining workers displaced by computers, robots, and other technological innovations, and by the migration of production to low wage centers overseas. In addition to new skills and knowledge, some suggest, workers also need greater motivation to excel not only as individuals but also as members of a team. Productivity in the era of human capital, writes a recent scholar, "will depend largely on collaboration, group learning, and teamwork."

Finally, one must consider the effects of decisions made by business managers themselves, especially those of the largest manufacturing corporations. According to one critic, professional managers, intent on a favorable reading of the "bottom line," have gradually become "paper entrepreneurs" since the mid-1960s. Avoiding the costs and risks of investments in fundamentally new products or processes, their innovations have been neither technological nor institutional. "Rather, they have been based on accounting, tax avoidance, financial management, mergers, acquisitions and litigation. They have been innovations on paper." Instead of creating new wealth, they have merely rearranged industrial assets.

The conglomerate merger movement that began in the 1960s is a case in point. Before then, American business enterprises as a rule confined their expansion to lines of business related to their original products, entering markets appropriate to their managerial, technical, and marketing capabilities in search of competitive advantage. The conglomerate enterprises born after the mid-1960s—Gulf & Western, LTV, Textron, Litton, United Technologies, Northwest Industries, ITT, and Teledyne—were entirely different. Multibusiness giants, they have grown by acquiring existing enterprises, often in wholly unrelated fields. ITT, for example, owns Wonder Bread, Sheraton Hotels, Hartford Insurance, Bobbs-Merrill Publishing, and Burpee Lawn and Garden Products. Conglomerates rarely, if ever, bring managerial, technical, or marketing skills to the companies they acquire because they lack any direct knowledge of these unrelated businesses. Their expertise is in law and finance, and their relationship to their subsidiaries that of an investor who diversifies to spread his risks.

Conglomeration has been taking place rapidly in recent years, with American companies increasing the amounts spent in acquiring other companies from $22 billion in 1977 to twice that sum two years later. Nineteen-eighty-one saw record-shattering expenditures of $82 billion for the purpose. Since conglomeration increases concentration ratios—that is, it increases the proportion of an industry's output accounted for by a few large firms—it follows that the movement must lessen the number of decisions affecting output and probably also the number of people making them. In sum, managerial emphasis has often in recent years shifted from cost-reducing and product-enhancing innovation through research and development to short-run profits from market manipulations of company assets. The consequence has surely been the placing of higher managerial premiums on expertise in law and finance than on engineering and other productivity-enhancing bodies of knowledge.

The causes of the decline in productivity are clearly complex. Just as surely, its consequences have been grave. Among them is an erosion of the average American standard of living. Real incomes began to slow their rate of growth in 1965, with real wages declining by one fifth between 1968 and 1981. In addition, exports of American manufactured goods have fallen as a percentage of world manufactured exports ever since 1963, and this is partly attributable to a weak productivity performance. Ironically, the industries affected are those on which the industrial preeminence of the United States has long rested, a superiority due to its ability to produce with growing efficiency standardized goods in high volume. They are its basic steel, textile, automobile, electronics, rubber, and petrochemical industries, together with other high-volume industries dependent on them. Increasingly uncompetitive, the American proportion of world automobile sales fell by nearly one third between 1963 and 1981. Sales of industrial machinery also declined by one third, agricultural machinery by 40 percent, telecommunications machinery by 50 percent, and metalworking machinery by 55 percent. Nevertheless, the United States has remained a net exporter of capital goods and of chemicals ever since World War II, and the surpluses have grown rapidly since the late 1960s.

Historically, the United States has been a net importer of consumer goods. But this was not the case in the years immediately after the Second World War, when, in 1947, for example, exports of consumer goods yielded a net surplus of $1 billion. The explanation lies in the relative impact of the war upon the United States and other industrial nations. The United States escaped with its factories, mines, and transport net intact, capable, in 1950, of producing approximately 60 percent of world manufacturing output. In contrast, industrial capacity in almost every continental European country and in Japan had been destroyed, and that of Great Britain crippled.

The distortion in the composition of trade was not destined to last. Public grants under the Marshall Plan of about $13 billion, by contributing significantly to European industrial and economic growth, paved the way to a return to traditional trading patterns. The European economies recovered and rebuilt capacity in the 1950s; in the next decade Japan entered competitive world markets in a major way; and in the 1970s several developing countries, aided by a gradual reduction of tariff levels after adoption of the General Agreement on Tariffs and Trade in 1947, and by relatively easy access to international capital through European,

American, and Japanese banks (and also by a new postwar institution, the World Bank), began making important contributions to manufacturing output and trade. By 1979, the share of the United States in world industrial production had fallen from 60 percent to 35 percent, and its share in world exports of manufactured goods from 29 percent (in 1953) to 13 percent (in 1976). By 1980, the share of the developing nations in manufactured goods had soared to exact equivalence with that of the United States, while Japan's rose in the 1970s from 6 percent to 10.5 percent. From a transitory position of early postwar domination of the export trade, the United States thus moved to one of rough equivalence with other industrial countries, in the meantime resuming its historical posture as a net importer of consumer goods.

However, the growth of industrial capacity in other parts of the world, together with roughly comparable cost developments, does not wholly explain the declining share of American manufacturers in world exports. As with agricultural exports, the relative values of national currencies must also be taken into account. During the years of postwar decline, the American dollar was overvalued in relation to other currencies, and in consequence, foreign sales of American goods were impeded, imports stimulated, and American firms encouraged to invest abroad. Because, however, of the peculiar role which the dollar came to play under what was known as the Bretton Woods System, devaluation of the dollar was for a long time effectively ruled out. The result was that the United States trade balance, after reaching a peak surplus in the early 1960s, began to deteriorate. By July 1971 the balance of payments deficit was rising at the very high rate of $23 billion a year, and this generated increasing pressure to abandon the system.

But this could not lightly be done. Under that system, adopted by a United Nations conference meeting at Bretton Woods, New Hampshire, in 1944, the dollar had become the standard in terms of which all other currencies were measured. The Japanese yen and British pound, for example, were valued in terms of the dollar, with the dollar itself being valued in terms of gold. If a foreign central bank wished to exchange its dollars for gold, it was agreed that it could do so at the fixed price of $35 an ounce. The convertibility of dollars into gold was the system's theoretical anchor. Because of convertibility, other countries were willing to hold dollars in their monetary reserves instead of gold. Bretton Woods, in short, adopted what was technically known as the gold reserve standard.

Unfortunately, the ability of the system to function began to deteriorate in the late fifties, weakened by increasing surpluses of dollars in foreign hands. The dollar glut bespoke growing deficits in the balance of payments and led to loss of American gold reserves. (Ironically, it was the outflow of dollars made necessary by the deficits which enabled the dollar to function as the principal reserve currency and medium for payment of international transactions.) Deficits mounted for three principal reasons. Government loans, grants, and military expenditures placed large quantities of dollars in foreign hands. So too did a growing deficit in the balance of trade. Rising prices in the United States in the later sixties made American goods more expensive abroad while cheapening imports. Finally, American firms began in the late fifties to increase their direct investments abroad. They did so in part because of greater prosperity abroad than at home. Had the opposite been true, they would have been more likely in ordinary circumstances to keep their capital in the United States, to expand domestic production facilities. However, circumstances were not ordinary. What changed them was the organization of the European Common Market in 1958. Fearful that the member countries might try to exclude competing American goods by high tariffs, many American firms elected to build or acquire plant and machinery behind the protective walls of the Market. Direct investments were especially prominent in European and Canadian manufacturing, petroleum, and mining and smelting facilities.

Those in manufacturing alone increased eightfold between 1950 and 1970, rising from $3.8 billion to $32.3 billion.

In sum, government expenditures, private direct investment, and the effects of inflation on the trade balance led to a dollar glut abroad. But while these developments made for growing deficits in the balance of payments, it is worth calling attention to the fact that it might have been possible to cover the deficits more largely by means other than the export of gold. Had the economic growth of the United States been stronger than it was, Europeans and others would have been attracted to the securities of American firms. Alas, it was not so. A massive gold drain began in 1958, the United States losing some $3.5 to $4 billion a year between then and the midsixties. The nation's ownership of $22.9 billion of gold in 1957 had represented nearly 60 percent of the free world's supply. By 1965 the amount had declined to $15 billion, the proportion to 35 percent.

Such losses fed the fires of doubt that the United States would continue to be able to keep its pledge to redeem its dollars at the agreed-upon rate of $35 for an ounce of gold. Speculators reasoned that the United States would be compelled to devalue the dollar, to raise the dollar price of gold. They were right. After a massive speculative run against the dollar, the Nixon administration decided in 1971 that devaluation was the only way out. It suspended indefinitely the official convertibility of the dollar into gold and in 1973 made the suspension permanent. Not only was the dollar devalued against gold. Nearly all the major industrial currencies were revalued against the dollar, the Japanese yen, for example, by approximately 17 percent. The purpose of the devaluation, it should be made clear, was to produce a major improvement in the United States balance of payments, including the trade balance, and to put an end to the disadvantage under which American export industries were operating, in the belief that this, together with a hoped-for reversal of capital flows, would improve the balance of payments. The Bretton Woods System of fixed parities was abandoned. Floating exchange rates replaced fixed exchange rates, with the price of dollars in terms of gold and other currencies henceforth being determined by the supply and demand for dollars.

Despite the devaluations of the early seventies, the dollar became strong once again in the eighties. What made it strong was the impact of large budgetary deficits on real interest rates. By 1987 the deficit, swollen by huge defense expenditures, coupled with unwillingness on the part of the Reagan administration to raise taxes, had reached a historic high of $173 billion. Because the government must compete with private borrowers for available savings, the huge sums borrowed by the government to finance the deficit kept interest rates high. These high rates, in turn, along with the perceived stability of the American economy, attracted foreign capital to the United States. Ironically, foreign investment made it possible to finance the gargantuan American budget without still higher interest rates. Capital-losing countries, on the other hand, complained because the export of capital reduced sums available for their own development needs. The reply of the Reagan administration was that a reduced rate of inflation was responsible for the dollar's strength, and it urged other industrialized countries around the world to follow the example of the United States!

If falling productivity and relative currency values go far to explain the decline in American manufactured exports as a proportion of world sales, they also throw light on the ability of foreign imports to win larger shares of the domestic market.

> By 1981 America was importing 26 percent of its cars, 25 percent of its steel, 60 percent of its televisions, radios, tape recorders and phonographs, 43 percent of its calculators, 27 percent of its metal-forming machine tools, 35 percent of its textile machinery, and 53 percent of its numerically controlled machine tools. Twenty years before, imports had accounted for less than 10 percent of the U.S. market for each of these products.

However, productivity and currency are not the only relevant considerations. Since the 1960s a major structural change has been taking place in the world economy. Access to capital, technological knowledge, and innovations, and global channels of sales and marketing, have permitted lesser developed countries to participate in that economy far more actively than before. Their participation, in turn, and that of Third World countries as well, has permitted an international rationalization of the location of production to take place. The globe is thus becoming a single marketplace, with goods being made wherever they can be made the cheapest. Real wages are lower in Third World countries, and many of them also have a favored access to cheap materials. In addition, the availability of data processing machines, microprocessors, and satellite communications facilities have made it possible for manufacturers to divide the process of production into separate operations that can be performed at different sites and then integrated into a single product. Such developing countries as Korea, Hong Kong, Taiwan, Singapore, Brazil, and Spain have been ideally suited to manufacturing standardized parts that are assembled into end products elsewhere. Sometimes, the process is reversed. Since 1970, for example, the United States has been increasing its exports of auto parts and its imports of complete cars, its export of industrial textiles and its import of consumer textiles. South Korea's textile exports rose by 436 percent between 1970 and 1975, while those of Taiwan and Hong Kong increased by 347 percent and 191 percent, respectively. Imports to the United States from developing nations rose nearly tenfold from 1970 to 1980, from $3.6 billion to $30 billion (in constant dollars).

One consequence has been an intensification of competition in the American marketplace, where, by 1980, foreign-made goods were competing with more than 70 percent of those produced in the United States. Another has been a progressive shift in competitive advantage in high-volume standardized production to the newly developed and developing countries. The upshot of these rapid changes was that a number of old-line American industries, including textiles, steel, automobiles, petrochemicals, electrical machinery, and metal-forming machinery, found themselves in trouble in the early 1980s.

Many of them had become stable oligopolies of three or four major firms. Unaccustomed to price competition, adhering to a system of administered prices and guaranteed wage increases, management often refused to allow prices to respond to market conditions. Technologically backward and reluctant to innovate, steel makers clung to open hearth and ingot casting techniques while their Japanese counterparts were investing heavily in superior basic oxygen furnaces and continuous casting. American automakers also held back, toying with changes in style while the Japanese were adopting new stamping technologies and experimenting with more efficient engines and pollution control devices. The competitive threat came not only from the Japanese but also from West German machine tool companies, French radial tire manufacturers, Swedish makers of precision instruments, and textile manufacturers in developing countries. The list of American companies experiencing sharply reduced profits in the early 1980s included ghostly giants of the past: United States Steel, General Motors, International Harvester, and RCA.

American producers in steel, automobile, consumer electronics, and other industries sought protection from imports by forming political coalitions with organized labor, petitioning the executive branch, lobbying Congress, and seeking support through the federal courts. Various sorts of trade restrictions followed, one example being the marketing agreement negotiated with Japan by the United States government limiting imports of Japanese color televisions to approximately 1.6 million sets a year, and similar agreements subsequently negotiated with Taiwan and South Korea. Besides quotas, protection has also taken the form of increased duties, and a wide assortment of government subsidies, special tax credits and depreciation allowances, and subsidized loans and loan guarantees. According to one computation, the total cost to the federal government of special tax provisions for the benefit of specific industries rose from $7.9 billion in 1950 to $62.4 billion in 1980. During the same interval, the cost of subsidized loans and loan guarantees, as measured by interest charges and loan defaults, increased from only $300 million to $3.6 billion. Altogether, government subsidies and tax expenditures increased from $77.1 billion in 1950 to $303.7 billion in 1980. In addition, government subsidies have taken the form of ad hoc bailouts of particular failing firms—for example, Lockheed and Chrysler.

Is this the way America should go? Should we look to government to protect the bottom line of firms and industries whose economic good health is judged to be in the national interest? Some think so. "Ultimately," says a recent writer, "America's capacity to respond to economic change will depend on the vitality of its political institutions." The United States must accept the fact that economic advantage in high-volume production of standardized products has moved to the developing countries. The challenge of the "new American frontier" is to promote the growth of "flexible system" production by technically advanced, skill-intensive industries, a highly integrated system that can respond quickly to new opportunities. The answer to economic decline, then, is to fashion "a new productive organization requiring a different, less rigidly delineated relationship between management and labor and a new relationship with government." What we need is an industrial policy.

Others disagree. Writing in 1983, Charles Schultze, chairman of the Council of Economic Advisers under President Carter, pointed out that the essential purpose of such a policy was the creation of an industrial structure different from what the market would have produced. In that case policy-makers would necessarily face a twofold task, that of protecting the losers and that of picking the winners. Protecting losers meant supporting major declining industries by such means as trade barriers, subsidies, favorable regulatory treatment, tax breaks, and subsidized loans. Protectionism, inefficiencies, and higher prices for consumers would soon manifest themselves. As for picking winners or providing various forms of government aid to specific companies and industries—fast growers, big employers, or technological leaders—Schultze wanted to know how government bureaucrats could be expected to be better judges of the likelihood of success than private investors. He feared such a policy would turn into a vast boondoggle for every industry with political clout.

The policy question was a significant political issue of the 1980s, and only time would tell the outcome of the debate. The debate itself, however, in Congress and out, appeared in the late 1980s to be approaching consensus on the need for government to join with private business firms in stepped-up efforts to retrain workers displaced by technological change and by the migration of production to cheaper areas overseas. Furthermore, even dedicated proponents of free market solutions also acknowledged the need for government to provide a safety net for low-income people, a net consisting of such income assistance programs as unemployment compensation, food stamps, and Aid to Families with Dependent Children.

Such an idea would have found few supporters before the debut of the Welfare State during the anguished years of the Great Depression. Most looked to a healthy economy to provide jobs and income and to private charity to help the victims of misfortune. The New Deal marks the triumph of a more compassionate philosophy, namely, that it is a legitimate responsibility of the federal government to aid in the provision of the minimal needs of the disadvantaged. Evidence of the new viewpoint took the form of enlarged governmental expenditures for such Social Security programs as those providing for old age, survivors', invalidism, and public health insurance, for workmen's compensation, unemployment insurance, family allowances, public assistance, and public employee programs. The welfare state of the age of Roosevelt was extended but not reshaped under Truman (who supported legislation making Social Security available to 10 million additional people, authorizing new public housing for the slum dweller, and expanding public power, rural electrification, soil conservation and flood control projects), and found its richest expression in the twentieth century thus far in the Great Society programs of Lyndon Johnson.

Some of the legislation of the Johnson years, such as medical care for the aged, had been bottled up in Congress since the Truman administration. Other programs bore Johnson's personal stamp, and of these probably the most important was the war on poverty. In 1962 Michael Harrington had written movingly about the 40 million or so people (one fifth of the American population) who had "dropped out of sight," who dwelt in a culture of poverty. They made up a more or less permanent underclass. They were the elderly, the nonwhites, the poorly educated, and unproductive small farmers; they were the inhabitants of urban ghettos and of Appalachia. "Poverty" is not only an absolute but also a relative concept, and one whose definition necessarily changes over time, but roughly half of all these groups were at or below the poverty line as defined by the Social Security Administration in 1964 (i.e., as having annual incomes of $3,000 or less to support a family of four).

Acting on the belief that poverty of this kind was impacted, that it was the result of social problems little affected by broad economic forces, and hence could not be eliminated by indirect methods which stimulated overall economic growth, Johnson put the weight of his presidential authority behind direct approaches to the problem. The Economic Opportunity Act of 1964, which established ten programs, among which were Head Start, the Job Corps, and Vista, represented the first concerted attack on poverty since New Deal days. Other major programs followed: Medicare and Medicaid, federal aid for elementary and secondary education, federal scholarships for college students, a multimillion dollar program for medical research, legislation providing rent subsidies, demonstration cities, a teachers corps, regional medical centers, vest-pocket parks, a rescue operation for the economically depressed region of Appalachia, and an assortment of consumer protection laws, including those designed to increase auto and highway safety.

Standing as a halfway marker between the Roosevelt and Johnson administrations, the creation of the Cabinet-level Department of Health, Education, and Welfare in 1953 symbolized the continuing enlargement of the federal presence in the area of human melioration. From 1950 to 1964, federal expenditures for these purposes nearly tripled, rising, in constant dollars, from $35.1 billion to $108 billion. Unhappily, the War on Poverty fell victim to the War on Vietnam, the escalating funding requirements of which induced Johnson, as early as the beginning of 1966, to reduce or eliminate his budgetary requests for the maintenance of civilian programs he came to regard as ones of lower priority. Nevertheless, the evidence of the past half-century of governmental interest in the preservation and improvement of human capital is unmistakable.

In this, the United States is not alone. While elements of welfare or Social Security programs vary from one country to another, reflecting differences in governmental structure, tradition, and historical development, the major industrial powers have devoted increasing portions of their gross national product to welfare objectives in recent decades. Despite differences in the nature of their political societies, all have responded to underlying social pressures engendered by an advanced state of industrialization. As Table 5 shows, however, government expenditures by the United States represented a smaller share than those of any other country except Japan. Even this proportion was subjected to deep budgetary cuts by the Reagan administration. The slicing of expenditures on education aid and loans, job training and retraining,

Table 5. Government Expenditures for Social Security Programs as a Percentage of GNP, Selected Countries, 1957–1977

COUNTRY	1957	1960	1963	1966	1971	1974	1977
Canada	6.5	8.7	9.4	9.0	14.8	13.7	14.6
France	14.3	13.7	15.4	16.6	n.a.	22.4	26.5
West Germany	16.6	16.2	16.9	18.4	18.8	22.5	26.5
Japan	4.3	4.7	5.1	5.6	5.6	6.4	8.7
Sweden	10.5	10.9	12.1	14.5	20.6	24.4	30.7
United Kingdom	10.0	11.0	11.1	12.3	13.5	14.1	17.1
United States	5.0	6.29	6.8	7.7	11.1	12.1	13.7

Source: David P. Calleo, *The Imperious Economy* (Cambridge: Harvard University Press, 1982), 96.

and nutrition benefits for expectant mothers placed in serious jeopardy the nation's future stock of human capital.

In the early 1980s the question of poverty also became ensnarled in statistical and definitional controversy. The Census Bureau reported that 34.4 million Americans whose cash incomes in 1982 were less than $9,862 for a family of four fell below the official poverty level. The poverty rate that year was 15 percent of the American people, up from 14 percent in 1981, and the highest rate reported since the start of President Johnson's antipoverty campaign in 1965. The director of the Office of Management and Budget, David Stockman, disputed these figures, however. In testimony before the House Ways and Means Committee in November 1983, he rejected the definition of poverty used by the Census Bureau and other federal agencies since 1964. "The official poverty count based on money income," he said, "substantially overstates the rate of poverty because it ignores $107 billion in in-kind medical, housing, food, and other aid that tangibly raises the living standard of many low-income families." When noncash benefits are counted as income, he added, the poverty rate for 1982 was reduced from 15 percent to 9.6 percent, the number of poor people from 34.4 million to 22 million. . . . The point was not a new one. Scholars had emphasized the relevance of in-kind aid nearly a decade before, if not earlier. The influence on policy was delayed and even now uncertain, but in 1983 the Census Bureau at least planned to issue future reports simultaneously displaying the official poverty rate, using the usual definition, and what the rate would be if noncash benefits were counted as income.

According to Stockman, poor people in 1982 fell into four categories. The elderly (sixty-five and older) formed 10.9 percent of the total, female-headed households 32.8 percent, young singles between sixteen and twenty-four years of age, 3.9 percent, and other adults between twenty-five and sixty-four years of age, 52.3 percent. The rising tide of economic growth would lift many boats, but not all. It would alleviate poverty for people in their prime working years but would be largely irrelevant to the elderly poor, many of whom had retired. Cash welfare programs, on the other hand, were of less value to young singles than to poor people in female-headed households, for whom government checks were of "critical and overwhelming significance." The conjunction of family instability, race and ethnicity, and poverty were painfully apparent. Only 56.1 percent of black families were husband-wife families in 1978, in contrast to 85.9 percent in the case of whites. In 1981, for female-headed families with children under eighteen, the percentages of families under the poverty line was about 68 percent for blacks, 67 percent for Hispanics, and 43 percent for whites. Unhappily, a task force appointed by President Reagan to investigate the question of hunger in the United States reported early in 1984 that "quantitative information about the extent of the problem is not available." In a final report characterized by the *New York Times* as one of "chilly, bloodless neutrality," the Task Force acknowledged "the sad truth" that "there is hunger in America," but concluded that "general claims of widespread hunger can neither be positively refuted nor definitively proved." Early in 1984 the nation awaited the course of action by a President who in November 1983 had said: "If there is one person in this country hungry, that is one too many, and we're going to see what we can do to alleviate the situation." The nation continued to wait in 1987.

As is evident from a comparison of the amount of cash income demarcating the official poverty line for a family of four in 1964 ($3,000) and 1982 ($9,862) something more than inflation has affected the definition of poverty. Undoubtedly, the most important additional ingredient has been the rising standard of living. "Need" today is defined at a higher level than in the past because of the very success of the American economic system in providing for the material wants of the average family.

> In 1900 15 percent of U.S. families had flush toilets; today [1976] 86 percent of our poor families do. In 1900 3 percent had electricity; today 99 percent of our poor do; in 1900 1 percent had central heating; today 62 percent of the poor do. In 1900 18 percent of our families had refrigeration, ice refrigeration; today 99 percent of our poor have refrigerators, virtually all mechanical.

It is this "upward trend in the reference standard" that makes the end of poverty "an ever-retreating goal, and an unachievable one." In sum, government has done much and must do more to alleviate the absolute poverty of hunger. But in the relative sense the Biblical admonition that "The poor ye have always with you" will continue to be true as long as American capitalism generates not only more and more goods and services but also the desire to have them. For in creating wealth it at the same time creates want.

Modern industrialization not only heightened consciousness of the need for increased public responsibility for the alleviation of absolute poverty. It also generated public response to its environmental consequences—pollution of the air by automobiles, factories, electric-power plants, and garbage incinerators, and of water by chemicals washed into the rivers by factories using it as a coolant and by oil spills which kill marine life and damage property, and by insecticides washed off numerous farms into the national water supply. The federal government first gave official recognition to the problem of air pollution in 1955, when the Congress enacted legislation authorizing research under federal auspices and technical assistance to the states. The Clean Air Act of 1963 then broadened the federal role by establishing a program of grants to the states to assist them in setting up or maintaining agencies for the control of pollution. Not till 1965, however, did amendments to this Act mention the automobile, the largest single source of air pollution, by authorizing the promulgation of federal standards for the control of emissions from cars beginning with model year 1968. Legislation enacted in 1967 strengthened substantially the powers of local, state, and federal authorities, and authorized the Secretary of Health, Education, and Welfare to enforce air quality standards in designated federally financed regions throughout the country.

Environmental alarms were sounding throughout the country in the 1960s in response to the warnings of biologists Rachel Carson and Barry Commoner, French oceanographer Jacques Cousteau, and others that the damage being done by industrial man might prove irreversible. Popular interest in ecology snapped into focus on April 22, 1970, with the celebration of Earth Day, a day marked by teach-ins, various clean-up projects, and adjournment by Congress to permit its members to address rallies across the nation. The next four years produced the broadest and most expensive environmental legislation in the nation's history. Congress at last established firm deadlines for the reduction of pollutants from automobiles, enacted a comprehensive water pollution control measure aimed at cleaning up the nation's waters by 1985, made petroleum companies liable for the costs of cleaning up oil spills, and acted on a host of other environmental issues, including the banning of hunting from aircraft, conservation of wildlife, reforestation of national forests, and the creation or expansion of national wilderness, historical, or recreational areas. It even shifted the priorities of President Nixon by appropriating more money for pollution control than he had asked for and less than he had proposed for defense!

It was the high point. At the same time that Congress was churning out environmental legislation in unprecedented volume, a new problem was emerging: shortage of energy. The issue became real for millions of Americans in the winter of 1972–73, when the United States suddenly seemed unable to muster enough fuel to heat its homes and power its factories. "Popeye is running out of cheap spinach," quipped former Commerce Secretary Peter G. Peterson. Then, between October 1973 and January 1974 the cost of imported "spinach" went up nearly 400 percent as a result of the embargo on oil shipments imposed by the Organization of Petroleum Exporting Countries (OPEC). More and more, it seemed that the solution to the nation's dwindling supply of power might be in conflict with the concerns of environmentalists.

As the first environmental decade came to a close, the race to clean up the country, begun in such earnest on Earth Day 1970, began to slow down. Economic concerns, as well as the problems of energy, were tempering the nation's commitment to a clean environment. Shrinking oil supplies, soaring inflation, slowing economic growth, and rising unemployment were forcing serious consideration of the questions "How clean? How fast? At what cost?" In the early 1980s the Reagan administration gave decisive evidence of its preference for renewed growth over environmental renewal; the Steel Compliance Act of 1981, for example, amended the Clean Air Act to allow steel companies to defer compliance for three years. Were rollbacks on environmental and workers' safety regulations, improved educational opportunity, and health, housing, and nutrition programs justifiable on grounds that these were too expensive "social luxuries"? Or did they rather represent foolhardy reductions in the nation's investment in human capital? That was one of the great political questions for Americans to confront in the late 1980s and beyond.

The answers given to those questions will go far toward determining the strength and resiliency of American capitalism in the twenty-first century. Healthy and well-educated working men and women are likely to become ever more important sources of the nation's economic well-being. That is because of the increasingly crucial role of scientific, technical, and managerial knowledge in economic growth. Even in the first half of the twentieth century, advances in knowledge contributed an estimated 40 percent of the total rise in income per person employed. In all likelihood, the contribution has risen since then and will continue to do so. For in the second half of the century, the American economy began to experience a Second Industrial Revolution, a revolution in the organization and processing of information and knowledge.

At the center of this revolution is the electronic digital computer. Unlike the calculator, the computer has a memory, a set of preprogrammed instructions or mathematical rules which it applies automatically to new data introduced at a later time. Like radar, jet aircraft, and other complicated high-technology developments incorporating state-of-the-art scientific knowledge, the electronic computer was a product of governmental need during World War II. The first large electronic digital computer (the ENIAC) was built to enable the army's Ballistic Research Laboratory to calculate trajectories for field artillery and bombing tables, a tedious task previously requiring large numbers of mathematicians using desk calculators. It was an enormous contraption, 100 feet long, 3 feet wide, and 10 feet high, and it contained about 18,000 vacuum tubes. Even though technical improvement was soon forthcoming, computers remained very costly after the war; they were difficult to program, and they were vulnerable to failure because of the dependence of their complex circuitry on vacuum tube technology. Many companies had both the knowledge and resources to build them, but great uncertainty over the size of the potential market made them reluctant to invest the substantial scientific, technical and financial resources required if they were to become commercial suppliers of computer systems.

Even the company that was subsequently to dominate the computer market, International Business Machines (IBM), held back at first. Under the leadership of Thomas J. Watson, Sr., IBM had grown from a small, struggling manufacturer of punch-card products and time-recording equipment in 1914, when it owned cash items amounting to $35,000 plus less than $200,000 in treasury bonds, which it used as collateral for short-term loans, to a firm whose American revenues in 1949 approximated $180 million. Watson was certainly interested in electronics—between 1937 and 1944 IBM had sponsored research in the techniques of electromechanical computation, and by 1947 had developed and built a partially electronic and partially electromechanical stored-program digital computer. But, faced with internal opposition on the part of engineers and executives, with continuing uncertainty whether there was really likely to be a demand for a computer, with technical problems, and with the fact that the traditional product line was very profitable, Watson hesitated. Perhaps his age—he was seventy-one in 1945—also had something to do with it. At any rate, it was his son, Thomas Jr., only thirty-six years old in 1950, who eventually authorized the development of a high-performing general purpose computer (the 701). Shipments began in 1953 at the rate of one a month, a production record unmatched at the time by any other company. Manufactured on an assembly-line basis, the 701 was from 10 to 100 times faster than the ENIAC.

It was also much smaller and cheaper; indeed, it was the first general-purpose computer that did not have to be built in the customer's computer room. Subsequent machines, both those produced by IBM and by such early competitors as Remington Rand and Burroughs, and by such later ones as General Electric, RCA, and Control Data, became still smaller and cheaper, and increasingly versatile as types of uses and users multiplied. Eventually, in the late 1970s Apple, Commodore, and Tandy emerged as leaders among firms manufacturing microcomputers. The technology of the industry had changed dramatically. First transistors, then silicon chips, replaced vacuum tubes. Chips no larger than the head of a thumbtack could hold the equivalent of 100,000 transistors, and work on a far larger integration of circuitry was proceeding apace.

It will be many years before the full impact of computers can be assessed: on business decision-making, the structure of the firm, labor unions and employment, the legal system, the home, the school, learning, leisure, and privacy. Yet it is already clear that its influence in some areas has become very great. The ability to link a personal computer with huge quantities of data stored in a central data base—by means of a modem, or modulation/demodulation device enabling it to communicate over telephone lines—helped transform information processing into information communication. Not only the curricula of hundreds of high schools and colleges, but the operations of small businessmen and professionals, have been affected. The business office is in the process of being changed radically: by the use of "teleconferencing" to save the time and expense of bringing together people from distant places for face-to-face discussions; by use of electronic mail, word processing, and even electronic filing; by calling upon the computer for such routine business functions as the assembly of financial data, and preparation of quarterly financial and actuarial reports, statistical analyses, and payrolls. Above all, the computer improves managers' ability to evaluate alternative investment projects, financing plans, production scheduling and inventory control. In sum, the computer has revolutionized the science of management. In manufacturing, it seems likely that the computer will more and more assist in product design, and in the control of welding robots and assembly line equipment. Finally, the public at large have familiar encounters with the effects of computers at the checkout counters of supermarkets and when they make flight reservations, rent an automobile, or buy an insurance policy.

It is sometimes said that the United States has been entering a postindustrial era since the end of the Second World War, that it is now best described as an information economy. If so, this would represent the most recent in a series of fundamental changes in the structure of the American economy. Change was slow at first, certainly relatively so, for agriculture dominated American economic life during its first three centuries. After the mid–1880s, the value of manufactured goods regularly exceeded that of agricultural products. From the point of view of national income generated by payments for labor, land, and natural resources, manufacturing continues to be the largest and most conspicuous sector. But its proportional size has declined somewhat in the years after the Second World War. In contrast, the service industries—trade, transportation and utilities, finance, insurance and real estate, and education, health, and government—have increased their share of national income. The provision of information alone, according to a recent calculation, accounted for 46 percent of the net income of the economy in 1967, and an even larger proportion, 53 percent, of all employee income.

Ever since the end of the last great war, industries producing goods—namely, agriculture, forestry and fishing, and manufacturing, mining, and construction—have employed fewer people than those producing services. In the two decades between 1947 and 1968, employment in services grew ten times as fast and brought about a massive shift from blue-collar work, including farming, to white-collar work, especially in professional, technical, and clerical jobs. Increasingly high levels of educational attainment accompanied these developments. In contrast to the prewar period, high school graduation became common among the young, with rising proportions of both men and women going on to college. The number of bachelor degrees granted doubled between 1966 and

1974, with masters degrees and doctorates increasing at nearly the same rate. As always, some fields of study enjoyed preferred status, law and business schools undergoing extraordinary growth. Engineering fared less well—until the boom in the popularity of computer science in recent years.

Other changes in the industrial distribution and composition of the work force are no less arresting. The share of state and local government in employment has doubled in the postwar period. By 1977 those governments were employing one of every seven workers, in contrast to one in fourteen three decades before. The most notable alteration in labor force composition has been the postwar influx of women into the job market, particularly married women with children. In 1978, 41 percent of the work force were women, nearly half of them less than thirty-five years of age, about one fourth between sixteen and twenty-four, one in six a college graduate, and over 70 percent high school graduates.

Some of these developments were not unrelated to the decline in industrial unionism in postwar America, for unions have historically been blue-collar phenomena. But it is also true that unions have rarely thrived in the absence of the support of the legal system. Between passage of the Wagner Act in 1935 and the end of World War II, union membership made a fourfold gain, but from 1947 to 1970 membership as a proportion of the total nonagricultural work force remained exactly the same. The Taft-Hartley amendment to the National Labor Relations Act in 1947 reflected a growing belief that the law should not only protect the right of a worker to join a union but also his right to refrain from joining one if he so chose. It was followed by a number of National Labor Relations Board (NLRB) and Supreme Court decisions favoring management's right to "free speech" in opposition to unionism. Encouraged by these rulings to contest NLRB elections, managements made extensive efforts to persuade workers to vote against union organization of the work place. They were often successful, however, because of the growing similarity in personnel practices between organized and nonorganized companies. Many large nonunion firms, for example, paid union level wages and maintained work conditions comparable to those in organized plants.

Unionism in the public sector has fared differently, growing rapidly in states with laws favorable to collective bargaining, and also at the federal level following the issuance of Executive Order 10988 by President Kennedy. The State, County and Municipal Workers union is the largest in the AFL-CIO. Public schoolteachers form one of the most highly organized occupations in the nation, and in most cities policemen and firemen negotiate over wages and working conditions. About half of the workers in the federal government are organized. These developments have changed the face of the American labor movement. They have also brought the United States closer to other developed nations, where unionism of government employees has long been practiced. There, as well as here, unions in the public sector rely on political rather than economic power to achieve their objectives.

Should business firms do the same? Should they rely upon government rather than upon the market in their effort to compete with foreign producers? Perhaps the question whether or not such a partnership or alliance should be entered into is the most important issue confronting the American political economy today. However—if a historian may be permitted to run the risks of prognostication—an alliance might well replace economic competition with political competition, might well politicize all economic decision-making, and in the words of a former chairman of Citicorp, Walter Wriston, create "an environment in which a corporation's well-being depends less and less on its ability to produce a saleable product or service and more and more on its ability to secure a favorable interpretation of some obscure paragraph in the Federal Register." Even worse, it might lead to an erosion of the soil of private ownership and control in which the power of political dissent sinks its roots.

There is one last consideration, by no means the least. While the public sector has played an important part in aiding the historical development of the American economy, the truth must remain that the overwhelming majority of decisions on what to produce, and how and where and when to produce it, have been made by private persons and businesses, that is to say, by the market. The powerful persistence of the nation's democracy is in part cause and in part effect of that truth. The high standards of living which most of its people have been able to achieve owe much to it too. Which is another way of saying that the wealth of the nation has been created by its people because they have been free to work, save, invest, and innovate. But they have been free to do these things only because they have believed it important that they be free to do them. In the end, then, the nation's wealth has been the product of the nation's values, and of the people and institutions in which they are embodied.

Index